The Russo-Japanese War at Sea 1904-5 Volume 1

The Russo-Japanese War at Sea 1904-5
Volume 1
Port Arthur, The Battles of the Yellow Sea and Sea of Japan

Vladimir Semenoff
Translated By L. A. B.

The Russo-Japanese War at Sea 1904-5
Volume 1
Port Arthur, The Battles of the Yellow Sea and Sea of Japan
By Vladimir Semenoff
Translated By L. A. B.

First published under the title
"Rasplata" ("the reckoning")

Leonaur is an imprint of Oakpast Ltd
Copyright in this form © 2014 Oakpast Ltd

ISBN: 978-1-78282-341-4 (hardcover)
ISBN: 978-1-78282-342-1 (softcover)

http://www.leonaur.com

Publisher's Notes

The views expressed in this book are not necessarily those of the publisher.

Contents

Author's Preface	7
PART 1: PORT ARTHUR	
Departure from St Petersburg	11
Impressions of Port Arthur	27
Personal Observations	42
Admiral Makaroff's Arrival	66
The Fatal April 13	85
After Makaroff's Death	106
Battle of Kintchao	125
The Beginning of the End	143
The Fleet Fights on Land	160
Our Last Days in Port Arthur	176
The End of the "Diana's" War Services	200
PART 2: THE VOYAGE OF ADMIRAL ROJESTVENSKY'S FLEET	
From Saigon to Libau	217
The Passage Through the "Belt"	241
Arrival at Vigo	260
Off the Cape of Good Hope	275

Author's Preface

And as Jesus passed by, he saw a man which was blind from his birth. And his disciples asked him, saying. Master, who did sin, this man or his parents, that he was born blind?—St John ix. 1, 2.

My book in its present form is considerably more complete than it was on its first appearance. The contents first came out as a series of essays in the *Russ* newspaper, and gave rise, at the time, to a number of articles and comments in the Press, in which these were generally referred to as "reminiscences."

Against such a conception of my work I must enter an energetic, protest. It in no way contains "reminiscences," but is simply the diary of an eye-witness, presented in the form of a narrative. Its whole value lies in this fact. It is material for the writing of history.

I kept a diary from January 30, 1904, to December 19, 1906 (even a little longer), and made daily entries, on specially important days even hourly. Everything I tell of here is based on the data of my diary. In every case, at the moment the event occurred I noted the time by watch; the general feeling at the time was noted somewhat later. My diary also contains conversations and remarks, which I wrote down whilst still fresh in my mind. Naturally, they stand in a very condensed form—mere headings sometimes.

It, naturally, also includes observations and explanations, which I added later. But then this fact is always specially noted. Moreover, I desire all the more to lay stress on the fact that this is not a narrative written from memory, but a diary, as I know from personal experience how unreliable one's memory is. This is especially the case in action. I have occasionally made myself a perfectly clear picture of this or that incident, which was decidedly influenced by the statements of others. When I then read over my diary again, I found my picture did not correspond with the notes made at the time. These short notes, however, were sufficient in every instance to enable me once more to bring before my eyes the correct picture of the event.

Here is an example of how one can forget details, even when they were really important, and had been personally noted in one's diary.

The Japanese state in their official account of the Battle of Tsushima (May 27, 1905), that at 4.40 p.m.[1] the destroyer division, commanded by Commander Sudzuki, attacked the battleship *Suvoroff*, which had sheered out of the line and was burning fiercely, that one of its torpedoes had hit the battleship on the port side aft, and in consequence the vessel had heeled 10°. None of those belonging to the *Suvoroff*, who were taken off by the *Buiny*, could call to mind that the ship had been hit by a torpedo. They even protested energetically that this could not have taken place. It was true, the *Suvoroff* was at that time a complete wreck, but still an incident like this was bound to have been noticed. Many of the *Buiny's* officers and men, on the other hand, testified that when their destroyer went alongside the *Suvoroff*, she was heeling 10° to port, if not more. The officers and men who came on board the *Buiny* from the battleship corroborated this. They remembered that it had been possible to get the admiral, who was unconscious, on to the destroyer by allowing him to slide down over the backs of several men. But these men had been standing on various projections close to the water-line on the starboard side, which was high out of the water.

When was this heel produced? Were the Japanese right in attributing it to a hit from one of their torpedoes? The battleship's people declared this to be inadmissible. Was it in consequence of the armour plates on the port side becoming loosened under the influence of the hail of Japanese shell, and the seams opening out? None of the eye-witnesses were able to state, even approximately, when this heel was noticed. I must add that we were only asked the question several months after the battle. I myself made the greatest efforts to think it all out and to reproduce the sequence of events from memory, but had to reply quite candidly: "I don't know any more." When I afterwards read over the laconic notes in my diary on the battle, I read:

3.25 p.m.—Strong heel to port; the upper battery is burning fiercely.

Instantly everything came back to me. This note proves that this

---

1. By our time it was 4.20. The Japanese reckoned their time from the meridian of Kioto, our squadron from the noon position of the day preceding the battle.

heel already existed at 3.25, that is, an hour before the torpedo attack with which the Japanese connected it. Without my diary I might perhaps have sided with the view of those who maintained that this hit by a torpedo had never been noticed in the heat of the action.

I won't boast about my memory (though I have been told that in this respect God had not dealt with me in a niggardly spirit), but it certainly is remarkable that one can altogether forget a fact which had been noted down in writing.

Let me once more emphasise this: this book is not based on reminiscences, but on a diary.

I will not, however, conceal the fact that occasionally, when under the influence of later accounts, I have been tempted to omit this or that passage, not to reproduce the judgment on this or that event, *which I had formed on the spot and at the time*. I have resisted this temptation. I said to myself: "It *was* thus." At that time we had these ideas, this conception. Perhaps we were sometimes mistaken, but these mistakes arose owing to what we had gone through and what we had felt. Do I, after all, mean to write a history of the war? No. I desire, in this work, to present to the reader a picture of the experiences of one who took part in the war, and who noted everything he observed at the time and place in his diary.

Up to now none of my old shipmates and comrades of the war has addressed himself to me with a request for any rectification.

If contradictions should be published as to any details, then they emanate from persons who, by order from above, are engaged upon the writing of History in the seclusion of their studies, and who base themselves in this labour on official reports, I do not propose to enter into any arguments with these.

Wl. Semenoff.[2]

---

2. Pronounced "Sem-yon-off."

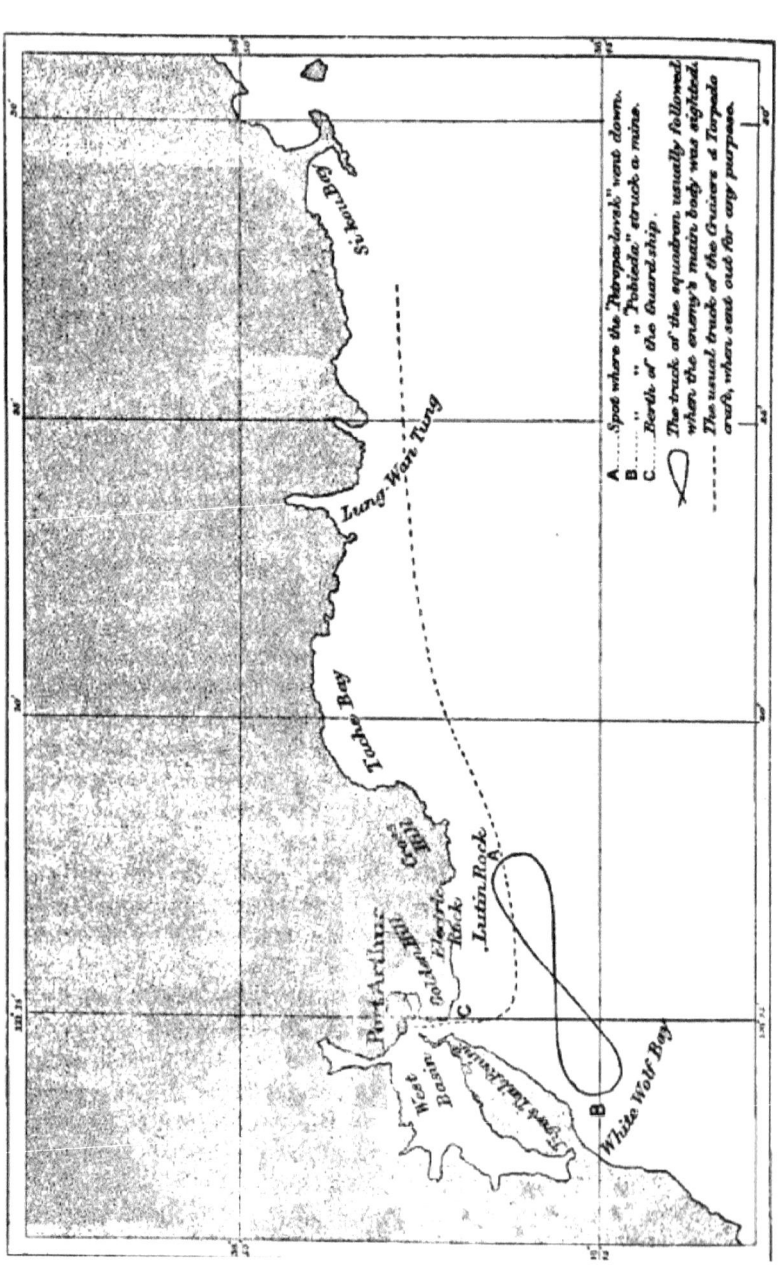

PART 1: PORT ARTHUR

CHAPTER 1

Departure from St Petersburg

"Now you have got what you wanted. God grant a happy issue!" With these words the admiral dismissed me. But I was already in the doorway when he added, in his usual rapid manner of speaking:

"Listen to one last piece of advice. Don't push yourself forward needlessly. One's fate, no doubt, overtakes one anywhere, and when volunteers are called for, of course one must respond. Simply do your duty, that is all. Don't push forward. There is nothing hard about death, but it is stupid to get killed to no purpose."

Almost the whole of my service, excepting two years at the Naval Academy, had been spent afloat in the Far Eastern seas. In the autumn of the year 1901 I was asked whether I would like a certain appointment on the staff at Cronstadt. This particular billet was combined with that of A.D.C. to the Commander-in-Chief, the Military Governor of the Port, (Port Admiral). As an old "sea-dog," I did not care for service on shore, in towns and in offices. All the same, I accepted with joy, for the Port Admiral at Cronstadt was then S. O. Makaroff.

I do not propose to give any description here of the admiral, who was to meet with such a tragic end. For long years he had to struggle against his enemies, who obstinately opposed all his efforts, and who were for ever placing obstacles in his path. When at last he was in a position where he was able to give full scope to his talents, his brains, his restless energy, for the good of his country, without any obstacles, and responsible only to his Imperial master, just then he was doomed to die. History will appreciate his worth.

I was not deceived in my expectations. It was no easy matter serving under Makaroff. Often there was no time either for eating or sleeping; but for all that it was a splendid life. What was especially characteristic in Makaroff was his horror of all "routine," and his hatred of the old office custom of devolving everything on others, of avoiding any and every responsibility, and therefore of never coming to an independent decision, but of passing on every paper to some one else, "to be dealt with." Whenever such an attempt at shirking a decision or allowing a question to drag on came to light, then it was that, in my opinion, the admiral, for once in a way, lost all control over himself. Then he often ran to the telephone himself, censured and gave orders to the persons concerned in the sharpest manner possible, and threatened to call them to account for their misdeeds.

I need hardly say that, as one accustomed to the direct methods of ship life, I deeply sympathised with the feelings of my chief, and was ever ready to assist him to the best of my abilities. As I said before, it was a splendid life.

But when war was in the air in the autumn of 1903 it went against the grain, however interesting my duties were, and I asked to be sent where my old squadron was preparing for war.

The first time the admiral regularly flew at me, upon which I became stubborn, and persisted in my request. Then he tried to talk me over. He said that if it came to war, it would be a difficult and lengthy business. Sooner or later we should all be in it. To push oneself forward now was a mistake. Here we should be overwhelmed with work, and his A.D.C. had no business to leave at such a moment. However, I did not give in, and assured him that if the war still found me on shore, any officer could easily replace me, for I should then be simply doing nothing, and continuously plaguing my superiors to send me afloat. This almost led to serious estrangement between us on two or three occasions. At last the admiral gave in, and had me appointed second-in-command of the *Boyarin*[1] from January 14, 1904. A fortnight passed in winding up my office work and handing it over to my successor. The leave-taking, with which this chapter opens, took place on January 27.

Before my departure I took leave officially of the different flag officers employed at St Petersburg, going last to Admiral R———. After the exchange of the usual official phrases, I could not resist asking him whether he thought there would be war.

The admiral looked away. "War does not always begin only with the firing of guns," he said abruptly. "In my opinion the war has begun long ago. Only those who are blind fail to see this."

I could not ask him for anything more definite, but I was alarmed

---

1. Fast, protected cruiser of 3,000 tons, and six 4.7-inch Q.F. guns—Trans.

at the admiral's sinister expression. My question had evidently touched a sore spot, which made him say more than he intended, or thought himself entitled to say.

"But I suppose I shall still arrive in time, before the firing begins?"

The admiral had recovered his composure. He did not answer my question, but wished me a pleasant voyage in the most friendly way, and I had to take my leave.

When I put the same question to several acquaintances of mine at the Foreign Office, I always received the same reply: "Don't worry; you'll arrive in plenty of time. We shall spin out this business till April."

My express started from St Petersburg on the evening of January 29.

A few friends had come to see me off. They all wished me *bon voyage*. The word "war" was not pronounced, but one felt it somehow in the tone of their good wishes. There was a certain solemnity in these last moments. We parted full of cheerful confidence in the future. How very different my return was to be!

However, that will all appear in good time.

As far as the Ural Mountains, and even beyond, the train was crammed with passengers. Outwardly, nothing exceptionable was visible in the demeanour of the public. But the further we proceeded East, the more this changed. Those who were only concerned with local business left the train by degrees at the intermediate stations, and the handful of people "going out" gradually foregathered. These could be divided into two categories: the one consisted of officers and others in government employ of every kind, the other of people of every profession and every nationality. The latter were the infallible indications of war. They were the vultures accompanying a military expedition, the sharks which follow a ship where someone is dying. Both categories recognised one another, and their respective members became mutually acquainted. Unfortunately, "we" were but few. The greater part of us was only going into Western Siberia. The last to leave at Irkutsk were a general officer and a captain of the general staff, who were travelling to some place on the Mongolian frontier. Beyond Irkutsk my only companion was a Colonel L——, who was to take command of a new rifle regiment to be formed at Port Arthur.

I well remember our passage across the ice of Lake Baikal. A passenger of the express has a right to a place in the clumsy railway sledge.

I did not make use of this right—why should one economise, when war was at hand?—but hired a fast *troika*.[2] It took me about half a day to cover the 28 miles across the frozen lake from Baikal station to Tanchoi station. It was a clear, sunny day, with a temperature of 5° to 6° F. below zero, and perfectly calm. The *troika* started at a gallop; but at the end of about 4 miles the horses relapsed into a trot. The driver turned round.

"Look here, your honour, halfway across there is a public house. Will you stand me a drink?"

"Maybe, if you drive well."

The driver bent forward and gave a low whistle, at the sound of which his three little horses started off at such a pace that clouds of "ice dust" rose high behind us. On Lake Baikal the famous Russian *troika*, of which the poet Gogol has sung, has still maintained its prestige.

In the clear, frosty air the hills on the opposite bank were distinctly visible. The seaman's practised eye seemed to have lost the faculty—the result of lengthy training—of judging distances. The hills seemed quite near. Apparently one could make out every little crack in the hillside, into which the snow had drifted. In reality these were deep ravines, and whole towns might lie buried in the masses of snow they contained.

A short time before a young, or at least young-looking general officer had started from Baikal station in just such a *troika*. He had evidently not made any special bargain with his driver, for we overtook him about 10 miles out. He was on the point of driving through the deep snow up to a detachment of soldiers, who were crossing the lake on foot. Officers and men, wearing their winter caps, their rifles over the right or left shoulder, were moving along contentedly over the thick ice—a cheering, inspiring sight. Turgenieff's *Dovolno* came into my mind. The herons are flying along under the heavens, replying with proud confidence to their leader's question: "Shall we get there?" with "We shall get there!"

Outwardly, this detachment did not perhaps present a very military appearance. Dressing and intervals were not well kept. But their light, swinging step, the cheery shouts and laughter sounding here and there in the column—all breathed the proud confidence described by Turgenieff.

I was not the only one to feel this. The general in front of me sud-

---

2. Sledge with three horses abreast.—Trans.

denly threw back his fur cloak, so as to expose the red facings of his overcoat,[3] and rose. "Your health, my lads!" he called out in a cheerful voice. "God be with you!"

"*Rady staratissia!*" ("Respectful thanks!") was roared back.

The general again shouted something, but I could not distinguish it. I was now alongside of these young, fresh, laughing faces. Officers and men replied to him and waved their caps or rifles. Again I had to think of the "We shall get there." My heart was beating faster. I thought of what was before us, with full confidence. Admiral R—— was right. This was already war.

At Tanchoi, on the other side of the lake, the express of the East Chinese railway was waiting for us.

Three engineers, who were inspecting the line. Colonel L—— and I, were the only first-class passengers. Of course we quickly made friends. As a matter of course, the political situation in Manchuria and in Korea formed the sole subjects of conversation. Opinions differed widely. The one said that war was inevitable. The Japanese had now been at work for ten years to strengthen their fighting powers, without being afraid of overtaxing their people. Now they were practically forced to make use of any favourable opportunity. Another maintained that if the Japanese had been at work for ten years to strengthen their fighting powers they would not stake everything on one cast. Failure would mean their end. And thus diametrically opposite deductions were drawn from the same facts.

On February 9 the colonel and I had a particularly warm discussion.

"They will never dare! Never!" he was exclaiming eagerly. "Why, it would be playing *va banque* for them, or even worse—a game already lost. Assuming even that they scored a success at starting, what would be the next step? Surely we should not throw down our arms after the first reverse? I could almost wish them an initial success. Just think what the effect of this would be! The whole of Russia would rise like one man, and never sheathe the sword until—"

"God grant it may be only a reverse, and not a serious defeat."

"Well, and if we do have a serious defeat? The effect can't last long. We shall simply wait until we have collected enough forces, and we'll drive them into the sea. You with your fleet will surely not allow the enemy to get home again. But what is the good of all this discussion? It will never come to that. They won't dare! There'll be no war!"

---

3. Special distinguishing mark of general officers.—Trans

"Well, I maintain that they have been preparing for this war for the last ten years. Now they are ready and we are not, and today or tomorrow they'll strike. You call that playing *va banque!* Very well; but why should they not risk it, if there is one chance of winning?"

"They have no chance."

"We shall see."

"Will you bet that there'll be no war? I'll stake a hamper of champagne."

"That would be no bet. We will say that you have won if the war has not begun by the middle of April."

"But why? I maintain there will be no war at all."

"All the easier for you to accept my proposal. Besides, you would otherwise never get your champagne. I should be the one to profit."

We shook hands over it laughingly. One of our travelling companions, who was also going to Port Arthur, asked us not to forget him when the bet was being paid.

Colonel L—— was a very interesting man. His nerves evidently played the principal part in his constitution. He was tall, big-boned, incredibly thin, and looked sickly. His powers of physical endurance depended entirely on his mood. Sometimes he would go for a walk without an overcoat with the thermometer below zero F., another time he would suddenly declare that there was a draught through the double windows, fitted with india rubber washers, and send to the dispensary for some *phenacetin*, of which he would consume fabulous quantities. A horrible, and quite uneatable Manchurian native dish he would eat "for the sake of science," but of the food in our restaurant-car he pretended that it was too heavy for his weak stomach.

On this particular evening he seemed to have made up his mind to convince me at whatever cost. He persisted in his attacks, until I commenced to undress in his presence, and finally went to bed.

"The agents of all the European powers agree in their reports that Japan cannot mobilise more than 325,000 men," he began again in the manner of a lecture, "and of those she must keep some at home."

"Do you believe these figures? Japan has a larger population than France. Why should there be this difference in the strength of their armies?"

"They haven't the organisation—no properly prepared contingents."

"They have been preparing themselves for ten years. Even the schoolboys are taught something of soldiering. Every schoolboy there knows more than one of our soldiers in his second year of service."

"They only possess arms and ammunition for 325,000 men."

"Then they will buy more abroad."

"Oh, nonsense—"

I turned out the electric light and rolled myself into my blanket.

"That is no proof," growled the colonel, and retired.[4]

About midnight we stopped at some station in Manchuria. I was fast asleep, when the colonel suddenly rushed into my compartment, shouting: "You have won!"

At first I did not understand him. "What? What's the matter?"

"General mobilisation through the entire viceroyalty and Trans-Baikal."

"Mobilisation does not mean actual war."

The colonel's only reply was a whistle. "With us, people are as alarmed at the order to mobilise, as old women are at a thunderstorm. There was always the fear of conjuring up war, by merely pronouncing that word. When therefore mobilisation is really ordered, it means that we are at war. It also means that the enemy has commenced hostilities."

"God grant a happy issue," I said, and crossed myself.

"Yes, yes; God grant it," he said moodily. "At the frontier we have 90,000 men. But only on paper. I know that as a matter of fact we shall hardly be able to muster 50,000 rifles and sabres."

Sleep was now out of the question. The passengers were all on their legs. We assembled in the dining-car. Strictly speaking, it was supposed to be shut up at 11 p.m., but this time the lights were kept going, and tea was to be had up to any hour. The railway officials crowded at the doors. Everyone was waiting for the next station, and everyone hoped for more details from someone else.

We passed two stations without our painful expectations being realised. It was said that a surprise attack had been made on Port Arthur; but no one knew anything for certain. At 4 a.m., at some station or other, a lady, the wife of one of the railway officials, got into our train. She told us that Port Arthur had been nearly captured. She was going to Harbin to draw all her deposits out of the bank, take away all her valuables from her house, and fly to Russia. She further reported that several days before all Japanese had disappeared out of the towns

---

4. The Japanese official reports of the sick, wounded, killed and dead give the numbers, not only in absolute figures, but in percentages. From these it can be seen that the Japanese armies numbered nearly one and a half millions.

in Manchuria. But they had not sold anything, and had hardly settled accounts with their clients. All their property they had handed over to their neighbours, and had said: "In a week, or ten days at the most, we shall be back with our armies."

The lady's stories gave rise to angry protests. Her audience would not believe all her dismal tales, and began to scatter.

"Damned old scarecrow!" growled the colonel. "It is not worth listening to her! Come on! Let's go to bed. Or, rather, just wait one moment—I want to fetch a little bromide from the dispensary."

The next day brought little that was new. However, the various reports gradually made it clear that the Japanese had opened hostilities against Port Arthur. Which side had got the best of it, we could not make out.

At Harbin we had a longer stoppage—about half an hour, so far as I remember. On stepping out on to the platform I found, to my great surprise, an old acquaintance from the Far East—our naval contractor, G——.

"Where are you coming from? Where are you going to?"

"I am coming from Port Arthur, Where I am going to, I don't know yet. I am helping as much as I can, accompanying the women and children, etc. Everyone is running away, and has lost his head."

Indeed, two long trains, bound north, were standing in the station. They had evidently been put together anyhow. There were carriages of all three classes, even some of the fourth class, generally only intended for *coolies*, and they were literally crammed with passengers. Not only all the seats were occupied, but all the corridors as well. Women and children were in the majority. Some carried very primitive bundles, some had put their things down anywhere, and amongst these there were *articles de luxe*, as well as objects of the most necessary daily use. One could see that these people had gathered together whatever they could quickly lay their hands on. Many of them did not even possess warm clothes. Numerous Chinese were doing a roaring trade at the carriages with old fur jackets, cheap tea-kettles, and suspicious looking provisions.

In payment they took alike money, rings, bracelets, and brooches. Their rapacity had taught them how to make a good profit out of the sudden panic. The local authorities, who had been taken completely by surprise, had enough to do with their own concerns, so that it was left to some volunteers to try and keep order. These were for the most part officers and officials; but there were also civilian passengers, ladies as well as gentlemen, who had not completely lost their senses, or who had recovered them. Hysterical cries were heard everywhere. Here someone was calling out despairingly for a doctor to attend a sick child, there another was imploring for help in heartrending tones.

"I know that kind of picture," some one suddenly said. It was one of our fellow-travellers in the express, a tall, robust-looking man. "It was just the same during the Boxer riots. Now, gentlemen, is the time for you to empty your portmanteaus. À la guerre comme à la guerre. I dare say we shall be able to make shift for ourselves, if we were to find ourselves in need by and by."

The right word at the right time has an astonishing power. Our portmanteaus were literally turned bottom up. *Bashliks*[5], Jerseys, fur caps, felt boots—everything went in a few minutes from the express train to that conveying the fugitives. These wretched people were touched, and grateful beyond words, and our hearts warmed up as they stammered their thanks.

G—— did not empty his portmanteaus, for the good reason that he possessed none, but his pockets instead. When these were empty, he made out cheques, which had the value of gold in Manchuria.

Before the express started again I asked him where he intended going. "Oh, with the fugitives."

At that we all began arguing with him. We told him that there was nothing for him to do in the north, but all the more in Port Arthur, where his presence was important.

Colonel L—— was specially insistent, but we all joined in, not quite without ulterior motives. We were, in fact, very anxious to keep in our company an eye-witness of the events in Port Arthur, for, in our eagerness to play the benefactors, we had not questioned him at all as to these.

At first G—— was inexorable. "No, gentlemen. War is your business. I am not a soldier, but a peaceful citizen, and have no interest at all in getting killed for nothing. You may go to the war. I shall go where there is no danger."

This was quite logical, but the official in charge of our train, a subaltern of the Army Reserve, at once proved the contrary.

"You may be quite sure, my dear sir, that there will be absolutely no danger at Port Arthur, so long as the Viceroy remains there. At the very first indication of unpleasantness in that respect, he will be off.

---

5. Hoods with long ends for tying round the neck.—Trans.

You could then always leave the place with him. Besides, if you were to give up your business there in times like these, surely you would suffer great losses?"

This argument convinced G——. As it was, he had already begun to shake off, in our company, that feeling of panic, of which, to a certain extent, he also had become a victim in that train of fugitives.

The express moved off to the southward. We took G—— with us into the restaurant-car for some tea, and listened eagerly to all his news. And what were we to hear? On the evening of February 8 the Japanese destroyers had attacked our squadron, without having previously sent us a declaration of war. Our ships were lying at anchor in the outer roads, without nets, and showing usual lights. It had ended comparatively well for us. It might have been much worse.

"And next morning I saw them where they had been stranded just below the lighthouse, the *Retvisan*, the *Tsesarevitch*, the *Pallada*—our squadron! The Russian squadron! Oh, gentlemen—"

G—— was silent, and put his hand to his forehead. I looked into his eyes and saw that his grief was genuine. He was a foreigner by birth, but had become one with us and the squadron, so that his feelings were no longer merely those of a tradesman. Formerly, with mild sarcasm, we used to call him "old friend." Now this term was taken seriously.

"What damage was done to the ships?"

"I don't know exactly. The *Retvisan* was hit forward, the *Tsesarevitch* aft; she nearly had her propellers smashed. And with all that, there is no dock which can take them in—not a single dock! The *Pallada*'s case is not so bad. She has a big hole, but is being repaired in dock. But how is such a thing possible? They say that money had to be saved. Very well; but then they should not always have reported that ' everything was in first-rate order.' Now, of course, they will build docks, money being no object. But it is too late. Oh, our squadron!"

"A man who is going to be beheaded need not lament the loss of his hair,"[6] said an old fellow-traveller in a surly tone of voice. "It is too late now for lamentations. We'll get out of this mess somehow. We'll undertake something or other—"

"We shall know how to die," came in the clear voice of a young subaltern of artillery at the next table.

"That is our speciality," morosely replied an old captain, who was sitting at the same table; "but it is a pity to do it without any object."

---

6. Russian proverb.—Trans.

"What else happened at Port Arthur?"

"What else? On the 9th they came, fired for forty minutes, and went away. What exactly happened I don't know. Whether they intentionally fired into the town, or whether we only got their 'overs,' I never enquired. Every soul who could bolted. It was said that if the fortress had been ready for war, it might have gone hard with them, but with us—"

The speaker broke off short, looked round nervously, and would not finish his sentence at any price.

"When you get to Port Arthur you will find out for yourself," he whispered in my ear. "You have got acquaintances there."

That picture of general panic had burst upon us too suddenly. Its depressing effect wore off, the further south our train took us. There was unusual animation at the stations, not to say restlessness, but it was orderly, without any symptoms of a scare.

All passengers got to share the general feeling which prevailed along our route. The colonel literally became twenty years younger. He forgot all his sufferings, and no longer took any interest in the weather, or even in *phenacetin*. The official in charge of the train was for ever proving to every one, though no one had contradicted him, that his superiors had no right to forbid his going to the front. He wanted to join one of the batteries of the East Siberian Division, in which he had served his time as a volunteer. There were quite enough people to take charge of military trains. He had to take his place as officer of the Reserve. "All my people are at the front," he cried. "They won't bring any disgrace on their corps." He seemed to pity us for not having the honour of knowing his battery.

"The first blow miscarried. That is very important," came from one of our companions in a bass voice. "We did not keep a look-out, but now the whole of Russia is at our back." Then he continued in a sarcastic tone: "Even if we have to retire beyond Lake Baikal, to clothe ourselves in the skins of wild animals, and to live on horrible Mongolian food, we will not lay aside our arms while a single enemy remains on our soil—nay, on the continent of Asia."

In the afternoon of February 12 we reached Tashitchao. The train stopped here a short time. The station was full of life and animation. A number of artillerymen rushed into the restaurant-car and hurriedly ate a few mouthfuls of anything they could lay their hands on. Whilst they ate, they told their tale in short sentences.

"We are going to Liaoyan—from there to the Yalu. They say the enemy has already been seen near Imkau. They are supposed to have landed. We have been shunted. The frontier troops did not wait for the train. They marched off. They consisted of a horse battery and two *sotnias,* (squadrons of Cossacks). We have a company of rifles with us."

No one ventured to ask what these two batteries, two *sotnias* and a rifle company could do if the Japanese had really landed at Imkau. It was clear they were doing what they could. That was enough.

When we reached Hai-Tchau during the night we were "called to arms." At this place the line passes close to the seashore, not more than 2 or 3 miles off. From' the beach reports had come in that many lights had been seen out at sea. One of the nearest outposts had seen parties of men, and half a *sotnia* of Cossacks, on guard at the station, had gone there. We could hear rifle fire. Perhaps they were Chunchuses, perhaps Japanese. It was a convenient place to destroy the line. Telegrams flew up and down the line. The 9th Regiment might arrive any moment.

"We are more than twenty here, anyway," said the stationmaster's son, a boy of fourteen, with a Winchester rifle on his shoulder. "We'll go into the blockhouse. There we can hold out an hour or two, until the soldiers come."

There was no lack of zeal and self-confidence. All we saw and heard made a fine, encouraging impression.

Kwantung greeted us next morning with a violent snowstorm.

At Nangalin station G—— left us. He was in hopes of reaching Port Arthur quicker by an ordinary passenger train. We of the express were tied to our luggage, and had to go *via* Dalny. This did not prove to be at all a simple matter. Owing to the sudden outbreak of war, the time-tables had been altered. The needs of the fortress and garrison had to be considered first. We reached Dalny all right at the appointed time; but instead of a stoppage of quarter of an hour, we were delayed four hours. Cabs there were none. Walking in this snowstorm was impossible. Moreover, we were expecting every minute to get permission to continue our journey to Port Arthur. Our companion, the big, warm-hearted man, had disappeared the moment we had arrived. Presumably he went to collect some news from his friends.

Colonel L—— and I sat down in an empty railway carriage and entertained one another with our lamentations over this tiresome delay.

The station looked utterly deserted in the snowstorm. Not a sign of that life, that fresh, healthy activity, we had found in the north. The faces of the employees who passed only expressed helplessness and anxiety; often one could detect the dread of coming disaster in them. We tried to stop some of them and to question them. Their replies were always vague, and they quickly moved on again.

"They are pretending to be busy when there is nothing to do," a civilian said as he was passing.

The colonel got ill once more, swallowed *phenacetin* and *bromide*, and abused Providence.

Towards noon the dull booming of single shots reached our ears, above the howling of the storm. "What is that?" I asked the conductor of the train, who happened to be passing.

"Why, don't you know? The dead from the *Yenissei* are being buried."

"We know nothing."

"The *Yenissei* ran on a mine she had laid out herself, and went down; the *Boyarin* also—"

I jumped up horrified.

"What? The *Boyarin*? What is the matter with her? I am on my way to join her—I am her second-in-command. Why don't you speak?"

"Speak! Speak! The devil take you!" roared the colonel. "Why, we are quite out of the world here."

"But, gentlemen, for heaven's sake, I can't—it is forbidden," wailed the conductor, and ran off.

Another hour passed in painful suspense. At last the whistle sounded and the train moved off. Just at the last moment our missing travelling companion jumped in. He threw his snow-covered fur coat into a corner, shut the door, and dropped heavily on a seat. "It's all over."

"What? With whom is it all over?"

"With us," he said fiercely, jerking out his words. "I know this sort of thing. In 1900 we had the same spectacle. Then also everything came as a surprise. We may as well throw down our cards. The *Tsesarevitch, Retvisan, Pallada* are *hors de combat* by torpedo attack. The *Askold* and *Novik* badly damaged by gunfire. The *Variag* and *Koreets*, they say, were destroyed at Chemulpo. The supply ships with ammunition have been captured at sea. The *Yenissei* and *Boyarin* are sunk by their own fault; the *Gromoboy, Rossia, Rurik*, and *Bogatyr* are 1,000 miles off at Vladivostok. The fortress is only being prepared for war after war has broken out. On the 9th only three batteries were able to fire. The forts were still laid up for winter, the garrison in barracks in the town. The recoil cylinders of the guns on Electric Rock were only filled at ten in the morning, after the hostile squadron had already been reported by the look-out ship. There you are! It's all over!"

He really never finished his sentences, but only jerked out fragmentary words. Many violent expressions of his impotent rage I have left out. But we, who happened to represent army and navy, listened attentively, and greedily took in every word of his, caring nothing for his violence. We felt somehow, without being quite clear about it ourselves, that he did not mean us generally, but some particular persons. Years of service had inoculated our flesh and blood with the sense of discipline. Without this we should certainly have joined in the denunciations of this strong, energetic man, who was flinging out his accusations so fiercely. And yet, strange to say, the more clearly our friend depicted our helplessness (as we afterwards found, he was right in the main), the more we felt an astonishing calmness coming over us, the more that torturing feeling, caused by ignorance and long-drawn-out tension, left us.

I looked at the colonel. He was leaning back on the cushioned seat, his hands buried in his coat pockets, and had a look which would not have made it advisable for anyone to offer him some *phenacetin*.

"We have been betrayed. Perhaps—at least we must assume this—not intentionally and knowingly, but we have been betrayed all the same," our companion ended, and drew a deep breath.

"If this is so, it can't be helped," cried the colonel; "but after all this is a, not very important, beginning. Behind us stands Russia. We are only the vanguard. We are nothing, but we shall do our duty."

This was the man, who only an hour ago had been so ill and weak. Now there was that same fine ring in his voice, with which that subaltern had called out: "We shall know how to die."

I regained my former confidence. At Nangalin there was again a stoppage of several hours. The restaurant-car had, for some reason or other, been left behind at Dalny and we had to get our food in the refreshment room at the station. It was a small room, grandly labelled: "First and Second Class Waiting-room." Into this were crowded all the people who were travelling through Kwantung and either wanted to reach Port Arthur or the Manchurian plains. Here the talk was neither of our failures nor of our future prospects. The crash of the torpedoes, which had robbed our fleet of part of its strength, the minute guns over the graves of our sailors, who in an evil hour had met with so sad a death, had not penetrated to this place.

While the storm was howling outside and piling up the snow on the new graves, within, in the close, smoky little room, corks were popping, and the talk was of government contracts, of fortunes which could now be amassed with little outlay, or of gambling.

We ate quickly, and hurried back to our train. Towards 11 p.m. we arrived at Port Arthur. The colonel was met by an officer of his new regiment. My other travelling companion found some colleagues, and I sat there quite alone. Both promised to send me the first cab they might meet, and I had to console myself with that.

I spent a horrible half-hour in a corner of the waiting-room, where I sat with my luggage. A company of Reservists who had not yet joined their corps were celebrating their last meeting here.

The petroleum lamps shone faintly through the tobacco smoke and the fumes of the kitchen. The floor was covered with dirt and melting snow which people had brought in from the street. This was mixed with puddles of spilt wine and beer, broken glass, fragments of bottles, and remains of food. Snatches of ribald songs mingled with the brawls of drunken men. In between, phrases were being shouted, which were meant to express high and noble sentiments; there was kissing and cursing. The company could not have been more mixed. Here were small landed proprietors, commercial travellers, coachmen; workmen's blouses alongside high, stiff collars, peasants' coats and peaked caps near fur-lined overcoats and good hats or even caps of cheap Chinese sable. Some wore long, flowing beards, others were clean-shaven, after the English fashion. I saw all this as in a bad dream, and tried in vain to picture to myself the feelings of all these future defenders of Port Arthur.

Who could tell? Perhaps what I took to be drunken shouts was in reality the outward expression of a warlike spirit thirsting for action. Anyhow, I greeted the Chinaman who came to report the arrival of my cab as a saviour.

My midnight wanderings in search of a lodging are of no interest. By next morning the storm had ceased. It was calm; there was a clear, cloudless sky and bright sunshine. At ten o'clock, when I went out to report myself to my superiors, the streets had turned into impassable swamps. Most cab-drivers had been obliged to give up their calling, as they had been called out as Reservists. The few who were left cheated their fares quite openly, asking as much as ten shillings for a five minutes' drive. During these early days their appetites had not yet been forcibly appeased. At that time the impenetrable mud had brought them in ten pounds per day, and more. This, however, by the way. During the state of fever, which seized upon everyone in those days, no one paid any attention to such trifles.

I had to jump from one dry spot to another, and walk round puddles, which had grown into small ponds. Horses and carriages whisking past bespattered me with mud. Amidst all these difficulties I tried to impress on my memory the whole picture, the mood of the town in general. At every turn I met vehicles marked with a small red flag.[7] Heavy artillery waggons were succeeded by the light two-wheeled carts of the riflemen. Horses, mules, donkeys, were dragging about the clumsy native carts. Military escorts were marching at their sides, with their great-coats buttoned up to the chin. Here donkeys were braying, Chinese and Korean drivers shouting at one another; there a coachman was making full use of the wealth of the Russian language. Cossack orderlies, almost standing up in their stirrups, were trotting about busily. Then again came troops with bands playing.

From the port one could hear the rattling of the steam winches of steamers discharging cargo. Sirens and steam whistles shrieked. Tugs were puffing and panting in front of strings of heavy lighters. Gigantic cranes stretched upwards into the clear air, like the antennae of some monsters. The penetrating sound of hammering on iron, loud shouts, and the hiss of escaping steam made a wild concert. In the distance were dimly heard fragments of the "*Dubinushka*,"[8] and the drawling notes of a Chinese song, from men pulling at a weight. Over all this was the pure sky, the resplendent sun, whilst the buzzing of the many-tongued crowd spread everywhere. It was a motley picture—people differing in race, speech, and manners. Still, one felt that in this turmoil, in this feverish activity, there was no confusion, no aimlessness. Everyone was carrying out his allotted task, and trying to do it well. The big machine "Mobilisation," of which in time of peace hardly the component parts were allowed to work, was now in full swing.

The bad impression of yesterday at Dalny, Nangalin, Port Arthur, the bitter talk of my travelling companions, gave way to pleasanter feelings. This mass of what had hitherto been utter strangers was now working for one common aim and object, and I felt happy at being one of them.

---

7. Commandeered by the military authorities on mobilisation.—Trans.
8. Russian popular song.—Trans.

Chapter 2

Impressions of Port Arthur

The first place I naturally turned to was the viceroy's [1] Naval Office. To begin with, I wanted to find out something of the fate of the *Boyarin*, which was of vital importance to me, and next to obtain some general information. Up to now I had not been able to make anything out of the rumours and gossip.

In the anteroom and the adjoining rooms immense packing-cases stood about. A number of clerks were busy packing them with bundles of official documents and various office utensils. An official superintended.

"What's up? Are you packing up?"

"No; we are just preparing for eventualities—however, pray excuse me." With this the official dashed off and flew at one of the clerks, who had made some small mistake, with obviously artificial anger.

The Chief of the Staff, Rear-Admiral Vityeft, had formerly been my captain for three years. He received me like a brother, embracing and kissing me. Then, however, he hastened to tell me, just as if he wished to stop all questioning, that there were still hopes of saving the *Boyarin*. I was to report myself as soon as possible to the admiral commanding the squadron; there I should receive all directions and orders. Meanwhile, he began to busy himself with all sorts of things. He turned over papers, placed sheets here and there, as much as to hint that he had no time for further conversation, being, in fact, tremendously busy.

Most of the officers of the staff were old comrades of my time in the Pacific Squadron, some even were my "term" as cadets. On leav-

---

1. Admiral Alexeieff, who was also Naval and Military Commander-in-Chief. Admiral Stark commanded the squadron under him.—Trans.

ing Vityeft's room I tried to get at them. As soon as I entered a room, no matter how idle they might have been, they at once sat down at one of the tables, busied themselves with some papers, and only gave utterance to vague phrases. Not that they in any way made themselves important as members of the staff. Nor did they forget old friendships. On the contrary, no sooner had I mentioned that I had been unable to obtain suitable lodgings, than I was deluged with the most friendly invitations. People who had only just pretended to be completely absorbed by the most urgent affairs, now became eager to send off orderlies to collect my luggage scattered over Port Arthur.

On board the *Petropavlovsk*, the flagship, the moral atmosphere was worse; it was depressed. I felt involuntarily "as if a corpse lay in the house."

The flag-lieutenants and other staff officers joyfully shook hands with me. They made endless enquiries about their friends at Cronstadt and St Petersburg, showed immense interest in my journey, but somehow always turned the conversation when I wanted to touch upon the present situation. The chief of the staff was even more busy than Vityeft had been. He took me straight in to the admiral.

Admiral Stark had changed little in the three years since I last saw him. He was still the old seaman; a little more grey than formerly, but his eyes, formerly so friendly and keen, now had something of weariness—a pre-occupied look. His amiable greeting and his orders gave the impression of being merely mechanical—the effect of habit. His thoughts were elsewhere. He hardly heard what I said. It seemed as if some invisible person were talking to him.

"Yes, yes," he said; "there is still hope. Yesterday we sent the captain and seventy men to look for the *Boyarin*. Perhaps—well, tomorrow you might follow with the rest."

I asked permission to start off at once with some vessel, a torpedo boat or tug.

The admiral was on the point of consenting.

"Yes, yes, of course—"

Then he suddenly seemed to remember something, and added in a weary tone:

"After all, no. It is all the same." With that he turned away and left the cabin without taking leave of me.

As soon as I was on shore again I went to the viceroy's house—or, as it is called, "Palace." There I wrote my name in the visitors' book and went home—that is, to the comrade who had invited me. Strictly speaking, I ought to have reported myself to the admiral second-in-command, but decided to put this off to the next day. "Was it not all the same?" My heart was heavy, and I felt the need of being alone.

My host had not yet returned from his work. I took off my uniform, sat down at the window, and looked about. Just in front of me rose up the massive "Golden Hill." It was crowned by the ramparts of our batteries, and over these flew the proud flag of Russia. "Where the Russian flag is once hoisted, it will never be struck," Nicholas I. said when the occupation of the lands of the Ussuri was reported to him. Until yesterday, yes, until this morning, I had believed this. And now, now I dared not answer myself Or still worse—a voice within me gave an answer, which I simply would not believe. To the left, in the east corner of the basin, lay the *Novik* in dry dock. Behind the grey roofs of the workshops and sheds rose a whole forest of slender masts, which belonged to the destroyers, tied up there alongside one another. Through the light haze illumined by the sun appeared the high sides of the *Petropavlovsk* and *Sebastopol*.

Further to the right, in the passage to the outer roads, over the roofs of the torpedo workshops, the masts and funnels of the *Retvisan*, which had grounded there, were visible. Still more to the right, behind the batteries, buildings, and the slip on the Tiger's Tail Peninsula, stood out the silhouettes of the remaining ships of the squadron. They lay there, closely packed together in the small portion of the western basin, where the dredging had just been completed. The sky was still cloudless, the sun as bright as in the morning; the noise and movement in the streets and the harbour had perhaps even increased; but this serene sky did not cheer me. It irritated me, on the contrary, as if it mocked at us. The bright sun by no means beautified the picture. It showed up the dirt in the streets and the rags of the Chinese coolies all the clearer. The sun blinded one; noise and movement only seemed to indicate senseless confusion. Whence this transition?

I was reminded of Andersen's old fairy tale. The fairy Phantasy whispers to the spectator in the theatre: "*See what a wondrous night! See the glorious moonshine—how everything lives in it.*" But the devil Analysis whispers in his other ear: "*That is no night and no moon, it is only painted scenery, behind which the drunken shifter is hiding. The enraptured singer there has only just had a dispute with the director over the increase of her salary.*" In the evening I went to the Casino. Hardly an officer, either of the navy or the army, was to be seen there, only now and then a member of the staff or of the port authorities. Officials and civilians predominated.

The air was full of rumours and tales, each one more improbable than the other. Only one thing was unanimously agreed to. Had the Japanese, (on February 8), sent, not four, but forty destroyers to the attack, and at the same time disembarked a division of troops, the town and the rest of the squadron would have fallen into their hands.

The conversations on this subject affected us all very deeply, but, strange to say, they were carried on in a sort of "academic" tone, as if things which, though important, had no meaning at the moment were being discussed. The chief question was: How will the viceroy get himself out of this difficulty? That he would succeed in doing so no one doubted—quite without irony. But how? By some cunning dodges, or at the cost of someone else—a scapegoat?

"No one can excuse Stark," said an old, hoarse port official, who had evidently drunk too much. "He is certainly a worthy man, but inexcusable. It is a thousand pities. And even now he is doing nothing."

"There you are mistaken," interjected a civilian official at the next table. "It is not so simple a matter as you suppose. Stark has in his pocket a document which makes it certain that he will be completely exonerated. And not only that: it will bring him thanks and reward. We of the staff know that quite well."

"Be quiet," interrupted his neighbour, with a sharp voice. "Stark has the document, not you. This business will run its course all right. No one cares a rap for you."

The civilian official said not another word.

The next morning, February 15, I was already on board the *Petropavlovsk* before the hoisting of the colours. Sad news awaited me. The *Boyarin* had foundered, so I had to look out for another appointment. This was not easy for an officer of my standing, but old friends in the squadron helped me. By chance, a billet was found. The captain of the destroyer *Reshitelny*, Lieutenant K——, was seriously ill, and had asked to be relieved. The correspondence which was necessary to put me into his place would usually have taken up three days. Now the business was settled in a few hours. The admiral had first to receive a report from his staff. Then the viceroy's naval staff had to be asked if anything stood in the way of my nomination. The staff had to submit the matter to His Excellency, and then send a reply. If in the affirmative, this was reported to the admiral, who could then make out my appointment, subject to the subsequent written approval of the viceroy.

All was arranged smoothly. I was my own orderly, and carried the papers from one office to the other.

"My friend, you now have your appointment in your pocket," said my old shipmate, on whom I had quartered myself. "This evening it will appear in the squadron orders, and as to the viceroy's confirmation, you need not bother. He does not concern himself with such trivialities. These he leaves to Vityeft, and he replied that nothing stood in your way. We shall submit to 'H. E.' the appointment already made out, and he will initial it with his green pencil, and that's all."

"A thousand thanks, dear friend, I will stand champagne at dinner today. And now I must go and call on K——. Perhaps he has some public money to hand over to me."

"Shall I invite anyone to dinner?" he called after me.

"Yes, of course."

I found K—— in one of the spare rooms of the casino. He was in bed with high fever, [2] However, he remembered clearly that he had no money on charge.

"We have only just commissioned; that is why there is no money. Provisions and stores must be on board.

You'll find everything in the account books—" He evidently tried to collect his fevered thoughts, but his wife, who was nursing him, gave me such an eloquent look that I quickly ended our service talk, wished him speedy recovery, and left.

At home things looked glorious. My host had prepared a gala dinner.

"The *Reshitelny* is in sight. Make room for the *Reshiteltny*."

"Gentlemen, let us sit down," said my friend. "We won't waste time on compliments, like a pack of young ladies, when fresh caviar and vodka are on the table," and so the meal began.

"I must tell you frankly," joked one of the guests, "that your destroyer is not worth much. She belongs to one of our unfortunate Russian imitations of the *Sokol* type. All the same, one likes what is one's own."

During the noise of the general conversation I told my host the result of my visit to K——.

"Well, thank God! the money is the principal concern. Who is going to bother himself with such trifles as stores? And why? To let it fall into the hands of the Japanese?" The wine seemed to loosen his tongue. He suddenly bent over towards me and rapidly whispered in my ear: "Take over the vessel as soon as possible. That is the main

---

2. He died at Harbin on the way home.

thing. Do it tomorrow. Report that you have found her in proper condition, and that you have assumed command. The matter has been rushed through. Turn it to account. When once an appointment is made it is more difficult to cancel it. Eh? You understand?"

The preceding nights had brought me little sleep. I was therefore sleeping like a corpse, when I suddenly became aware of someone tugging at my shoulder, crying: "Your Honour! Your Honour!"

"What's up?"

"The admiral's office is calling up on the telephone. They seem in a great hurry."

Through the window the day was breaking. It was evidently still very early.

"They are in a hurry—a great hurry," repeated the orderly.

"Hullo! I hear. Who's there?"

"Your appointment came out last night."

"I know—I know."

"Can you take over command at once? Your destroyer is to go out at seven. She is now getting up steam." (I looked at my watch. It was 6.35.) "You are to be at the disposal of the second-in-command. He has hoisted his flag on board the *Amur*, (mine-layer). You will get your orders from him. What shall I report to the chief of the staff? Can you do it?"

I was called upon to go on board a destroyer that I did not yet know—the devil knew what kind of a one!—and be off at once. What nonsense!! Then I suddenly remembered the conversation of the evening before: "Take over the vessel at once. The matter has been rushed through. Turn it to account." Instead of refusing energetically, I shouted into the telephone:

"Of course I can. Report to the admiral that I'm off this minute. Please let the duty steamboat fetch me at the landing-place."

My host had got up also at the ringing of the telephone. With his assistance I threw everything that I needed into the first portmanteau I found, and in a few minutes I was at the landing-place. The servant followed with my gear. Five minutes later I was on board the *Reskitelny*.

The torpedo lieutenant, two sub-lieutenants, and the chief engineer received me. There was no time for ceremonies. I mentioned my name, and went straight to the bridge without going below.

It was seven o'clock. At the signal station on Golden Hill the signal was already flying: "*Reshitelny* proceed out of harbour."

"Thank God!" I thought, and ordered: "Cast off bow hawsers!"

The destroyer was a handy little vessel. Although I did not know her at all, I safely wound my way through the crowd of shipping in the East Basin. Then I ran through the entrance, passed the *Retvisan*, which was surrounded by a lot of vessels rendering assistance, and proceeded with the destroyer *Steregushtchi*, which followed in my wake, to the outer roads. The *Amur*, with a rear-admiral's flag, *Gilyak*, and *Gaidamak*, were awaiting us.

The only order I received from the *Amur* was the signal: "Take station four points on the starboard quarter." And so we shaped our course for Talienwan.

The weather was suspicious and dull. Snowflakes were floating in the air. I sent for the lieutenant, and asked him if there were any deviation tables. He did not know, as he had only come on board yesterday. I then asked the senior sub-lieutenant. He had been on board quite a long time—that is, two whole weeks. He reported that since the last commission no one had touched the compasses. The magnets were in the same places as last year.

"Then our compasses will show us a nice sort of course," I said jokingly. Inwardly, I did not feel at all in a mood to joke. The falling snow might get so thick as to hide the coast from view, and then I was tied to the *Amur* like a blind man to his guide, if I did not know the deviation of the compasses.

Towards ten o'clock we were near the San-chan-tau Islands. These lie at the entrance to Talienwan Bay.

Amur signalled: "Destroyers to search Kerr and Deep Bays." She herself and the other two vessels reduced speed. We had to increase ours. I was the senior. *Steregushtchi* followed me.

This, my first cruise, has remained fixed in my memory.

In such moments a man understands and takes in everything, even insignificant incidents: he arrives instinctively at decisions, and on thinking them over again later, finds that they fulfilled logically the requirements of the moment.

Kerr and Deep Bays were well known to me from former times. I required neither compass nor chart. I only needed to look at the characteristic capes and rocks. Here the enemy might be hiding. I had orders to search the bays. What was I to do if I sighted the enemy? Nothing had been forbidden—therefore I must attack.

"Full speed ahead! Clear for action!" I shouted from the bridge.

The men hurried to their stations.

"You mean to attack if we get the chance, sir?" I heard the torpedo lieutenant ask near me.

"Certainly!"

His eyes brightened up, and I could see how much my decision went to his heart.

"Clear away the horizontal rudders. If we have to deal with destroyers, I intend to fire surface-runners."

"On which side?"

"Just as it may come. Train one tube to starboard, and the other to port. By and by you must keep a sharp look-out."

"Aye, aye, sir."

The engineer came up on the bridge.

"Be ready to work up to full power," I called to him before he had time to ask.

"Are we going to attack?"

"I don't know yet."

We were going 16 knots. Astern the *Steregushtchi* was going so fast that spray and foam were sent high up on her bows.

The dark mass, lightly covered with snow, of the rocky promontory which hid the bay from our view, came nearer and nearer. If there was anyone behind it, we would come as a complete surprise. Perhaps someone was also on the look-out on the other side. How our hearts beat in suspense!

No one there.

Both destroyers steamed through the bay on a curve, went out into the open sea, and searched the next bay in the same way.

Again no one. All our keenness was thrown away.

As soon as I had reported by signal that both bays were clear of the enemy, *Amur* ordered *Gilyak* and *Gaidamak* to stop engines and wait for her, while she went in herself to lay mines. We, the destroyers, were to follow her, slightly on the quarters. We were to fire on and sink any mines which might have been badly placed, and have come to the surface, thus revealing to the enemy the whereabouts of the line of mines. This convoying the mine-layer was very dull work.

When we returned to the place where the two vessels were to wait for us, we did not find them. We steamed backwards and forwards looking for them, but were obliged eventually, as night came on apace, to go into Dalny without them. At Dalny we found the *Vsadnik*. Next morning, on enquiring by telephone, we heard that our two consorts, not being able to find us in the snowstorm, had returned to Port Arthur.

Whether they did so on their own initiative or by superior order, I do not know. I confess that this simple solution of their task did not specially please me. After the sinking of the *Yenissei*, we only possessed one mine-layer, the *Amur*. She had to be preserved. That was why she had been given the two above-mentioned gun-boats and the two destroyers as a protection. And now she had only the two latter with her. Moreover, the *Gilyak*'s 4.7-inch guns were our principal strength.

The *Amur* went into the inner harbour. The destroyers had to watch the northern and southern entrances. It was horrible lying there at anchor. The tide was running either towards the entrance or out of it, keeping the vessel permanently broadside on to the heavy sea running from the southward. I had learnt during my long experience how to wedge myself into a bunk, but now we were rolling so heavily that one could no longer sleep. Perhaps we were thus more useful as guard-ships, but we suffered greatly.

The sad experience of the *Boyarin* was, as it seemed, not in vain. Orders were given to lay out the mines in Talienwan Bay strictly according to plan.[3] The next morning the harbour boats began the preparatory work of placing beacons. These were carefully charted and the mines were laid between them.

On February 18 an incident occurred, trivial in itself, but which irritated me greatly.

I had gone alongside the *Amur* to coal. When nearly finished, the admiral sent for me.

"Can you start at once?"

"Yes, sir,"

"The boats are coming back for some reason or other. They have orders to return if they see anything suspicious. Go and see what is the matter. If there is nothing, let them continue their work."

"Aye, aye, sir."

A few seconds later my vessel was steaming out of the harbour towards the boats which were slowly returning.

When alongside of them, we stopped.

"What's up?"

"A Japanese torpedo-boat appears to be in sight to seaward."

"How many?"

"One."

"A large one?"

"We could not make out: she is too far off."

---

3. The *Boyarin* had struck one of the Russian mines.—Trans.

It was evident that they had either been mistaken, or sighted something else. The weather was clear, without fog or snow. What should a single hostile torpedo-boat be doing here in these circumstances in broad daylight? If, however, one had gone astray by accident—so much the worse for her. I did not hesitate for a moment.

"Return to your work. I'll drive off the enemy."

The clumsy steamboats, with the row boats in tow, turned slowly. Meanwhile, the *Reshitelny* hurried towards the passage between the San-chan-tau Islands, against the spray of a very high but short sea.

Again "Clear for action!" Once more officers and men hurried to their stations in cheerful excitement.

We reached the open sea. The horizon was perfectly clear. We could see 10 miles, and there was nothing in sight but a Chinese *junk*. Her square sail, which was foreshortened, might at a distance have been taken for a funnel. The old seaman at the helm could not suppress a confidential remark: "Your Honour has no luck," he said; "this is the second time."

"Perhaps there is another one, and she is only hiding behind a point," mumbled the sub-lieutenant at the engine-room telegraph.

I did not think this likely, but the two remarks appeared to be the *vox populi*—that is, of the crew. I should have considered it a great mistake not to encourage this ardour for the fray.

"Well, we'll have a look. Perhaps he'll come out. He shan't hide from us. Full speed ahead! "

The engine-room telegraphs rang out. We ran up to one point, then another, but no sign of anything.

"They dare not face the daylight. We have been kicking about three days and have met no one," some voices amongst the crew were heard to say:

"We've got no luck at all," complained the sub-lieutenant.

We re-entered the harbour of Dalny to report to the admiral. On the way we were met by the *Vsadnik*.

"Remain under weigh near the entrance and protect the boats," she signalled.

We turned, and rolled about in the swell all day. When I got back to my billet in the evening I went on board the *Amur* to make my report. The admiral received me very curtly. After he had heard my report he said:

"You only had orders to enquire, look around, and report, and not to embark upon adventures."

"But, Your Excellency, on the information which reached me, I considered myself justified in taking action."

"You had no right to risk your destroyer. You are bound not to endanger the safety of the vessel entrusted to your care."

"What!" I thought; "not to risk anything? Warfare surely means permanent risk to men and ships. Every torpedo-boat attack is a desperate venture, even in the most favourable conditions, if looked upon from the point of view of praiseworthy caution. Not to endanger one's vessel? Why, we do that even in time of peace, so as to be ready for war. If we are to guard our vessels from a meeting with the enemy we had better hide them in some inaccessible harbour. But then, in the devil's name, what is the fleet there for?"

"*Risk nothing!*"—that was the maxim to which they clung, Alexeieff at sea, Kuropatkin on land.

How often, in the course of the war, have I had to think of this maxim with bitter anger? Later on we were forced to risk something. Meanwhile, we had had a whole string of failures, had indeed thrown away a great part of our fighting strength, and had allowed the first enthusiasm of our men to evaporate. Mukden and Tsu-Shima are the consequences of this maxim.

Then, of course, I could not guess how the war would end, but it must be owned quite honestly: in my diary it is clearly indicated, that inwardly I grumbled quite as much as so many around me did aloud, although I had, outwardly, to "bring them up" as in duty bound.

When I returned on board, I of course did not mention a word of my conversation with the admiral. Zeal, love of fighting, spirit of enterprise, I considered the foundation of success, especially in a destroyer. These happened to be present in my officers and men in a specially high degree. According to my view, it would have been criminal to kill these qualities by telling the men that we were to "risk nothing" (that is, that there was to be no hostile meeting), and that we were not allowed to "expose the vessel confided to us to any danger" (that is, to the enemy's projectiles).

On February 20 our labours were at an end, and we returned to Port Arthur. The whole time we had seen no Japanese, but we had suffered a good deal under the constant changes of weather. On some days the thermometer stood at 37° and 38° F., in spite of the wind, on others it went down, in calm weather, to 20°. Then the harbour was covered in a few hours with a crust of ice, which, however, remained so thin as to form no obstacle or danger even to a destroyer.

In those days our mines developed a very unpleasant quality. They had been tested in protected ports, such as Transund in the Baltic and Tendra Bay in the Black Sea. There they thoroughly answered all requirements. But here they lay in bays subject to both the rollers of the open sea and tidal streams. A small error in construction made them here dangerous alike to friend and foe. The steel wire mooring rope, which joins the mine to its anchor, and is intended to secure the mine in place, is rove through a small hole in one part of the anchor. These holes are made by machinery in all the anchors, and no one remembered that they had sharp edges. In a seaway, however, and in alternating currents, the mine moved, and with it the mooring rope. The latter became gradually worn through, and the loaded mine, fitted to explode at the slightest touch, drifted about at sea.

Once such a mine drifted up in front of the hut of a Chinese fisherman built on the edge of the water. The mine bumped on the rocks of the coast, and nothing remained of the hut and all it contained. Another floated in a calm up on to a flat beach and was left high and dry by the receding tide. A military patrol discovered it and decided to remove it. When the men began to drag it away, the mine naturally exploded, and of the twelve men of the patrol only one escaped by a miracle, and was able to report the circumstance. Of course, we were constantly exposed, as were the Japanese, to the danger of hitting one of these mines drifting about at sea.

As we left Talienwan we saw two of them, and had to destroy them.

At Port Arthur, a heavy blow awaited me.

I had just secured abreast of the coal shed and begun coaling, when an officer arrived alongside in the duty steamboat and informed me that, by order of the Viceroy, he had been appointed to the command of the *Reshitelny*. At the same time I had been appointed second-in-command of the *Angara*.

"The destroyer is, I suppose, to have some rest now?" asked the new captain without leaving his boat.

"What? Rest? She is to fill up with coal, then go to the dockyard to make good some defects developed during the night (they are in the engine-room), and to have steam up by 8 a.m. tomorrow to go out into the roads—kindly take over the command."

The "novice" at once altered his tone. He came up on deck, and began to shake me warmly by the hand.

"You don't say so. I never expected *that*. I'm in no way prepared.

Pray do me the kindness to take the vessel to the dockyard after coaling. This is the first time I have been on board of her, and I can't be expected to take her through this mass of shipping at dusk, or even at night."

I was so stunned by this naive remark that I answered mechanically.

"Very well. Be off. I'll do it."

The steamboat departed in haste.

When I had secured the *Reshitelny* alongside the other destroyers at the slip, and was preparing to leave her, it was already pretty dark. I had not much to pack—a handbag—all my other gear had remained in the house of my friend, whom I had to leave so hurriedly. As it was so late I intended sleeping again at his lodgings and starting on my new duties in the morning.

In the cabin the officers were assembled to say goodbye, as is customary. They clinked their glasses with mine and emptied them, but their good wishes were somewhat vague. It seemed that in the short space of only five days we had become good friends. The parting was not easy; I had to end it quickly.

"Gentlemen," I said, "I have only been your captain a very short time, but I thank you for your services. Everything was excellent. One must not quarrel with one's fate. I shall now rust away on board a transport. But for you I wish that on the first coloured chocolate box pictures that are made during the war, the photograph of the *Reshitelny* may appear."

"Many thanks. We will do our part. But what do you say? You are ordered to a transport?"

I hurried on deck. By contrast with the bright light in the mess it seemed doubly dark. (As it was war time we were not allowed to show any lights on deck.) Only the messenger showed the way to the gangway with a shaded lantern.

"And the men?" asked the lieutenant, who had seized my hand just as I was about to step into the boat.

When I turned round I had already got accustomed to the darkness, and saw that rows of men were standing along the ship's side.

"Why this parade? Surely this is not necessary. It is night, the men must sleep."

"I have not ordered it. They have come of their own accord to say goodbye."

I took a few steps along the front.

"Thanks for your services, my brave lads. God grant that you and your destroyer may soon meet the enemy and give you glory in the fight. Goodbye."

"Respectful thanks," [4] sounded back from the ranks, somewhat confusedly, but so heartily—I was glad it was dark.

The customary embrace of the boatswain's mate, a last grip of the hand with the officers, a few strokes of the oars, and everything seemed far, far behind me.

"What has happened? Why have I been superseded?" I shouted to my friend of the staff. "Surely you told me that all was in order."

"Yes, but—"

"No; you listen first. I have given up my good billet at home for the sake of the war. If I had wanted to join a transport, one starting from Cronstadt would have done as well. The transports at Cronstadt are just as fine as those at Port Arthur. I have not come out here for that sort of thing. In time of peace I have always served in fighting ships, and now in time of war I am to join a transport. What is the meaning of it? Couldn't a worse man be found for the *Angara*? Such a post is hardly a coveted one, I should think."

"Peace! Curse as you like, it remains as it is. Everything was in order, as I told you. When the draft appointment was submitted, it was, as usual, a mere formality. Then he suddenly struck out your name with his green pencil. 'The other is senior,' 'He' said. Vityeft tried to stand up for you, and asked where you were to go. You had been sent out as a second-in-command. 'To the *Angara*,' was the reply. He at once wrote it in himself. He forgets nothing."

That night I did not sleep well, hardly at all.

My want of seniority was evidently a mere pretext. Amongst the destroyer captains were many who were considerably my juniors. But what was the real cause? Did "he" now, in his present position and in time of war, bethink himself of an old story? Years ago a certain lieutenant had declined to blow "his" trumpet. That young officer had told "his" A.D.C. that his pen was as little for sale as his sword. If he were even base enough not to forget such like personal affairs in times of peace, now we had war, and in the face of this all else must give way. Honour, duty, conscience demanded this.

"It can't be," I thought, and threw myself about in my bed. "We are now at war—a real war, not merely Chinese riots. In war one lets volunteers fight in the front rank."

---

4. When superiors address their men they are taught to answer thus in unison.—Trans.

I involuntarily thought with bitter wrath of an anecdote which is told of one of our best known admirals. He was once second-in-command to a very autocratic captain. On the latter saying: "While you are serving me, you must do this differently," he replied: "I am not serving you, but *with* you I serve His Majesty the *Tsar*. You are not rich enough to keep me in your service."

In Port Arthur at the time of the viceroyalty such views would have been considered rank heresy.

When the day broke, I was already up, and no sooner were the viceroy's offices open, than I was there.

Admiral Vityeft received me at once, but seemed still more busy than at my first interview.

"It is not right of you to be so excited about the *Angara*" he tried to calm me. "She is by no means a transport, but already attached to the cruiser division. Perhaps she will be told off to most important duties. The vessel has only just been taken over from the Volunteer Fleet and has a somewhat mixed crew. We count on you to put things right there. Very responsible and difficult duties await her executive officer."

"If the service is so honourable, you will easily find candidates, who are older and worthier than I. I don't aspire to this at all. I was appointed second-in-command of the *Boyarin*. She has gone down, and it would be absurd for me to demand to be appointed to another ship in a like capacity. I don't think of it. But I merely ask to be sent to a fighting ship. That is what I have come for. You know me. I am an old navigator and know every spot hereabouts. Can't I become navigating officer, or even watch-keeper? I shall be content with anything."

The admiral had never been a good diplomatist, and now ceased acting. He leaned over the table and raised his arms in a helpless attitude.

"What can *I* do? Just consider: he wrote it *with his own hand*, and with his *green pencil*."

What I thought when I left the office I would rather not say.

At the door I was stopped by one of my old friends. "Makaroff is appointed to the command of the Pacific Fleet," he whispered in my ear.

"What! And what about you people?"

"We depart—are you satisfied? Now you won't remain long in the *Angara*. But say nothing of this. It is still a secret."

I squeezed his hand in my joy, and began my new duties with a lightened heart.

CHAPTER 3

Personal Observations

On board the *Angara* I found myself for the first time associated with men who had witnessed the catastrophe of February 8,[1] and the action of the 9th. As I became their messmate and was no longer a stranger asking information of strangers, I learned full particulars.

Here I must make a small digression. I do not intend to give a history of the war in this book. The history of the war can only be written when the archives which are now closed, are opened, and their secret reports and documents are made accessible to the public. Until then we must content ourselves with published reports and private sources of information. In the former much has, of course, been left out or cut out, as the circumstances demanded. One of the most reliable private sources of information is, I believe, my diary. I kept it from January 29, 1904, the day of my departure from St Petersburg, until my return there on December 19, 1905.

The entries consist not only of all events which I witnessed myself, but also of accounts of eyewitnesses, who were still fresh under the impression of the events. In it I have not merely confined myself to facts. Above all, it appeared important to observe the mental attitude of the men who had taken part in these events. Here, in this book, I will, as well as I am able, describe, with photographic accuracy, the feelings which we experienced. I will tell of the hopes, the doubts, and the disappointments which we had to experience in the course of events.

The impressions which I had received during my first days at Port Arthur were most strange. It seemed as if the dangers amidst which we lived did not affect public opinion to any great extent. I noticed that

---

1. The torpedo attack which began the war.—Trans.

everyone was dreading something, but not disaster for the squadron or fortress. There was also no question of personal dread of danger, but people seemed concerned at perhaps being made to suffer owing to the Government getting into an unpleasant position.

"How is the affair going to end?" "Who will be picked out as the culprit?" "Am I also going to be dragged into this dirty business?" Questions such as these seemed to perplex every one high and low.

I must here observe that the population of Port Arthur consisted almost exclusively of State employees, or such as were closely connected with the government. The weal or woe of these people naturally depended entirely on how matters stood with the government. That was why I had never been able to obtain from any one detailed answers, when I enquired for particulars or even the causes of the first catastrophe. All remained silent, or said that they knew nothing, or they suddenly remembered most pressing business which obliged them to break off the conversation. If they were to give an account, they would have to take sides, and that was "very dangerous."

Everyone knew, apparently from the experience of previous years, that a bold word, an independent opinion, immediately reached a certain destination by mysterious paths, and that the rash individual, who often did not even know what he was accused of, suddenly felt the punishing hand. It would be false to affirm that this state of mind was produced by an iron discipline. Discipline is the conscious and voluntary submission to law. Discipline obtains, where old and young obey, not from fear, but for the sake of conscience. At Port Arthur, one saw only fear, pale-faced fear of the almighty, irresponsible government.

Tongues were at once loosened, when the news of Makaroff's appointment reached the town. Notwithstanding all efforts, it could not be kept secret. Now it was quite evident what discipline is worth, if based on fear. I could surely not be counted amongst the adherents of the viceroy; but even I found more than once the language of these very gentlemen, who only yesterday were "his most devoted," rather too strong.

To me the Pacific Squadron does not merely mean a collection of ships. I had spent almost my entire sea service in it, and for me it was a living thing, permeated with a single-minded spirit. With it I had grown up, and it was dear to me. On my journey here I felt as if I was going home. I had already served in this squadron when it was at its beginnings. During my last five years of service there, I witnessed its apogee under Dubassoff and Hildebrand. Its gradual decline I was not called upon to see. I was only a witness of its end.

"How could such great changes have taken place during the three years of my absence?" I asked myself. "How could this great organisation fall into such a state of decomposition?"

At Cronstadt I had, of course, heard of the institution of the "Armed Reserve of the Pacific." I knew that the votes for keeping ships in commission had been cut down, and that the ships in reserve had only twenty days at sea in the year. The rest of the time they were floating barracks. Finally, I was aware of the constant changes amongst the officers. All the same, I had preserved my faith in the "squadron."

I thought this would all pass away. Owing to unfavourable conditions, some defects had cropped up, but one needed only to alter these conditions to put everything once more to rights. Now in war, I thought, those gentlemen who had played with their duties would disappear, and the old officers would once more join "their" ships. The grand old life in the squadron was then bound to arise anew.

I well remembered how we had idolised "our ship "in the squadron. I had known an officer who had had already three years' service as lieutenant and who still did duty as "second watch-keeper," [2] as he had not been relieved. When he had to move up as "first watch-keeper," he protested, as it would mean leaving "his *Nakhimoff*." Another lieutenant, with fifteen years' service as a commissioned officer, was nominated as "Senior Gunnery Lieutenant" [3] of a battleship in home waters. When, however, he heard that "his *Donskoi*" which had only just returned from the Far East, was to go out again, he entreated his superiors to send him back to her. In the end he was made happy by becoming once more watch-keeper on board "his" old cruiser.[4] I could produce such examples in large numbers, but I fancy these will suffice. The fiery youths were formerly ever ready to demand satisfaction, sword in hand, for any insult offered to "their" ship. The men had recourse to the simpler method. They fought, when they met on shore, and thus settled the question as to which was the best ship.

Let not the reader imagine that this was in any way a bad sign. By no means. If the good elements held these views, they arose from the conviction that their ship was bound to be the best, provided each one threw his whole strength and energy into the service of "his" ship. At

---

2. Presumably under another lieutenant.—Trans.
3. There are two in big ships.—Trans.
4. Gunnery lieutenants occupy a more important position on board than the watch-keepers, irrespective of seniority.—Trans.

every evolution, every exercise, hundreds of jealous eyes watched the other ships. Woe betide the ship which these strict and experienced judges found out in the attempt to cheat. This emulation between ships was of great benefit to the squadron. Each ship did her utmost to prove herself the best of the company. A man was just as proud of his squadron as of his ship. Everything that took place in other waters was closely followed. We wanted to beat all other squadrons.

When I had been three years navigating officer of the *Dmitri Donskoi*, Admiral Dubassoff sent to ask me whether I would like to join his staff as senior flag-lieutenant. The question found me quite unprepared. It so upset me that I asked for twenty-four hours to consider the matter. Back on board, I consulted the captain, the commander, and another old messmate, whether I might leave the ship without committing treason. After lengthy discussions, we came to the conclusion that I was not bound to refuse. After all, I was *not* to take up a higher appointment on board another ship—that would have been treason towards the old *Donskoi*—but was in future to serve the squadron as a whole. Our *Donskoi*, it was felt, was certainly the best ship of the entire squadron, but still only one amongst many.

I had thought of all this, and preserved my faith in the "squadron." I believed its old spirit was still alive. I did not know all that had happened out there at the foot of Golden Hill in Port Arthur to kill this spirit, during the three years I had spent at Cronstadt. If a captain loves his ship truly, he must not neglect to attend to the smallest defect in her. He must report it, and see that it is made good. In time a small defect may become the cause of a very big one. But if a captain at Port Arthur did his duty in that manner, he was an "inconvenient subordinate." The viceroy desired, as long as he reigned, to see no other reports than those in which it was stated that "everything was in the best condition." Then he was able to report most respectfully that "the fleet confided to his care was completely prepared for war, and would valorously repel every attack of the enemy."

Were we serving the viceroy and not His Majesty? Were we not merely subordinated to His Excellency, but subjects of the emperor alone? Are not, in the eyes of the "Supreme War Lord,"[5] the youngest bluejacket and the commander of a squadron equally the servants of the Crown and country—quite independently of their relative position? Anyone who dared to hold such views as these was looked at askance in Port Arthur.

---
5. The sovereign, as the head of the army and navy.—Trans.

In justice to the viceroy it must be admitted that whatever he wanted he carried through. In his immediate surroundings he soon had only his own creatures. He cared nothing for the "common herd." These did not require to be handled with gloves. But in the body of officers every feeling of cohesion and solidarity was stifled by constantly moving them from ship to ship. If an officer duly subordinated himself to the authorities, he could serve in a harbour craft and yet advance more rapidly than another who was wearing himself out in doing his duty with the utmost zeal on board a fighting ship.

When I reached Port Arthur the second time, one never heard, either at the Casino or on board ship, the beautiful old terms "our ship," "our squadron." All interest was centred on "getting on" quickly. A man would say: "So-and-so was in luck!" and speculate as to places with higher emoluments, or where he would be more immediately under the eye of the authorities. Sometimes, indeed, I heard that someone was proud of belonging to the garrison of Port Arthur. But in the mouth of a naval officer this did not sound well. Makaroff once said: "A naval officer should only feel at home on board." The turning of ships into floating barracks has produced fine fruits.

I was horrified at all this. It was hateful to see this collapse of the personnel of our squadron. Only in a very few ships some remnants of the old traditions had been preserved. Still, I stuck to my hopes, and perhaps I was not wrong. The outer pressure need only be removed to awaken the spirit of the squadron out of its sleep of the last three years. The flame was glowing under the ashes. There were indications of this. "Above," the stillness of the grave was still preserved. The office work went on in the old style, as if nothing had happened; but the joyful news already flew through the ranks—Makaroff had started from St Petersburg. I now resume my narrative.

The truth of the rumours I had already heard at Harbin interested me, of course, most. They were probably being disseminated all over Russia by now, through the fugitives. "Is it true," I asked, "that the squadron was guilty of absolutely incomprehensible carelessness? Was it, in fact, lying at anchor in an open roadstead with all lights burning, without steam, without torpedo-nets being out and without any guard vessels? Is it a fact that at the moment of the attack not only many officers and captains, but the admiral himself, were ashore to celebrate the latter's birthday?"

This conversation took place on board the *Angara* with one of my new messmates.

"We of the *Angara* are certainly in a position to form an unbiased judgment," he said. "We only joined the squadron quite a short time ago, and are not bound to it either by tradition or common service. We could indeed consider ourselves slighted, as we are not serving in a man-of-war, but in an armed merchantman. Therefore to reply without reserve: the first part of your question is bitter truth. The only excuse one can find is that the squadron is not to blame for this criminal carelessness, which you mildly call incomprehensible. The second part is gossip, which has been launched into the world with the very evident intention of burdening Admiral Stark with the entire responsibility. This was bound to happen at the outset. When the first staggering news flew through the town and fortress, one heard the ugly word 'treason,' on all sides. Thank God it was never uttered aloud! It might have been awful.

"The old gentleman was passing through a bad time, but he was equal to it. He resisted the temptation to defend himself publicly against all the accusations which were hurled at him. So he kept his famous document in his pocket, and only reminded certain persons of the existence of the paper. The 'brave' calumniators at once became dumb. They had probably received orders to hold their tongues. In this attitude of Stark's there is something of the old Roman, is there not? *Pereat mea gloria, vivat patria.* However, my Latin is weak; but judge for yourself. If he had then said: ' I did not receive permission to prepare against an attack—here is the proof,' not a stone of the Viceroy's palace would have been left standing by next morning."

"So that the second part of my question is untrue?"

My messmate shrugged his shoulders.

"From the moment that the whole squadron was assembled in the roads, orders were given that the entire personnel was to be on board from sunset (about 5 p.m.) until next morning. Communication with the shore during that time was prohibited. This was the only measure of safety the Admiral commanding the squadron was able to take on his own responsibility and without the viceroy's permission. This order was strictly carried out, especially on February 8. Had we not seen the steamer with which the Japanese Consul from Cheefoo took away the Japanese subjects from Port Arthur? She anchored almost in the centre of the squadron and hurried away before dark. It was quite evident to every one that this meant war. Or do you imagine that we had not understood such a sign? Would every ship have been at 'man-and-arm ship' stations? Should we have got off so cheaply after all, if the entire squadron had not been warned?"

When I had this conversation, it had already come to our knowledge by private, but perfectly reliable, information from Cheefoo, that, in addition to the consul, a Japanese naval agent had been on board the steamer which called at Port Arthur on February 8. This agent had been living for some years at Cheefoo. At that time he was, of course, on board the steamer "unofficially," and is said to have landed at Port Arthur disguised as the consul's servant. The steamer had ample time, whilst she was at anchor in the roads, to mark the berths of our ships on her chart. At sea she met at a rendezvous the Japanese Squadron, and transferred the pseudo-servant with all his news.

"For the night of February 8-9, an exercise at repelling a torpedo attack had been ordered. Four of our destroyers had gone to sea for this purpose. This circumstance assisted the Japanese greatly.

"I don't know who had ordered this ill-fated exercise. At any rate it was put off, and the destroyers had received orders to go to Dalny. This alteration in the programme was not communicated to the squadron. When, therefore, about 11 p.m., torpedo-boats were sighted to seaward showing lights, they were naturally taken for ours. It is even maintained that one of the boats signalled the name *Steregushtchi* quite correctly. Now that was precisely the name of one of the destroyers which had gone out. This story, however, does not sound very credible. At any rate it was only the exploding torpedoes and the bugle calls on board the torpedoed ships that showed everyone what these boats really were."

"Did we have steam up? Were the torpedo-nets out? Were all lights out? Was there no service of guard and look-out vessels?"

"What are you talking about? Don't you know that the admiral could not order these things off his own bat, but that the Viceroy's approval was necessary?"

"Then, why was this not obtained?"

"Not obtained? How often was it not asked for? When verbal discussions produced no results, the admiral submitted a written request. On this document is written with the green pencil: 'No; not yet.' Now various explanations are put forward. It is said that it was feared lest our warlike measures should be taken as a provocation and hasten the rupture. Others say that on the 9th the recall of the minister and the solemn declaration of war with Divine Service, parade, and public proclamation were to have taken place. Unfortunately, the Japanese were one day in advance."

"What was the impression produced by the attack? What influence did it have on the spirit of the squadron?"

"The impression was, of course, depressing, but there was no sign of panic. You know that we beat off all subsequent attacks. How heavy were the losses and damages did not become known at once. The *Retvisan*'s bows went down a little and the *Pallada's* stern. The night was so dark that we did not notice this. But it was an unpleasant moment when the *Tsesarevitch* went into harbour, heeling 18°. We thought she would capsize. And the general feeling? Well, the first attack was over and the Japanese had retired. We had just ceased fire, when our good-natured, fat, little friend S—— turned towards Golden Hill, with clenched fists. Tears of rage stood in his eyes, and with a choking voice he cried: "Did they expect this, these infallible, high and mighty gentlemen, these. . . . ?" (His words cannot be repeated.) Most people thought the same."

"And what happened on the 9th?"

"Nothing very much. After the attack, we, of course, all got up steam without signal. The damaged ships at once went up harbour. But their leaks made them steer badly, and not one reached the place it intended to. All three piled up side by side on the bank off Tiger's Tail Peninsula, just under the lighthouse. Next day the *Tsesarevitch* and *Pallada* were towed off and brought in, but the *Retvisan* is still hard and fast. She has a hole in her bows. There the water is pouring in, and slowly but surely spreading all over the ship through the ventilating shafts. The *Retvisan* has a special system of ventilation, approved by our technical committee. The shafts have specially constructed spherical self-closing valves, which the inrush of water flattened out. It is therefore impossible to isolate the damaged compartment. Until the leak is provisionally stopped, we must thank God that the ship is aground.

"We were lying there early on the 9th with steam ready. When the torpedo attacks had ceased, our cruisers were sent out to scout even before daybreak. The *Boyarin* came back first and signalled: 'Hostile vessels in sight and approaching.' A little later the *Askold*, which was already in action, with the Japanese cruisers chasing her, closed and reported: 'The enemy's main body is approaching.' We lay at anchor in three columns, our *Angara* being the easternmost ship of the southern line, in a very exposed position. Soon we required no signals. We saw with our own eyes the entire Japanese fleet appear above the horizon, and yet we remained lying there. The admiral had been sent for by the viceroy in the morning to receive instructions, and had not yet returned. We did not know that then. You may imagine what we went through."

"Were no reports sent in?"

"What? Hah! hah!" My friend laughed bitterly. "Don't you know that Golden Hill can take in all signals first, as it can see much further than the ships in the roads? The signal station is in direct telephonic communication with the viceroy's palace. Presumably, he said: 'No; not yet,' and continued the discussion. Anyway, how can we know what went on there? When the chief of the staff saw that the enemy would soon be within range, he signalled: 'Weigh and form single line ahead.' He did not wait for the admiral, and when the latter came out at last he had to follow in his steam barge. He boarded the flagship after she had already begun to go ahead. We had no regular battle. We only exchanged shots for a while with the enemy. They fired well. Their first two shells fell close to the flagship. They also fired at Electric Hill, where the 10-inch battery had been cleared away. The latter, with its high site and position finders, had the advantage, and seemed to make good practice. The enemy fired for forty minutes, and then steamed away. Our spirits rose. Then the signal was made to chase. The *Askold* and *Novik*, our two fastest ships, were already after the enemy, when Golden Hill suddenly hoisted flag F ('Negative the last signal'). They had to return, and we steamed up harbour in order of fleet numbers. And here we are still."

I could hardly take all this in.

"The *Angara* also took part in the action. Owing to the great distance, she can hardly have caused the enemy any damage with her 4.7 guns. She herself suffered a good deal. There were dead and wounded on board here. We had a critical moment when the rudder chains were shot through. For a while we had to steer with the screws. The port boats were mostly destroyed, and our funnels and ventilators riddled. This all came from projectiles which burst in the water close to the ship. The only shell which struck the steamer direct—it was, moreover, a 12-inch shell—fortunately did not burst. It passed through the ship's side, the deck, several bulkheads, and ended in a first-class cabin. Here it destroyed a bunk, on the spring mattress of which it came peacefully to rest. It sounds like a made-up story, but it is true all the same."

I don't quite believe in these promised cruiser services of the *Angara*. Why, even the real cruisers had nothing to do. The maxim: "Not to expose ships to any danger, not to risk anything," with which I had already become personally acquainted, was no independent *dictum* of the rear-admiral second in command. Probably he had instructions from above. Of course, I kept my pessimistic thoughts to myself. Not only did I not communicate them to any one, but I even tried to raise the spirits of the crew. My object was to make all work hand in hand in preparing the *Angara* for her future activity. Work there was in plenty.

The *Angara* (ex-*Moskva*) was one of the best steamers of the Volunteer Fleet. The Admiralty had only taken her over when the war broke out. She had received an armament of six 4.7-inch and eight 6-pounder Q. F. guns, filled her holds with coal, and drawn a few men from different ships, which were added to her crew. That completed the auxiliary cruiser.

The whole internal organisation, including the Watch and Quarter Bills, which give each man his place and his duties under various conditions, was in a rudimentary state. I had to attempt, besides, to give, with such means as were at hand, some kind of protection, if only against splinters, to the vitals of the ship, such as, for instance, steering-gear, the main engines, the pipes of the fire service, etc. The chief thing was to reduce to the smallest minimum all the woodwork and other inflammable material on board. The *Angara*, that is, the *Moskva*, had on board the entire luxurious fittings of a passenger steamer, which could easily produce a regular bonfire. It was lucky that the 12-inch shell of February 9 did not burst, when it embedded itself in a first-class cabin. Everything would have been alight there at once.

In these endeavours I met with the unexpected, though quite formal, opposition of the captain. He maintained that the viceroy must first be asked. A few days before hostilities broke out His Excellency had visited the *Angara* and given an order that the auxiliary cruiser was at the same time to serve as his yacht. Should he be forced at any time to make a journey by sea, he would embark in her with all his staff. It must be noted that the viceroy's staff in time of war numbered ninety-three persons (admirals, generals, superior officers of both services, and civilian officials). The *Angara* was indeed the ship best fitted to receive him. At first we were even to lock up all the first-class passenger accommodation, and not touch it, without orders. The captain and officers were to occupy the modest accommodation set apart for the steamer's own officers.

When it was found that these spaces were all required for the warrant officers, offices and issue rooms, the captain and officers were permitted the use of certain first-class cabins. But this was not conceded without the condition that nothing was to be spoilt.

"What is the meaning of this condition?" growled some of us. "Do they think we have never travelled first class? Are they afraid that we shall smash the looking-glasses and ruin the furniture?"

When I had the doors of the saloons on the promenade deck and of the luxurious special cabins opened, I was amazed: these spaces were crammed with armchairs, small chairs, couches, tables large and small, and piles of carpets and curtains.

"How is such a thing possible? Why, here are bonfires ready laid."

"This is according to my orders," explained the purser, who accompanied me. "Everything is to be ready in case the viceroy and his staff embark."

It recalled my schoolboy days and Ilowaiski's book of history. On the battlefield of Marathon were found the chains with which Xerxes, the ruler of Persia, had intended binding his Greek prisoners.

We also had a certain amount of work in which the assistance of the dockyard was necessary. As regards the latter, every supporter of time-honoured red-tape habits would have been beside himself with joy if he had seen the calm of the dockyard routine. It was as if the war did not concern the dockyard. When a captain sent in a defect list of the most urgent and important kind, it still took, as formerly, from seven to ten days before all formalities had been complied with. One might have thought that it was not a case of war between Russia and Japan, but that two South American Republics were at loggerheads.

There existed certainly one way of eliminating these delays, which were caused by adhering to the regulations. It was freely used in time of peace, and was not at all a creation of the war. One had only to address oneself to an old acquaintance. I was already serving in the squadron when Port Arthur was first occupied, and had witnessed the founding of the town and port. In consequence, I was enabled to render the *Angara* many a small service by the above method, when the chief engineer, the gunnery lieutenant, or the paymaster made urgent requests. On one occasion I had been running about in the steamer from 5 a.m. (I always get up with the ship's company) until noon, and I was footsore and weary. After lunch I was just going to lie down, so as to get some rest during the men's dinner hour (until 2 p.m.), when the chief engineer entered.

"What is it?"

"Oh, I beg your pardon if I disturb you, but you are yourself so anxious that these holes in the watertight bulkheads should be made tight. It must absolutely be done. My defect list has been in three days, and nothing is done. Now X—— is an old friend of yours. The work is in his department. Won't you say a word to him personally? I don't ask for myself."

My chance of a rest was gone, but, heartily wishing everything and everybody to the devil (for the good old engineer knew this was not personal), I started off.

Two or three words sufficed to settle everything. Whilst orderlies and messengers with the necessary orders rushed off, I sat down at my friend's table so as to get at least that amount of rest, and lit a cigarette. I could not help asking him a few questions.

"Is there no such thing as a war routine in your department? Why does everything still go on in the old red-tape fashion?"

"My dear fellow—no blasphemy—let heaven and earth perish, if only our accounts remain."

"Oh, bosh! If a 12-inch shell were to burst in your shop there would be nothing left of it."

"Quite so. There is no better voucher than the hole made by a 12-inch shell. Up to now, however, we have not had one. Consequently, the regulations must be complied with."

"But this moment you have given directions, without anything in writing."

"That is quite a different thing; I did it to please you. You have given me reasons, and I believe you. I see that in this case I shall eventually get something in writing. I am as certain of it as if I already had it in my pocket. If it were not for that, I should never do such a thing."

"That means that if it had not been *me* you would not have done anything?"

"Unless the defect list had followed its proper course, no."

I got quite excited. "But if the war makes it imperative?" I cried.

"The course which urgent defect lists have to go is clearly laid down."

"You are joking."

"Not at all. Anyway, don't excite yourself; it is very bad for your health. I'll give you an example. Stark was nearly tried by court-martial. However, it ended all well for him. Why? Because he had something in black on white. You know that he sent in a report to the effect that he considered certain precautions to be necessary. It is said that on February 8 he went to the viceroy's naval office and asked about his report. He was told that on it was noted the decision: 'No; not yet.' He took it away with him. If anyone were to say to him afterwards: 'You ought to have done something,' he could answer: 'I could not; it was prohibited.' At that time no one noticed this, and when the sad business occurred they wanted to put all the blame on him. He, however, tapped his pocket and only said: 'If you like I can show this paper to everybody.' No, my boy. What is written is sacred. If you possess something in black on white, you stand there as pure as snow. In the other case it will go hard with you, as with the Swedes at Poltava."[6]

"How cynical! And what does your conscience, your sense of duty, tell you? It is sad to have to hear such things."

"Why, you are as innocent as the well-known boy who was old and big and still believed that papa and mamma found their children in the garden under the cabbage leaves, or that the stork brought them in neat little baskets. Well, *au revoir*. If you again want anything, come straight to me."

On February 22 the repairs of the *Novik* were completed. She came out of dock and the *Pallada* went in. When the torpedo exploded some very interesting observations were made on board. The doctors said that the men in the adjacent compartments, into which the gases penetrated, were poisoned. But the symptoms of poisoning only made their appearance the next day. When the men affected went to the Sick Bay they complained of having caught a chill. They said: "I have pains in my chest," or "I have got such a cold that I can't breathe." It was a fact that they had inflamed *conjunctivae* and *bronchi*. One of the young doctors called the complaint concisely "Something like *glanders*." Of nine men four men died, and in great agony. It was clear that in the torpedo heads there was no *pyroxiline*, but some new explosive, melinite, lyddite, *shimose*—or heaven knows what.

"Therefore bear in mind, gentlemen," dogmatised our very youthful disciple of Æsculapius on board the *Angara*, "if a shell or mine bursts near you endeavour not to breathe. Hold your breath so as to prevent any gases from entering the body."

Neither the *Retvisan* nor the *Tsesarevitch* could go into the old dock. The new dock was not completed. It was hoped, however, to repair them with cofferdams. As the reader may not know what a cofferdam is, I will briefly describe one.

A huge box is constructed, of which two sides out of the six remain open; that is, the upper one and the one that is to be placed against the hole in the ship's side. Its shape must, of course, correspond ex-

---

6. A Russian saying; the Swedes were annihilated at the Battle of Poltava.—Trans.

actly to the shape of the ship. When ready, the box is sunk and placed against the ship's side. The flooded compartment is then pumped out, and the pressure on the outside of the box becomes so great that it adheres firmly to the ship and does not drop off. A new ship's side is thus, as it were, built on outside. Between this and the damaged side there is now an empty space into which one can climb from above, as the upper edge of the box is some feet above the surface of the water. Repairs are then executed just as in dock. Naturally, the work is more difficult.

It was not difficult to construct such a cofferdam for the *Retvisan*. The ship had been hit in the fore part, and here the ship's side is nearly flat. But whether it would be possible in the case of the *Tsesarevitch* was doubted by many, even specialists. That the shape of the stern was complicated was not the real difficulty. One of the screw shafts had to pass through the cofferdam. This was the great difficulty. A small error in measurements or a mistake of a few inches in placing the cofferdam would bend the shaft, and then: "Goodbye, battleship."

Great hopes were centred round Constructor K—— and his workmen from the Baltic Works, who were to come out to Port Arthur with Makaroff. Altogether one always consoled oneself in every difficult situation with the thought: "Makaroff will soon be here."

On February 22 the *Askold* and *Bayan* went to sea. But they soon came back. I did not discover what they went out for. They saw nothing of the enemy. On the 23rd the *Amur* went out. She was to lay mines in the bays of the west coast of Kwantung. She got back safely. The weather was very fine, calm, clear, dry, with a bright sun.

On February 23 I had again been on my legs all day. I was therefore sleeping the sleep of the just in the night of the 23-24, when I was awakened at 2.40 a.m. by the sound of guns. I at once rushed on deck. From the *Angara's* bridge we had a capital view of the *Retvisan* across the low part of Tiger's Tail Peninsula. She was grounded there on a bank below the northern slope of the Lighthouse Hill. The *Retvisan* was working her searchlights and firing, but only with the guns of the primary and secondary armament.[7] Her fire was intermittent, and gave the impression of uncertainty. It was also evident that the fortress searchlights were looking for something at sea. In the nearest batteries, into which we could see from the rear, luminous points were moving about. Men were running about with lanterns and clearing for action; but the guns were still silent. From seaward no response came to

---

7. Twelve-inch and 6-inch guns.—Trans.

our firing. All the officers of the *Angara* had assembled on the bridge. None of us could understand what was going on. If the Japanese squadron was approaching, the batteries along the sea front would undoubtedly have opened fire. If it was a torpedo attack the *Retvisan's* light Q.F. guns would also be firing.

The night was frosty, but quite calm. In the intervals of firing there was an oppressive stillness, which gave the impression as if every one in the town and on board the ships was holding his breath, to listen for every sound which could give some indication as to what was going on out there.

"Quick, quick—the turret! quick, quick!" was suddenly heard in a high, penetrating voice from the *Retvisan*.

From the first hill of the Tiger's Tail Peninsula came another voice, a powerful bass, through the stillness of the night: "Are you asleep at No. 3? Don't take your eye off the sight, you pheasant from Irkutsk, etc., etc."

To us who were listening with strained nerves, the words at such a moment seemed grotesque. A nervous titter ran through the rows of officers on the bridge, and the men along the bulwarks, and remarks were exchanged.

"Even in action S—— does not forget his 'quick, quick!'"
"Our friend there possesses a great command of language."
"Which one?"
"The one on Tiger's Tail."
"He gave it him properly."
"Probably a Siberian. They are all like that."

Sometimes the firing ceased, sometimes it started off with renewed fury.

An hour passed thus.

Suddenly, on the outer side of Golden Hill, there was a greenish golden flash. All guessed at once: "That was one of the 10-inch from Electric Rock." Also a 6-inch Canet in our friend's battery thundered out, and then the whole sea front joined in. The *Retvisan*, in the glare of the incessant flashes of the guns, looked like a volcano.

From outside, no response. It was a little after four in the morning. What on earth was going on? Between the thunder of the heavy guns, we could now hear distinctly the rattle of musketry and the sound of machine guns.

Were they trying to effect a landing? An open attack? No one could give an answer to these questions.

Suddenly the sounds of a bugle came across from the east basin. It was sounding "action," and was at once repeated on board all the ships.

He who has never heard the call to action in war will hardly be able to understand me. It is impossible to describe the effect produced by these sounds when the buglers of all ships sound off at the same time, accompanied by the roll of the drums. There are good reasons for our keeping to the bugle ever since the days of Peter the Great. There is something cruel, animal-like, in these screeching, ear-splitting sounds. They turn one's blood cold, and deaden all capacity for thinking. Harmony is absent. Every bugler starts on his own note, regardless of the others. Chaos, horrid discords are the result—the right kind of music for the moment, when man is to forget that he is man. He is to awaken the animal slumbering within and plunge into the orgies of death, in a drunken rage for destruction, as into a feast.

"Please have the landing parties ready in any case," said the captain.

"Landing parties to muster!"

It was as if the entire crew of the *Angara* had only one thought, and as if this order represented their unanimous resolve.

No sooner had the boatswain and his mates repeated my order, than the small-arm men, hastily buckling on their belts, were already falling in. The boats' falls were ready for lowering, the boats' crews were on their thwarts, life-lines in hand, and all merely awaited a sign to lower the boats into the water.

Quite suddenly thick clouds of smoke, in which darkened flames shot up, arose from the other side of Lighthouse Hill. Perhaps an explosion had taken place there. We had been unable to hear anything with the roar of the guns. The sky was getting more and more red every minute.

"There is a fire. But what is on fire? After all, the coast itself can't burn."

Our uncertainty was now increased, as the firing had become weaker after the outbreak of the conflagration, and ceased altogether at 4.40 a.m.

When day broke, we saw "flag-wagging," (morse-signalling), going on busily in every ship. Everyone wanted to know what had happened in the night.

The news we received was so unexpected that sceptics would not believe it at all.

Towards 3 a.m. the searchlights had noticed four or five steamers, which were approaching Port Arthur from seaward. The steamers were heading so boldly, so calmly, for their goal, that they were at first taken to be the colliers and supply ships we were expecting. The *Retvisan* was the first to have doubts, and opened fire on them. It appeared strange to her that these steamers had formed single line abreast, just as if they were intending to steam altogether into the narrow entrance of Port Arthur. For merchant ships it would have been more natural to form single line ahead, that is, in each other's wake, as at Port Arthur, and especially at night, only one ship at a time could pass through the entrance. The further proceedings of these mysterious craft had strengthened the suspicions of our people. They did not anchor, nor did their sirens shriek, when they were fired upon. Instead of this they resolutely continued their course.

However, when suddenly a number of torpedo boats, which had up to then been hiding behind the steamers, dashed out and attacked the *Retvisan*, every doubt vanished. At that moment fire had been opened all along the line, as witnessed by us. We were told that one steamer was sunk in the roads, that another had run upon the rocks at the foot of White Wolf Hill, whilst a third had not been able to face the furious fire, and had fled seawards.

Two, which had steered straight for the *Retvisan*, had penetrated furthest. One went a little too far to starboard and sank under Golden Hill. The other went too far to port, and ran up on the southern slope of the Lighthouse Hill, about 200 yards from the *Retvisan*. Here she had caught fire, and this was what we had seen.

In the *Angara*'s ward room there were violent debates. No one thought of rest after this sleepless night. Opinions differed violently.

"I believe we have fired at our own ships. It wouldn't be the first time either. Why were the batteries silent so long? Probably steamers were expected that very night," said the pessimists.

"Why didn't they anchor at the first shots?"

"Anchor in 40 fathoms? They hoped that we should at last recognise our mistake."

"And what about the torpedo-boats?"

"That is yet another explanation why they steamed on so obstinately. They were being chased by Japanese torpedo-boats. How else can you explain these steamers? Fire-ships are no use against a modern iron-clad. After all, the Japanese aren't bigger fools than we."

"The role of fire-ships was only a secondary consideration. Their chief object was certainly to block the entrance."

"That would be a silly idea."

"The Yankees also tried to block Santiago."

"The attempt failed."

The dispute was ended by positive information, confirming the fact that the steamers were Japanese. We had succeeded in making a few prisoners. The small crews had left the ships at the last moment in boats and tried under cover of darkness to gain the open sea, where torpedo-boats were awaiting them. The calm weather and smooth sea had assisted them greatly in this attempt.

Behind Lighthouse Hill, columns of thick smoke were still rising. Although it was daylight, one could still see from time to time a glare of fire.

I got leave from the captain, and went off in our steamboat to have a look at the steamer.

The plan of the Japanese did not appear to me to be at all as silly as some of my messmates on board the *Angara* had maintained.

The steamer which had grounded about 200 yards from the *Retvisan* under Lighthouse Hill, I estimated to be of about 4,000 tons. If she had rammed the half-wrecked battleship the latter could hardly have been saved. The blow of the stem itself though, would hardly have had much result. But a modern battleship possesses coal bunkers, much inflammable material, and above all magazines and shell rooms, for which the immediate neighbourhood, ship's side to ship's side, of this huge fire-ship would have been very dangerous.

I was told that it was only by chance that the steamer did not reach her objective. The storm of fire and iron which raged around her did not destroy any of her vitals. She calmly ran on parallel to the coast-line of the Tiger's Tail Peninsula, and headed straight for the centre of the battleship, which was pouring shell into her. Just short of her goal a small projectile or splinter cut the chains from which the port bower anchor was hanging. The anchor was neither torn away nor destroyed, but only let go. It held, the steamer sheered to port and grounded. The coal in her bunkers had been saturated with kerosene, so that water was powerless against the flames, which had to be smothered with sand. In amongst the coal small mines had been placed. These exploded from time to time, and interfered with the work of putting out the fire. This did not go on without causing some casualties. It was like working on a volcano. Underneath the coal there might also be a big mine which would cause still greater dangers.

Far away on the horizon the outlines of three torpedo-boats were in sight.

The *Novik* was already leaving the harbour; and steamed past me. She was evidently intended to drive off these scouts. I was unable to watch her performance as my leave had been short, and I had to return to the *Angara*.

At 8.30 a.m. a group of light Japanese cruisers came in sight to the south-east. They were the *Chitose*, *Kasagi*, *Takasago*, and *Yoshino*.

These four cruisers were the first division of scouts. At Port Arthur they were christened the "Greyhounds." Every one knew that when the "Greyhounds" appeared, looked round, and then disappeared, the Japanese main body might soon be expected.

At that time this rule had not yet been established. Therefore only the *Bayan* and *Askold* were sent out, to support the *Novik*.

These three cruisers, however, returned very soon, for in the rear of the "Greyhounds" almost the whole Japanese fleet hove in sight.

From the *Angara*'s berth we could, from the bridge, see the sea horizon towards the south-east. We could look out between Lighthouse Hill and Golden Hill. It was just in that direction that the Japanese hove in sight.

I had a curious feeling, as the outlines of these battleships, so well known to me, stood out more and more clearly against the blue background.

"Those are now my enemies. But why? We were quite good friends a short while ago." Thus I thought quite involuntarily. War is something too gruesome, mysterious. One's mind at first fails to grasp its meaning.

"That's the *Asahi*. Her captain is Nomoto, my old friend. If we were now face to face, he would surely smile good-naturedly as of old and call out: 'Good morning, my dear fellow!' Now he is clearing away his guns out there, and is only awaiting the moment when his admiral will open fire. Then he will deal death and destruction amongst his old friends with his 12-inch guns. And why? How insane it all is!"

The piercing sounds of the bugle "Action" dissipated these dreams instantly. A voice within me was saying: "If they would only come near enough for us to take part in the battle with our 4.7 guns."

There was no battle. The Japanese only approached near enough to get a view of Port Arthur, and then steamed away to the westward.

We thought the Japanese would go into the Gulf of Petchili during the night, so we sent a destroyer flotilla[8] there.

Between moon-rise (about 1 a.m.) and 4 a.m., the Japanese destroyers delivered a whole series of torpedo attacks against the *Retvisan*. They did not succeed. On the morning of the 26th our boats returned. They had also not had any success, but the *Vnushitelny* was lost. This boat had no luck. She only met the enemy in broad daylight, when not only was an attack out of the question, but she had to fly. The maxim *"Risk nothing!"* had perhaps a hand in it. The *Vnushitelny* had been delayed by something, and the Japanese cruisers then cut her off from Port Arthur. The destroyer ran into Pigeon Bay, but here she was no longer under protection of the coast batteries. The Japanese destroyed her by gunfire without the least hurry, just as at target practice. At last the captain himself sank his burning vessel. He landed with his crew, and reached Port Arthur safely on foot.

On the same day, February 26, the Japanese Squadron again appeared before Port Arthur. Again the *Bayan*, *Askold*, and *Novik* were sent out. They remained within range of the batteries, and together with these fired at the Japanese. Electric Rock and a battery on Tiger's Tail Peninsula joined in. Our ships soon returned into port, as the forces were too unequal. They had no losses. Towards 1 p.m. the Japanese also disappeared.

In view of the increased activity of the enemy, orders were given for the ships having no special duties (the *Angara* amongst the number) to land their small-arm men. These amounted altogether to about five hundred. They were intended to reinforce the garrison. It should be noted that at that time the field army proper—infantry and guns—occupied positions at Tsin-Chau, Nangalin, Dalny, and other intermediate places. The orders were that in future parties were to be landed daily.

During the night there were several alarms. About 11 p.m. the coast batteries and the *Retvisan* opened fire. This was replied to from seaward. We heard the whizzing of the shell, and saw distinctly that one burst on the southern slope of Golden Hill. Later, about half-past three, Electric Hill fired, and about half-past four the Mortar battery on Golden Hill. What had happened we could not find out.

Whether the viceroy was still in Port Arthur during these days,

---

8. The destroyers at Port Arthur were divided into two flotillas. The first consisted of the larger and better French and German built boats, the second of ours, which had been built after the *Sokol* type. For active operations, only the first counted; the second mostly did guard and patrol duties.

or whether he had already left for Mukden, I do not know. There is nothing about it in my diary. As he never took part personally in any of the engagements, no one in the squadron took any interest in what he did, with the possible exception of the flag and commanding officers.

During the following ten days no Japanese showed themselves. What were they doing? Where had they gone? These questions forced themselves on many a one; but no one tried to clear up the mystery. The squadron slumbered in the basins of Port Arthur.

"They ought to send us out scouting," growled the young ones in the mess of the *Angara*. "Our old tin box isn't good for anything else anyhow."

These bold ideas suddenly came to nought. We received orders—to disarm.

The official orders ran approximately as follows:

> It has been established that the successful repulse of the Japanese fire-ships must primarily be ascribed to the light Q.F. guns of the battleship *Retvisan*. The coast batteries which protect the sea front and the entrance to the harbour possess too few of these guns. The battleship will be towed off at the next opportunity and taken into the basin. As the defence will require reinforcing, two batteries are to be erected on the seaward slopes of Golden Hill and Lighthouse Hill respectively. In consideration of the fact that the fortress does not possess the necessary *matériel*, it is directed that the cruiser *Angara* shall hand over her 4.7 guns to the new batteries. The guns are to be mounted as low down as possible, that is, close to the surface of the water, so as to give them a maximum danger zone. It is intended thus to obviate the drawback under which the remaining high-sited guns of the sea defence, with their large angle of descent, suffer. In consequence of the above, etc., etc.

We started on our labours with heavy hearts.

The batteries were built by our own people, and our officers had to superintend the work. They received their instructions from the military engineers. The wooden and iron portions of the temporary gun-mountings were made of anything available, partly on the spot, partly in the dockyard.

We now went through hard times. Nearly half our ship's company was permanently employed in the batteries or in the landing parties. The latter not only remained ashore all night, but sometimes the whole twenty-four hours. The Chinese villages were frequently surrounded and searched. It was remarkable with what certainty the Japanese invariably avoided our floating mines. This and other circumstances made it clear that every measure taken on our side was accurately known to the enemy. For one thing the Chinese were the culprits. They hated all foreigners, and for money were as ready to serve us as the enemy. Then again, we discovered in the first days of the war, in the midst of the native population, a considerable number of disguised Japanese. When we arrested a suspicious individual, our people generally began by tugging at his pigtail. The latter frequently proved to be false.

However, not even a real pigtail was always a proof of the owner's nationality. It turned out that, in this respect also, the Japanese had prepared themselves for the war for a long time. They had sent their agents years in advance to South China—for instance, Canton. These people there grew pigtails, learnt Chinese, and eventually sailed to Kwantung disguised as Chinese, in search of employment. In such cases they deceived even our most experienced and most zealous (that is, sufficiently well paid) Chinese detectives. It required a very sensitive, so to say musical, ear to detect the very slight difference between the speech of a Cantonese speaking the North China dialect, and a Japanese who had lived for years in Canton and then speaks North Chinese.

Very often the spies were found out from their carrying a signal lantern fitted with a movable shade (a system something like the French *ratière*). A peasant or dock labourer often excited suspicion merely from the possession of such a lantern. When a spy signalled with it, it was almost impossible to catch him. He established himself amongst the rocks of any small cape or point, directed the beam of his lantern on a prearranged bearing to seaward, and communicated his news by Morse flashing to the hostile scout hidden in the darkness of the night. Our coast patrols had literally to stumble on such a fellow before they could catch him. If the spy turned off his light in time and hid amongst the rocks, he could not be found. Then the most attentive watchman could pass along the coast-line, amply provided as it was with every kind of hiding-place, without his suspicion being awakened in the slightest degree.

Of what went on on land we only heard little afloat. It was said that the fortifications, which had not yet been armed, or even constructed, when the war broke out, were now being completed systematically. A part was being equipped in haste, a part even reconstructed. The information as to the latter was not very clear.

The weather began to change. February in Port Arthur is somewhat like the Russian April. With a clear sky and a calm, or light wind, the sun was so warm in these latitudes that we walked about on deck with our overcoats unbuttoned. But it sufficed for a strong northeaster to blow to bring forth fur coats and caps. For example, on February 27 we had a thunderstorm with hail and then a temperature of 20° F. On March 3 we first had a southerly wind with 40°, and then suddenly a snowstorm, which heaped up great masses of snow on the deck

The squadron was quite numbed in its inactivity, but everywhere there was a state of anxious expectation. Every newcomer who might have heard something through the railway telegraph was bombarded with questions: "'Where is Makaroff?'" "When will Makaroff be here?" He had reached Mukden on March 1, and was to remain there a few days to consult the viceroy.

This news produced a great sensation.

"This is not the time for much palavering."—"Why all these formalities?"—"Probably they will now begin to ask for decisions from St Petersburg, and when once they begin to write it is all up," pestered the hotspurs amongst us.

"Makaroff won't stay there making speeches. Makaroff won't stay at Mukden longer than absolutely necessary," replied the more sober-minded.

The sub-lieutenants of the *Angara* had always been capital officers, but now they began to surpass themselves. In consequence of their duties with the landing parties or the work at the new batteries, they sometimes had to go without sleep for twenty-four hours, and hardly had time for meals. When they returned they were fresh and cheerful, and ever ready to go off on some new job, without .any rest. The cause of this extraordinary zeal for the service was soon revealed to me. Each of them chose a suitable moment for a private conversation with me. He then appeared in my cabin, and after a few introductory remarks, it came out that he wanted to get away from the "transport" and join a fighting ship.

All these conversations ended something like this: "The admiral knows you well. You are also well acquainted with his staff. Shifting about a sub-lieutenant is a small matter. If I felt that I had been misbehaving myself, the thing would be different, but as it stands—well, pray judge for yourself. Isn't it a shame to be serving in a transport now in time of war? Surely they could find a billet for me on board one of the men-of-war."

The dear, keen youths! I thought and felt exactly like them.

CHAPTER 4

Admiral Makaroff's Arrival

At eight o'clock on the morning of March 7 the Commander-in-Chief of the Pacific Fleet, Vice-Admiral Makaroff, arrived at Port Arthur. As Vice-Admiral Stark was still in the *Petropavlovsk*, he hoisted his flag provisionally on board the *Askold*. When it was first seen there, many of our people took off their caps and crossed themselves. A feeling of solemnity seemed to have seized upon every one.

The cofferdam for the *Retvisan* had been completed some days ago, but when the attempt was made to put it in place it was found that it only covered the hole very imperfectly. The mighty turbines of the pumping vessel were unable to pump out the battleship. The defective parts had to be examined by divers and temporarily made water-tight. Just on the day of the new chief's arrival this work was successfully completed.

The battleship floated, and was towed by tugs into the west basin, where it was secured between buoys close to, and to the northward of, the *Angara*.

"A good omen," was the verdict in the wardroom. On the lower deck they said: "Do you see, no sooner is he here than everything goes right. He'll stand no nonsense, my friend. He makes everything go."

At first, of course, Admiral Makaroff was taken up entirely from morning to night with the taking over of his new duties. He had to familiarise himself with the local conditions and the state of affairs generally, to have consultations with various commanders, etc. The very little free time at his command he utilised in going on board the various ships in turn. Naturally, he could not be expected to visit the *Angara* at once.

Makaroff's inspections were very short, and always of the same kind. The admiral came on board, received the captain's reports, had the officers presented to him, and then greeted the men.[1] Then followed an inspection of the decks below, upon which the admiral once more walked down the ranks. Every time he had a few words for some of the men. One man Makaroff would remember from a former ship, or some cruise together; another was asked what he had done during the last fight; or he started a conversation with one of the gun-layers. He would be asked by the admiral how many rounds he got off during the action, and in what time, and whether he had been able to keep his sights on. In this he called for replies and opinions, and sometimes even argued it out with the man. It ended with: "*Au revoir*, my lad! God grant us a happy issue," and he moved on.

There was nothing very remarkable or extraordinary in all this, but every word, every movement of Makaroff's, was at once known throughout the squadron. Although the admiral had not as yet given any real proof of his capacity, his popularity rose, as if by magic, from day to day, or more accurately, from hour to hour. The great mass believed in Makaroff, believed that he was the right man in the right place. Whole legends arose about his alleged plans.

It did not matter that these legends generally proved to be false. If one did not believe them entirely, one was only too ready to believe them to be feasible, and that was very important. The squadron had at last found its proper leader, and its old spirit arose anew. It appeared to me as if my hopes were not deceiving me. The pressure of these last years had been incapable of completely stifling the spirit of the squadron. When its hour came it was bound to throw off all obstacles and to open up its path in its old strength and beauty. In these days my not have dared to say: "It is all over with us."

"How about our guns? Shall we re-embark them, sir?" the boatswain asked me one day in that tone of mingled respect and familiarity with which a boatswain asks the executive officer about the captain's intentions.

"What guns?"

"Ours in the batteries."

"What do you mean?"

"I was only thinking, sir, that if they send us to the Cape—"

"What Cape?"

"The Cape of Good Hope, to capture contraband. We can't do that

---

1. Inspecting officers always call out "Good morning!" or "Your health, my men!" to which the whole crew shout back a prescribed reply in unison, and keeping accurate time.—Trans.

very well without guns."

"Where did you get this from? "

"They all say it, sir. The admiral has ordered it. Every cruiser, such as she is, has to be put to some use."

This was perhaps somewhat far-fetched, still, it was very fine.

From Vladivostok the news came that the cruisers had been at sea from February 25 to March 7, but without any result. They had suffered the whole time from heavy snowstorms. A small Japanese steamer had fallen into their hands.

On the evening of March 8, we "heard" the Japanese, that is, our wireless stations received unintelligible messages.

At dusk we saw from the *Angara* that both destroyer flotillas (all we possessed) were going out.

"Oh! This 'risk nothing' won't go down with old 'Beardy.'"—"'Little Grandfather' is quite another fellow," was said amongst my messmates.

"Beardy" and "Little Grandfather" were terms of endearment,[2] which had been bestowed upon Makaroff during his earliest days at Port Arthur.

Towards seven o'clock on the morning of March 9 the first destroyer flotilla returned to Port Arthur. They had not succeeded in finding the Japanese Squadron. Instead of this they came upon a Japanese destroyer flotilla in the dawn, when they were already in sight of Port Arthur. Between them and the Japanese a hot engagement commenced, and at quite close quarters. They even fired surface-running torpedoes at each other. The *Vlastny* maintained that she had sunk a Japanese destroyer with a torpedo of this kind. In return she had her engine disabled by shell fire. Our losses were: the flotilla commander wounded, an engineer scalded to death, as well as one dead, and several wounded amongst the men. All news was invariably communicated to the squadron by "flag-wagging."

In the second flotilla, the *Reshitelny* and *Steregushtchy* had no luck. They did not find the hostile squadron during the night and were cut off on their return journey. The enemy was twice as strong as they. Our boats tried to break through, and a hot fight ensued. They were very near boarding one another. One Japanese was said actually to have leaped across on to the deck of the *Steregushtchy*. He killed one of the officers with a cut of his sword, but was instantly knocked down. The *Reshitelny* got through. On board her consort a torpedo exploded

---

2. The admiral wore an exceptionally large beard.—Trans.

in the stern tube. Probably it had been struck by a hostile projectile or shell splinter. The boat's stern was terribly mangled. The Japanese at once turned away from the *Reshitelny* and threw themselves with all their might on the *Steregushtchy*. They beat down all resistance and took her in tow, but when they tried to tow her away to the southward she sank.[3]

Though the *Steregushtchy* was lost, the first flotilla had also accounted for one of the hostile boats. The fight brought no victory, but also no defeat. At the most one could only be depressed at the thought that our destroyers were so worthless. Fully half their number took no part in the expedition. They were lying in the East Basin, making good small defects, which cropped up almost daily. Nor were they sufficiently trained for their special duties. The boats lost one another when they were out at night, they did not know how to find the enemy, etc., etc. All the same, this enterprise had been the first bright deed, and it therefore did not by any means produce a bad impression in the squadron. On the contrary, one was proud of it. The cause lay in a circumstance insignificant in itself, but which represented something so unheard of in Port Arthur that at first one could hardly believe it.

When the signal station on Golden Hill reported that our destroyers were engaged with the Japanese, the Askold and *Novik* at once went out in support. The *Novik* led.

"Is the admiral by any chance going out himself?" everyone asked, highly interested. The officers fetched their binoculars. On board the *Askold* Makaroff's flag was not flying.

"Well," it was said, "that is quite natural. He can't expose himself to such a danger. The *Askold* is, after all, only a protected cruiser."

"The *Novik* has hoisted the admiral's flag!" shouted one of the signalmen.

There was great excitement everywhere. The men left their breakfast and rushed on deck, the officers fought for glasses. Doubt was no longer possible. At the only masthead of the *Novik*, this toy vessel, which looked more like a torpedo-boat, the flag of our commander-in-chief was flying.

Exclamations of surprise flew through the ranks of our men. The officers clearly showed how greatly they were pleased.

"He wouldn't wait until the *Askold* was ready; therefore he goes

---

[3]. We learnt from the Japanese reports that the *Steregushtchy* was half destroyed, and that all the officers as well as most of the men were killed. The survivors sank their vessel themselves by opening the Kingston valves.

out in the *Novik*. By Jove, this is splendid!"

In reality, Makaroff's decision was nothing at all extraordinary, but merely what ought to have happened. The old maxim "risk nothing" was buried at that moment, and a new principle arose in its place.

The destroyer action took place about 10 miles from Port Arthur. The *Novik* and the *Askold* did not arrive in time in spite of all their efforts. The *Steregushtchy* had already sunk when our cruisers reached the scene of the action. They at once started chasing the hostile destroyers. In doing so they ran upon the entire hostile squadron, which was steaming towards Port Arthur, and had to turn back. Happily, the two vessels were in full possession of their steaming powers. With our other ships this only figured on paper. The Japanese battleships and armoured cruisers could not catch the two cruisers. Only the "Greyhounds" were able for a while to chase them with more or less success.

We in the harbour heard with great concern that firing was going on out at sea, but both cruisers got back safely.

This return nearly became a triumphal progress. Thousands of men stood crowded on the decks of the ships, on the ramparts of the forts, and along the harbour embankments, and every one anxiously followed the movements of the *Novik*. The fast little vessel manoeuvred cleverly through the narrow passages in the entrance; but the general attention was not fixed on the ship herself. Everyone wanted to see the proud flag of St Andrew, with an admiral's distinguishing marks, which the cruiser flew at her masthead.

An accidental success in action would not have had the significance of this moment. The admiral had conquered all hearts at one stroke and could henceforth be justified in speaking of "my" squadron. Everyone was his, body and soul.

To this episode must undoubtedly be ascribed the grand composure with which the squadron underwent the bombardment which followed on the same day. It was perhaps not the only cause, but it certainly contributed towards it by the extraordinarily strong impression it made on the masses. All the same, our situation was by no means a good one.

The Japanese Squadron, before which the *Novik* and *Askold* had to fly, steered at first on a westerly course, as if it meant to pass Port Arthur. It soon got out of sight behind Liao-ti-shan Hill. A single cruiser remained off the entrance of the harbour, but outside the range of our forts. Soon after 9 a.m. there arose suddenly between the ships in the west basin a gigantic column of water. A sharp detonation was heard at the same instant, which had nothing in common either with that produced by the firing of a big gun or the explosion of a mine. Immediately everyone left his work and looked around aghast. Again and yet again the same thing happened. All at once it all appeared clear to us. The Japanese battleships, which were circling about 8 or 9 miles from us, were firing at us indirectly across Liao-ti-shan. Not a single fortress gun could interfere with them. Evidently our Ministry of War, as well as that of the Marine, had, before the war, thought such a thing to be impossible. Otherwise some one would surely have built batteries to meet such a contingency, or have made the necessary preparations in the squadron for replying to such high-angle fire.

As soon as the bombardment commenced, Admiral Makaroff ordered suitable measures to be taken in hand at once. But this was no easy task, and could not be done in a few hours. The chart had to be divided off into squares, marks for laying on selected, posts of observation to be established, and a simple system of signalling from them drawn up. For all this several days were required. We could not help asking ourselves: what were we really thinking of before the war? It is curious how history repeats itself. In the Turkish war our infantry had to improvise for themselves wooden sights for the longer ranges and fix them on their rifles. Since then twenty-five years had passed, and again we see ourselves forced to improvise from our own resources additions to our gun sights for firing at very great ranges. Some ships were in any case unable to use high-angle fire. Their mountings were not so constructed as to allow the necessary elevation being given.

The Japanese evidently had suitable mountings and a trained personnel. Their shots were very well placed. A single shell would have sufficed to put any battleship out of action, as the projectiles struck with a very large angle of descent. The 11-inch mortars of the Japanese proved this at the end of the siege.

The hostile battleships manoeuvred without hindrance south of Liao-ti-shan. When each reached the right place, she quietly laid her 12-inch guns, and neither fleet nor fortress could make any reply to their fire.

The only escape from this deplorable situation would have been for us to go to sea. We had been in possession of Port Arthur for seven years before the war broke out. In all this time we did not manage to complete the grand scheme of deepening the inner harbour and the entrance. The big ships could only go in and out at high water. At low water the insufficient depth kept our ships more securely locked in port than the most powerful enemy. On March 9 low water at Port Arthur was at 9 a.m., therefore the Japanese had selected precisely that hour for the commencement of their bombardment.

The reader has surely had the experience at one time or other in his dreams of lying helpless, while a heavy weight was threatening to crush him to death. This crushing weight could easily be thrown off if one had the use of one's limbs. But one is, as it were, tied down, unable to move a limb, and only one's thoughts are at work. And even these thoughts are not free. They can only ask: "How much longer can I bear this?" One would like to be rid of them altogether.

Such was our situation during the bombardment on March 9. The word "bombardment" exactly describes it. There was no question of a fight. At other times the defender at a bombardment is able to reply shot for shot, even if in a less favourable situation than the attacker. Here it was, for one of the parties, merely a very convenient target practice, free from all danger. The other party provided the living targets.

The bombardment of March 9 was my "*baptism of fire.*" However, I won't bore the reader by describing what I then thought and felt. After a war, the first impressions of the enemy's fire have been described and minutely analysed by so many writers that I need not waste another word. I will confine myself to describing the events and my observations of others. I have conscientiously noted them in my diary.

I do not know how the crews of our squadron would have behaved two weeks earlier under such a bombardment. Their attitude on March 9 was so exemplary, that I have come to the conclusion that Makaroff's arrival and his short trip in the *Novik*, as just described by me, were the causes.

Against the 12-inch shell which came down nearly vertically, there was no protection on board any of the battleships, still less on board the *Angara*. But against the very small splinters of shell bursting near by, a bulkhead or merely the ship's side sufficed as a protection. Consequently, we ought to have ceased all work on deck and sent the men below. This was not done in a single ship. Of course, I mean only the ships I could see. We were lying so close together at our buoys in the west basin, that the space between the lines of ships was only a trifle over 200 yards, whilst there were only about 60 yards between ships in the same line. I was therefore able to observe a good many ships. And if a panic had broken out at some distance from us, it would have spread quickly to the other ships, crowded so closely together, and reached us.

Nothing of the sort happened. Life on board the ships and in the harbour went on as usual. It had apparently been realised that after all it was impossible to defend ourselves, and therefore every one acted as if he did not notice the shell which was pitching around him. The chimneys of the workshops belched forth clouds of smoke and steam as usual, and in the harbour the daily busy routine went on. Tugs were towing about lighters and floating cranes, and the steam-boats of the men-of-war were going hither and thither, some alone, some with row boats in tow.

This happened to be the very day on which the mounting of our 4.7-inch guns in the new batteries below Golden Hill was to be completed. Our men had already gone there in the early morning, and did not knock off work, although they were quite unprotected in the batteries. , Towards half-past ten our steam-boat took out the dinners of the working party as usual. When it returned and had come alongside, one of the men was led out, supported by others under his arms.

"What's up?"

"On our way out, sir," reported the coxswain, "a shell burst quite close to us. The cook's mate got a flesh wound. We have probed it; the bone is all right, and he can move the foot. He said himself: 'Don't make a fuss, but mind the soup doesn't get cold, otherwise the men will swear.' We have bandaged him up well."

Happily, the wound was not serious. Towards eleven o'clock the men went to dinner and the officers had breakfast. At that time the enemy's projectiles were making particularly good practice. I was standing on the upper bridge of the *Angara* when the *Retvisan* was struck by a shell. (The distance between her stern and our bow was between 40 and 50 yards.) The projectile only damaged her side near the port midship gangway. It burst here, and destroyed two boats that were lying alongside. One of them burst into flames. The pumping vessel *Silatch*, which was also secured there, was covered with shell splinters.

"That was a near shave," I thought; "half a dozen yards more to the right and the shell might have got into the after 12-inch shell-room."

On board the battleship people were running about excitedly. After a while she cast off her bow hawsers, and had her bow, which had gone down perceptibly, towed round to starboard by the *Silatch* into shallow water. We afterwards heard that the bursting shell had damaged the cofferdam covering her big hole forward. A few minutes later another projectile struck the *Retvisan*. This time she was hit on the starboard side (now facing south), near the water-line abreast of the after-turret. The armour held. When smoke and spray had disappeared we saw merely a brown spot where the shell had struck.

"The *Retvisan* has no luck," said the officer of the watch near me.

At this moment one of the servants announced that breakfast was ready, and I went down into our mess.

We were more lively than ever at breakfast. I should never have thought that our party possessed such brilliant wit. It was a long time since I had enjoyed such pleasant company, and listened to the conversation with so much interest. Much sarcasm was levelled at the fact that we of the *Angara* were exposed to quite an uncalled-for amount of danger. If the Japanese had known where the disarmed *Angara* was lying they would never have fired in that direction.

"They are wasting their ammunition; they might just as well fire at the water as at us."

"Are you speaking *pro domo sua?*" asked the gunnery lieutenant with dignity. "I presume I am worth a trifle more than one Japanese 12-inch shell."

Towards the end of breakfast we organised a little *jeu d'esprit*. The first-class saloon on the upper deck was used as ward room. At the open door an orderly was so placed that he could see where the shell struck. After each explosion we had to guess where it had struck—in the water, on shore, to starboard, to port, ahead, astern, far off, etc., etc.—judging by the nature and force of the detonation. Every attempt to get a view through one of the windows at the sides was prevented by energetic shouts of "No cheating!"

The report of the umpire at the door decided.

It was fine to see the carelessness and cheerfulness of these heroes. The threatenings of death they turned into a harmless game. Such is the strength of patriotism. I wrote in my diary:

> Is it pride or love of glory that does all this? If Makaroff were not here, and the old maxim, 'risk nothing,' were still in vogue, these people would probably be hiding behind traverses made of coal bags. Now they show off before one another. Each one watches carefully for one of the others to betray his emotions. They laugh at the young blue-jackets, who stoop when a shell splinter whistles in the air. These show no shame. They say: 'It

came so suddenly,' or 'I was not looking out, and did it unconsciously.'

Here the "suggestive" influence of a strong will over weaker ones was clearly shown. The former is able to exercise this influence, and the others really mean to do the same thing. They obey, not from fear, but for the sake of their consciences.

The meal was coming to an end, and we were drinking our coffee. I could not help laughing heartily over the rage of our chief engineer. The poor fellow heard very badly with his right ear, and therefore was a constant loser at the game. He heard everything with his left ear, and therefore thought every time that the hits were to the left of him. This amused the sub-lieutenants hugely, and they declared that if the Japanese would only bombard us twice a week, the "Chief" would have to pay for drinks all round.

Suddenly there was a hit quite close. The explosion was so violent that a hand-bell on the table jumped up and rang.

I snatched up my cap and ran on deck. Happily, all had gone off well. The shell had pitched into the water about 20 yards off our port side, abreast of the fore-bridge. Its splinters had made a few holes in the boats and ventilators. On the bridge there was some damage, but no one was hurt. The Japanese were apparently again firing in our direction. The next projectile nearly grazed us, but did not burst. The water which it threw up simply swamped our deck. A group of men standing there were completely soaked.

The men shouted and laughed cheerfully.

"Have you ever had a Japanese bath?"—"Water is very different from splinters."—"If that had been a splinter my new shirt would have been spoilt."—"Hah, hah! he's in a funk about his new shirt."—"Naturally, his thick skull won't be hurt by any splinter."—"Just you wait. A splinter may hit something else besides the skull."

"Clear out!" called out the boatswain. "The orders are that no one is to be on deck who has nothing to do there. Clear out!"

The men moved on reluctantly. "What does he want? He himself goes on to the bridge with the gentlemen. Where are we to go? We have got to be somewhere. How did old 'Beardy' do it this morning? He said: 'If I fall, I give an example.' And we are to hide?"

On our port bow a shell burst just under the stern of the *Diana*. Her men were running about, and some screwed the fire-hose to the rising mains. Another shell plunged into the water alongside the

Kasan, which was secured just ahead of us.

"That was nearly a hit," we joked. "Thank God! a miss is as good as a mile."

The *Kasan* signalled to us for a doctor. Her own was sick. They evidently had men wounded.

A "portmanteau"[4] hit the parapet of the mortar battery on Golden Hill.

When the flood was at half-tide, towards 1 p.m., and the squadron could have commenced to go out of harbour, the Japanese retired. Thank God! no ship was seriously damaged. The squadron lost about thirty in killed and wounded.

It might have been much worse. The ships of the squadron and the harbour craft. Government as well as merchant steamers, were crowded together in the basins. The clear surface of the water was barely twice as much in area as the aggregate deck space of the vessels exposed.

At daybreak, towards 4 a.m. on March 10, all the men-of-war began moving out to the roads. Admiral Makaroff had ordered this. On this occasion it was shown once more what a leader in whom his subordinates have faith, and who has faith in himself, can accomplish. Up to now, the tugs, both government and private, had borne all the responsibility in moving our ships. It was so laid down in the rules and regulations elaborated at Cronstadt and approved by the Admiralty. In times of peace these rules may have been quite wise. The captains were too fond of working their engines, and this interfered with the masters of the tugs, who were not accustomed to this. But the result was that the whole squadron was unable to get out of the basins and into the roads during one tide. The resources of the port were too limited, and two tides had to be waited for—that is, it took nearly twenty-four hours to get to sea. Makaroff changed all this by issuing new regulations.

Henceforth the tugs were merely to "assist" our ships in the manoeuvres. They "helped" us to turn in the narrow parts, and "endeavoured with all their powers" to render us assistance in tight places. If they did their business well, they were not likely to be called to account for any damages. The captains, on the other hand, were enjoined

---

4 "Portmanteau" was the name at Port Arthur for the long Japanese shell. Does not such a projectile, 1 foot in diameter and over 4 feet long, look like a portmanteau filled with explosives? They contained 106 lbs. of melinite or *shimose*. We had no shell of the kind.

not to shirk their responsibility. They had to keep in view their paramount duty of getting their ships out in the shortest possible time. To this end all available means were at their disposal. Whoever, with the best intentions, did not manage to carry out this task, merely showed his ignorance and inexperience. Whoever clung to the letter of the instructions from dread of responsibility proved himself culpable.

The admiral developed this idea very fully at a meeting of flag officers and captains, at which the masters of tugs and the port officials were present.

The result was that the entire squadron went out of harbour on March 10, during the early morning high water, in two and a half hours. When it was high water again that evening, it re-entered the port between 5 and 7 p.m. We hardly believed our eyes. Our young officers were beside themselves with joy.

"The tugs are working like Trojans. Look how smartly they come alongside, how quickly they carry out their job and then hurry off to the next ship."

These vessels richly deserved this praise.

The enemy had completely disappeared. Our squadron carried out evolutions as soon as it was outside. Admiral Makaroff had issued tactical orders immediately upon his arrival at Port Arthur. These orders contained rules as to the cruising and battle formations of the squadron, fundamental principles as to the use of the gun armament, and directions as to what ships were to do in special circumstances in action. Up to then we had had no such orders. As the Japanese did not put in an appearance, these exercises on March 10 were carried out as in time of peace. They produced a sad result. Two battleships rammed one another. The *Sebastopol* was damaged. It appears that she was rammed right aft. However, orders were given not to talk about the incident.[5]

"Those are the results of our being kept in Reserve so long," grumbled some of my messmates. "We want to go to war, and don't know yet how to keep in the wake of the next ahead. We are, after all, only floating barracks."

---

5. The *Sebastopol* was rammed by the *Peresviet*. Luckily, she made no water. The result of the blow was only an insignificant crack in the outer skin plate. Besides that one of the blades of the starboard propeller was bent. This blade was afterwards exchanged by means of a bell-shaped cofferdam. The *Peresviet* twisted her stem slightly, and some water got into the foremost compartment. She was repaired. On the same day the *Sebastopol* rammed the *Poltava* very slightly, the latter also having a plate cracked.

"Makaroff will make good all this."

"God grant that there may be time!"

Admiral Makaroff had brought with him, besides the constructors and workmen of the Baltic Yard, a number of other specialists. Amongst these was, for example; Colonel M—— and several workmen from the Obukoff gun factory. All branches of the service received a fresh impetus. The cofferdam for the *Tsesarevitch*, the feasibility of which had hitherto been doubted, was taken in hand energetically. In place of the *Retvisan*'s old cofferdam, which had been found useless, a new one was built. In the gun sheds there lay, quite unnoticed, a number of guns and part of their mountings which had been looted at Tientsin in 1900. From these several were picked out, missing parts of the mountings were made anew in the dockyard, and eventually there were forty new guns at the disposal of the land front. The mountings of the battery on Electric Rock were improved, increasing their arc of training by 5°. In the port a great deal was accomplished by volunteer artisans and divers of the Reval Salvage Company. The admiral thought of everything and forgot nothing.

March 14 became a "red-letter day" for me. I was invited to breakfast on board the *Petropavlovsk*. After breakfast the admiral took me into his cabin and told me plump and plain, as was his fashion, what he intended to do for me.

"When I left St Petersburg I heard that you were in command of a destroyer. I know you, and knew that you would not give up this appointment for any other. When I was getting my staff together I did not therefore count on you. Now you have got another appointment, but my staff, as allowed by establishment, is complete. Would you like to be attached to the staff as a supernumerary? After all, that is better than serving in a transport. It would give me much pleasure."

I apologised for my candour, and replied as briefly. We were at war, and I did not like being attached to the staff without special functions. I did not aspire to high honours, and only asked to be appointed to a fighting ship, it did not matter which.

"I thought so," the admiral laughed; "you are an incorrigible fellow. Unfortunately, no destroyer is free. Well, a vacancy will, no doubt, turn up somewhere. Go to Michael Paulovitch,[6] he has got something up his sleeve for you. It is a pity you won't come on the staff as supernu-

---

6. Rear-Admiral Michael Paulovitch, son of Paul, Molas, Makaroff's Chief of the Staff. He went down with his chief in the *Petropavlovsk*. Amongst acquaintances the surname is rarely used.—Trans.

merary. However, that is your business."

I tried to soften the effect of my blunt refusal. I said I was truly grateful for his sympathy with my sad position on board a transport. I had been so long an ordinary ship's officer (as opposed to serving on the staff) that these duties were what I liked best, and it was therefore, etc., etc.

"Oh, nonsense!" interrupted the admiral. "We know one another. I can understand you, and in your place would, perhaps, act in the same way—God grant a happy issue!" With his usual ending he dismissed me once more.

Very glad—I know all about it," said the chief of the staff, when he received me. "I have already told you off. You are going to the *Diana* as second-in-command. It is certainly no very grand billet. Your ship belongs to the "Goddesses" built in Russia.[7] No other appointment for you was vacant. You will have to work hard. There is an enormous amount for you to do there.

How true Admiral Molas's words were I only understood when I had been on board the *Diana* some days. My journal contains not a line about these days. There was so much for me to do that I hardly had time to eat and sleep. The cruiser had been commissioned on January 30. Previous to this she had been eleven months in the Reserve. If on leaving Cronstadt (autumn 1902) she had carried a normal complement, she ought now to have had on board men belonging to two annual contingents, who had never gone to sea in her. These two contingents would aggregate about one-third of the complement. As a matter of fact, 50 *per cent*, of the whole crew were peasants dressed as blue-jackets. A single cruise from Port Arthur to Vladivostok and back was the entire sea experience of a good half of the remainder. Manners and customs had grown up amongst the men, which were anything but man-of-war-like.

Even in barracks things were different. I could have imagined myself to be, not on board a warship, but in a small village. At every kind of work one never heard a proper word of command or a clear order. The petty officers "begged" the men to do this or that. Not even the boatswain knew how to act as a superior. He requested the "children" to go to the work in a friendly way. Everything was carried out in a hurry and superficially. I don't exaggerate in the least. These were

---

7. *Pallada, Diana, Aurora*.—Protected cruisers of 6, 600 tons, 13,000 H.F., 19½ knots (nominal), eight 6-inch and twenty-two 12-pounder Q. F. guns, 3 funnels.—Trans.

facts. The *Angara* had certainly not received the best of the men of the various ships of the squadron, though these were in commission, but her crew of odds and ends was, compared with that of the *Diana*, faultlessly trained. It was an endless trouble to eradicate the patriarchal tone which had grown up in the *Diana*, and to infuse some military spirit into the life on board. The dirt on board was incredible, especially in such holes and corners as a casual inspection might overlook. Such a result was quite natural after eleven months in Reserve. During that time the cruiser had become a floating barrack, but a good barrack it could never become.

On board a ship's crew lives so crowded together and under such totally different conditions as compared to the shore, that order and cleanliness inside and outside are the first conditions of any well being. Order and cleanliness can only flourish when the entire organisation of a ship in all its parts is in full working trim. To turn a ship into barracks is an impossibility. While in Reserve—of course, I don't refer to short periods for making good defects—every ship goes back. Slowly but surely the good tone and the activity of the personnel, as well as the good condition of the *matériel*, decline, until the ship ceases to be a man-of-war. Life on board then begins to resemble one of those long Polar nights, during which the strongest and most energetic men fall a prey to depression, however much they strive after artificial distraction. The monotony produces boredom, and boredom causes discouragement. Eleven months on board in Reserve means about the same thing as eleven months imprisonment *en masse*. I said that on board the *Diana* I could imagine myself in a small village. Such conditions as existed on board her can really only arise in prisons where supervision is lax and easy-going.

I broke with all these traditions, which had already produced bad effects. Of course, I had to demand many a thing of which the men had long since lost the habit. Consequently, there was a certain amount of reluctance. Happily, I was most energetically supported by the captain, who had only taken over the cruiser two or three months before I joined. The greater part of the officers also supported me with zeal and intelligence. This was especially important.

We could perhaps have brought the ship's company of the *Diana* to work by force, and perhaps even to learn this or that. But that would not have sufficed. It was necessary to make these indolent, dull-witted creatures grasp the utility of their work. They could not be left in the belief that all that was demanded of them was the mere caprice of all-powerful superiors, whom they were bound to obey in compliance with laws which they did not even know. Makaroff's arrival was of great help in all this. Gradually a change took place. There arose the spirit which leads to victory—faith in the leader at whose command one gladly faces death. It only remained to instil into the men the fact that death was not the main thing, but victory; that it was not sufficient to be able to die, but that one had to know how to fight. They had to learn to fight, and to grasp the necessity for keeping everything on board ship, down to the smallest detail, in good order and readiness for war. Gradually their dullness and discontent gave way to their instinctive love of fighting, and this had to be brought home to them.

It gave a deal of trouble, and there were some failures, but in time everything got better. The chief merit lay with my messmates. It was a labour of love to them to break down the stone wall between forecastle and quarterdeck. They mixed with the men, and missed no opportunity of making it clear to them that we all, from admiral to recruit, had the same task. Nowhere is the connection between superior and subordinate more apparent than in a fleet. Nowhere is it easier to make this clear to the men. Equality in the face of death binds closely. In the army one can protect the lives of the leaders more than that of the so-called "food-for-guns," the rank and file; in a fleet this is not possible. The higher a man's position on board, the greater his personal danger. Between the commander of an army and the commander of a fleet there is a tremendous difference. The one directs the battle without being exposed to much danger to his person; the other leads his force himself into action in his flagship. The enemy's whole fire is concentrated on her, and he is the first to risk his skin. The sailor is not *sent* into action, but *led* into action, which is a very different thing.

And that is why Makaroff's "run" in the *Novik* produced such a tremendous effect. The consciousness that leaders as well as subordinates were exposed alike to the chances of being killed, can be made to exert an extraordinary influence, if the crew are properly educated up to it. If this has been done, then the men look upon every order received more in the light of valuable instructions coming from an older and more experienced comrade. When forced to work they don't do so because of the compulsion, but because they realise the object of the work.

To introduce such conditions on board my cruiser was my keenest endeavour, and I was fortunate enough in finding amongst my comrades men of the same ideas. On board our ship there were no special hours of instruction, but the officers, as I have just mentioned, gave up their whole time to their subordinates. In reality they took more trouble in learning to know the men they were to command in action, than to instruct them. Often they only explained this or that order in a few words, or they gave a few brief elucidations on any theme the men might happen to be discussing, and, as it were, quite *en passant*. The effect was tremendous. I often felt a real pleasure when I saw how the men seemed to fall in with our views.

I observed this, for instance, when the petty officer in charge of a shell room reported to me that the place was damp, and asked for some men to make covers for the projectiles. "The shell might otherwise get rusty and damage the guns in action." Formerly many of the crew thought that cleanliness was a caprice of their superiors. In fact, they never noticed anything but the grossest filth. Now they realised all at once what cleanliness meant. One had only to point out that a man, in being wounded, might fall on to the deck and get dirt into his wound. Now dirt produced gangrene, and gangrene in a very slight wound might lead to the loss of the whole limb, or even to death.

Personally, I always wound up as follows: "Work hard so as to learn how to fight. If in battle you don't kill the enemy, he will kill you." This simple philosophy always appealed to them.

Amongst the ships of the squadron the *Diana* was no exception. It is true that not all the ships had been kept in Reserve for eleven months before the outbreak of the war, but many were in a similar plight. The arrival of the beloved admiral, who set such an example in his own person, produced a new spirit. The strenuous, zealous activity of all officers and other superiors made it possible to complete the theoretical education of the men much more rapidly than in times of peace. But nothing could replace the lack of practical sea training. The time which had been wasted in this respect was irretrievably lost. The peasants in blue-jackets' clothes and the gentlemen in naval uniform might become heroes, but not experienced seamen. Long years would have been required to turn our floating barracks into a squadron, ready for war. Our sad experiences on March 10 proved this clearly enough. Admiral Makaroff had taken up his command for the purpose of leading us into action. He found himself under the necessity of first teaching us the simplest movements. The evolutionary exercises took place as in times of peace, without an enemy in sight. And yet ships rammed one another. Was this the fault of the captains, who now took their ships to sea for the first time?

It was too late to deplore these omissions, and there was nothing left but to give the squadron at the last moment such training as was possible.

When the officers of the *Diana* spoke to me about the manoeuvring on March 10, they always referred also with shame and indignation to a certain cruise which the squadron had carried out to Shantung and back on January 30, soon after the ships had been brought up to sea-going complements. It was generally known as "the cruise of the Argonauts."

As regarded the gunnery training of the individual ships, things were not so bad. With the unanimous cooperation of all parties, from the captain to the youngest blue-jacket, a good deal could yet be done in this respect.

The admiral developed this idea in some detail at the next meeting of admirals and captains. He said that everyone was bound to devote himself with all his heart to his special task, no matter how trifling it might appear. Individuals were not to do this, simply because they were ordered to, but because they ought to be penetrated by the great importance of faithful devotion to duty. Only thus was any success conceivable. The gun-layers ought to be impregnated with the idea that one lucky shot might destroy the conning tower of a hostile battleship, and thus decide the battle. If the gun-layer knew this, he would ever keep it before him and be sure always to aim carefully. That was the bedrock of it all. If men were really determined, they would be able to do it.

"It is too late now to start on a systematic training," said the admiral; "every captain, every specialist, in fact every officer who has charge of any department or part of the ship, no matter how trivial in itself, must hunt out with the utmost keenness any and every defect and work seriously at its removal. Let superiors and subordinates assist one another in this. Don't be afraid of making mistakes. Even a piece of work which starts on wrong lines and has to be given up bears fruit. Inactivity must remain barren of results, even if due to justifiable doubts as to the utility of the work. Remember that we do not know what time we have for our preparations. It may be months, it may be hours, nay, minutes, which still separate us from the final issue. Don't waste time by brooding over things. Bring out everything you may possess in knowledge, experience, and initiative, and do what you are able. What we can't complete will have to remain incomplete, but whatever *can* be done, must be done. Everyone—understand me well—everyone must be penetrated with the importance of his particular task. Even the least of us should realise how great the responsibility is which our country has laid on him—God grant a happy issue!"

Everyone set to work with frantic zeal. Never, not in the palmiest days of the Pacific Squadron, have I seen such enthusiasm.

Only a portion of the west basin had been dredged before the outbreak of the war. The remainder was still shallow, and was uncovered at low water. The ships which were lying crowded together in the deepest part of the basin utilised these mud flats. Here they planted numerous small targets, varying in shape and colour, and fired at these from morning to night with sub-calibre guns. The gun-layers had thus an opportunity of practising laying on an object correctly, and of finding and maintaining the range, with frequent change of object.

"All guns to fire at the red target!" came the gunnery lieutenant's order from the conning tower. "The stern group on the black target!"—"The battery on the brown target!"—"All guns on the round target!" etc., etc.

It may be thought that exercises, like this repelling of an imaginary torpedo attack, did not possess any very great value. But what emulation it produced! I could hear how in the men's messes as well as in the ward room, nothing else was talked of but who had made the best practice that day. Involuntarily I thought of the emulation in former times between sailing ships, even between the masts of the same ship. Now the same picture was presented when the gun-layers hotly argued the point, the officers commanding groups made sarcastic remarks to one another, and the gunnery lieutenant spoke heatedly about some ship having cheated. In the midst of all this zeal I felt happy at heart, I felt that I was once more in my old squadron.

CHAPTER 5

The Fatal April 13

On March 18 the placing of the *Tsesarevitch's* cofferdam was begun. The unfortunate and damaged old cofferdam of the *Retvisan* was removed, and a new one built. Meanwhile, the battleship lay across the basin, her stern secured to a buoy, her bow resting on the bottom near the water's edge. The hole was being provisionally closed by divers, and the pumping vessels were continuously at work keeping under the water. It was said that great difficulty was experienced merely in preventing the water from rising. Slowly but steadily the ship sank deeper and deeper into the soft mud which forms the bottom in the west basin. In spite of this, however, no one doubted that the repairs of the *Retvisan* would ultimately succeed.

"Makaroff goes there nearly every day, and the captain neither eats nor sleeps, but works night and day." This was sufficient guarantee that all would go well.

I have already mentioned that we expected great things from a detachment of workmen from the Baltic Yard. These people's connection with the government was purely a matter of business. They formed a self-contained section of their company's personnel, and were not interfered with in any way by our bureaucrats. (See note following).

★★★★★★

Note:—Our expectations were fulfilled.
The detachment of workmen from the Baltic Yard only consisted of an engineer, Mr K——, a foreman, a, draughtsman, one hundred and eighty-nine workmen, and two clerks. During the siege, four of their number were killed, one died of scurvy, and eleven were wounded.

Compared with the masses of men which the Imperial Dockyard of Port Arthur had at its disposal, the number of these Baltic workmen was very small. The following is the work accomplished by them:—

Repairing the under-water damage caused by mines or torpedoes to the *Retvisan, Tsesarevitch, Pobieda,* and *Sebastopol* (in the case of the latter, twice over). All these repairs were carried out by means of cofferdams.

Repairing underwater damage from a mine to *Bayan*, and the best half of similar damage caused by a torpedo to the *Pallada*. Both these ships were repaired in dry dock.

Repairing damage caused to the *Amur* by being rammed. For this purpose the ship was only heeled.

Changing a damaged screw-blade of the *Sebastopol* by means of a bell-shaped cofferdam.

General repairs to the *Peresviet, Sebastopol,* and *Retvisan* after the battle of August 10.

Repairing hundreds of shot holes of every kind on board our ships during the bombardment from the land batteries.

Repairing the destroyers *Reshitelny, Rasyashtchy, Lieutenant Burakoff Beshumny, Storoyevoy,* and several others.

The Imperial Dockyard only provided the necessary amount of unskilled labour. There was really no need for this, as the military authorities disposed of any number of men as good. What was of real importance was that the dockyard authorities did not dare to interfere with the skilful work of the "Baltics." This enforced passive attitude was probably more useful than their active assistance would have been.

I should further like to mention that the Baltic detachment brought with them five railway car loads of material, implements, and instruments. Amongst these were pneumatic, electro-pneumatic, etc., etc. tools, such as we had not up to then possessed at Port Arthur, the chief naval base of our battle fleet.

Naturally, these workmen had been carefully selected.

★★★★★★

On March 20 our wireless stations "heard" the Japanese. That night the destroyers were sent out, but saw nothing of the enemy.

The night of March 21–22 was clear, but there was no moon. During this night the searchlights of the fortress repeatedly came upon suspicious objects out at sea. Between 12 and 1, and again towards 4 a.m., the batteries opened fire. The fire was not very brisk, and was not replied to from seaward.

At 5.45 a.m. the general signal was made: "Raise steam for full speed."

Towards seven o'clock, as soon as there was sufficient water, the squadron began to move out of the basins. The cruisers, owing to their light draught, went out first. The *Novik* and destroyers, of course, led. (The latter did not go by divisions, but as the circumstances best suited.) Then came the remaining ships, in such order as fitted in best with their berths. When we (*Diana*) steamed out at 8.25 a.m., the *Askold* and *Bayan* were already circling in the roads.

Far away to the southward, about 10 or 12 miles off, the masts and funnels of the Japanese ships appeared above the horizon. We could make out that these were the Japanese battleships and armoured cruisers standing towards Port Arthur in two columns. To the south-east, but much nearer, were the "Greyhounds."

By 8.45 the enemy's armoured ships had approached up to 8 miles, when they altered course to the westward.

"They want to go to Liao-ti-shan and chuck about 'portmanteaus' again," was the joke on board the *Diana*. "They won't hit anything; we have taken care of that."

The weather was glorious: a clear sky, thermometer 37° F., no sea and no swell. A faint breeze was blowing from the south-west.

At nine o'clock the hostile squadron passed out of sight behind the Liao-ti-shan Hills. A single armoured cruiser remained off the mouth of the harbour. Evidently she was to watch how the shells pitched.

At 9.35 the Japanese battleships began to circle south of Liao-ti-shan, just as they did on the previous occasion, and to fire their 12-inch guns at Port Arthur when they reached a certain point. They were probably not a little surprised when they discovered that this time they were not to do this with impunity. We replied. The *Retvisan*, *Peresviet*, and *Pobieda* fired from the basin. Our ships even had a slight advantage, for the Japanese fired under way, whilst ours did so from a fixed place, the position of which was exactly known, just like a shore battery.

Meanwhile, the hostile armoured cruisers steamed past us demonstratively, as though to challenge us to fight. We did not respond. Towards ten o'clock the *Petropavlovsk*, flying the commander-in-chief's flag, steamed out into the roads. When the Japanese noticed that our squadron was leaving the basins which were exposed to their bombardment, they concentrated their fire on the entrance. Their practice there was very good. At 10.20 the *Poltava* came out at full speed. Twice a shell struck the water so close to her as to cover her with water and splinters. Luckily, the ship herself was not struck.

At 10.40 a.m. we heard cheering on Golden Hill. The signal station reported by Morse flags that one of the Japanese ships had apparently been hit.[1] This the Japanese did not seem to like. They ceased bombarding and steamed away from Liao-ti-shan, In doing so they carefully kept out of the range of our forts.

Towards eleven o'clock the hostile cruisers approached to 57 cables,[2] evidently with the intention of challenging us. They were five in number, as opposed to two battleships, one armoured cruiser, and two protected cruisers on our side, not counting the *Novik* and the destroyers. The admiral steered towards them in such a way as if trying to cut them off from their main body.

At 11.30 a.m. the 12-inch turrets of the *Petropavlovsk* opened fire.

The cruisers never replied to our fire, but steamed off to the southward towards their battleships, at high speed. The latter, however, made no haste whatever to come to their assistance. Evidently they wanted to avoid getting within the range of our forts.

Moreover, the *Sebastopol*, *Peresviet*, and *Pobieda* were just then coming out to support us. The two last named had the deepest draught, and were only able to leave the harbour at the top of high water.

We ceased firing, as the enemy was so determined not to come within reach of our fortress guns. At 11.20 a.m. the flagship made the signal: "Stop engines. Ships' companies to go to dinner." The cooks of messes ran to the galley with their dishes. "With old 'Beardy' there is no loafing. It used to be very different," they were heard to chatter cheerfully as the dinners were being served out.

The next high water was after dark. It was on account of this, and also because the Japanese had retired, that the admiral made his squadron go up harbour again at once. Towards 12.30 the first two ships, the *Peresviet* and *Pobieda*, received orders to that effect. Whilst they were doing this the remaining ships advanced towards the Japanese. They were to cover the movements of these two ships, which the enemy, owing to the great distance, would anyhow not be able to make out

---

1. We heard later on that it was the *Fuji*. A 12-inch shell had hit her fore-turret.
2. 11,400 yards. In the Russian Navy the long ranges are always indicated in cables. One cable = 200 yards.—Trans.

clearly. The Japanese probably thought that we meant to face this unequal contest. They retreated southward, evidently with the intention of drawing us out to sea. We chased the enemy for half an hour and then turned back. The *Sebastopol, Petropavlovsk,* and *Poltava* went up harbour before the tide began to ebb. The cruisers followed them in. By 3 p.m. we were back at our old berth in the West Basin. The whole thing was a *tour de force*. During a single high tide nearly the whole squadron had gone out, manoeuvred about, and gone in again. Only a short time ago we required *two* high tides, that is, nearly twenty-four hours, merely to go out.

The feeling amongst the crews was as if we had scored a victory. We certainly had not beaten the Japanese, but we had overcome our own slackness and want of enterprise.

During the night of March 24 we occasionally received Japanese wireless messages. It was intended to send the cruisers out scouting next morning. We were greatly pleased, and in hopes of perhaps coming upon one of the "Greyhounds," but at 4 a.m. there was a thick fog: we could not see a cable's length, and had to abandon all hopes of any adventures. Towards noon it cleared a little, but came on as thick as ever later on.

March 25 brought real spring weather with a temperature of 55° F. in the shade. All hands in the dockyard and on board ship were as busy as bees; the *Tsesarevitch's* cofferdam was at last placed: it was now possible to move the battleship into the East Basin, closer to the dockyard. Thanks to the energetic labours of our experienced divers, it had been possible to close up temporarily the hole in the *Retvisan's* bottom: the ship was pumped out and floated once more.

On March 25 the admiral took his squadron to sea during the early high water: this was soon after daybreak. Makaroff merely meant to practise manoeuvres: unfortunately, he was forced into this by our insufficient training. The squadron stood to the southward and to the westward, and carried out various evolutions: their execution was very poor; sometimes it was indeed a sorry sight. "The 'Argonauts,'" growled the navigator.

Towards 9.30 several vessels hove in sight. They were standing on a north-westerly course, across our path, and were made out to be merchant steamers: a fourth was following a short distance astern. The *Askold* received orders by signal to stop and examine the steamers: they were British on the way to Niu-Chwang in ballast; they were allowed to go when nothing suspicious was found on board.

At 10.20 a.m. we made a better haul: the squadron was just passing North and South Hwang-tching-tau. These are the largest islands of the Maio-tao group which lie nearest to Port Arthur. The *Novik* was despatched to see if everything was all right in the Sound. Just as she could see round the Cape, she sighted a small steamer, not flying any flag, and towing a *junk*. When the steamer caught sight of us she tried to escape; but to get away from the *Novik* and her destroyers was not so easy. A few shots were first fired across her bows and under her stern; when this produced no effect a shot or two was fired into her, and she was finally forced to stop. A portion of the passengers (or crew) tried to get ashore in the junk; they were all captured. They consisted of twelve Japanese and nine Chinese; the steamer was Japanese, of rather less than 1,000 tons. She was called *Haien Maru*, and had been chartered by the special correspondent of the newspaper *Asahi*. Now she was employed, as was pretended, in transporting dealers in wood and fish to the different islands. This was obviously a pretext. The sparse woods of Kwantung had long since been seized for the defence of Port Arthur, and in the sea, mines were caught more often than fish. The steamer had been so damaged by our fire that she was unable to steam with her own engines; when the attempt to take her in tow failed, she was destroyed.

All these details we only heard after our return to Port Arthur; at the time we only saw the *Novik* and destroyers were going slow, and then, when they reached the Sound between the islands, that they suddenly dashed ahead for all they were worth. Before we had time to make out what kind of vessel they were engaged with, their victim was already in flames; the latter had stopped, and our vessels surrounded her.

Everyone was pleased with the *Novik*. "The *Novik* is a first-rate little ship: she sees and brings up everything: a regular retriever," was the general verdict.

Soon after this episode we wheeled about. Towards 2 p.m. we re-entered the port.

Whilst we were manoeuvring about, the *Amur* was detached to lay mines. She steamed away in the direction of Talienwan: she probably went to Melanhö Bay.

During the night of March 26-27 the Japanese repeated their efforts to block the entrance to Port Arthur. The attempt began at 2.20 a.m. It was the same sight as the first time; with this difference, however, that no one was in doubt as to the intentions of the steamers: fire was opened instantly all along the line.

The *Retvisan* was, indeed, not at her old billet, but in her place the *Bobr* and *Gilyak* lay in the entrance; and from the foot of Golden Hill the new battery, with the *Angara's* 4.7-inch guns, was firing.

Two of the "blocking-steamers" ran aground on the beach immediately below this battery. When they were still steaming ahead, the destroyer *Silny* delivered a plucky attack on them. Quite indifferent to the hail of our shell, she steamed up close to one steamer and fired her torpedoes at quite close quarters. The torpedoes hit, but were unfortunately placed. None of the steamers were so damaged as to sink at once. One, for instance, had her whole stem shattered, but the collision bulkhead held, and the steamer went on.

Two other steamers kept a little more to the left; one sank before she had come up to the lighthouse, the other grounded precisely at the spot where the *Retvisan* had struck.

It was said that there were more steamers besides these. One portion was supposed to have been sunk by our mines, another by our gunfire, and the remainder had lost heart and fled to seaward. Rumours of this kind must be received with very much caution.

It is astonishing how many hostile vessels are always destroyed in night attacks. Everyone has this weakness. No one is boasting, but everyone is so firmly convinced of the truth of what he reports, that he is ready to take his oath on it.

Next day, just as it was getting light, the entire Japanese squadron came in sight on the horizon. At 6.30 a.m. the "Greyhounds" came up quite close with the greatest boldness. However, it sufficed for one of our coast batteries to "show its teeth" to drive them away to the proper distance.

Our squadron was on the point of going out of harbour. The Japanese were thus able to satisfy themselves that their second attempt to bottle us up had failed like the first.

Towards 8 a.m. we were already in battle formation. With the *Petropavlovsk* leading, we cruised about in the bay between White Wolf Hill and Cross Hill, (See chart further on). Our object was to tempt the enemy to come closer; but he was not to be caught. Until 9.30 a.m. his armoured ships, accompanied by the "Greyhounds," steamed up and down on the horizon. Then they disappeared in a south-easterly direction, without having attempted an attack on the squadron, or a bombardment. We anchored, to wait and see whether they would return. When nothing happened, we calmly returned to the basins about 2 p.m.

In order to stop any further blocking attempts on the part of the enemy, we laid out two floating booms in the roads. Such boom defences, or, at least, the material for them, ought to have been prepared in time of peace. Now it was impossible suddenly to procure all that was needful. We had to make use of what was available, and console ourselves with the faint hope of perhaps being able to strengthen the boom by and by, if circumstances permitted.

The admiral tested these booms himself, but the results were not very brilliant. The boom was only able to stop small steamers of 1,000 to 1,500 tons, if built with a straight stem (that is, vertical to the surface of the water). Steamers with over-hanging bows got over the boom, though with difficulty. When the *Angara* (11,000 tons, slanting stem) was tried, she passed over the boom, with her engines stopped, as if she had never noticed it. The vessel pressed the boom bodily under and kept her way right up to the mouth of the harbour. With two or three steamers of the *Angara*'s size, the Japanese could bottle our squadron up in Port Arthur. We therefore had to think out some better means of defence.

The fact that the entrance into the harbour ran quite straight without any bends constituted a great danger. "Blocking-steamers" which, by chance or intentionally, headed the right way, could reach the entrance even with their engines disabled and the rudder shot away, as was proved by the *Angara*'s trial. In consideration of the magnitude of this danger, Makaroff ordered two steamers of the East Chinese Railway Company, the *Chailar* and *Charbin*, to be sunk across the channel. They were placed to the westward of the centre of the fairway, near the banks of the Tiger's Tail Peninsula. A little further up the steamer *Shilka* was sunk, but to the eastward of the centre of the fairway. In this way, ships on entering were forced first to keep to the east side of the fairway, then to turn to port, back again to starboard, and then only to steer the usual course. This manoeuvre, at night, blinded by searchlights and under fire from the guard-ships and batteries, was, to say the least of it, very difficult. Moreover, the "blocking-steamers" aground on the beach below Golden Hill formed a new obstacle.

The protection of the entrance was further strengthened, as far as possible, by a suitable disposition of the cruisers and gun-boats as guard-ships. On the shoal off Lighthouse Hill a "fire-ship" had already stranded. She lay there almost exactly on the spot on which the *Retvisan* had grounded on February 8. This steamer was used as a breakwater. The *Gilyak* placed herself behind the former and tied up to her. She thus formed, together with the coast batteries (armed by the *Angara*) to the right and left of her, the first line of defence. Further back, to the right and left of the entrance, our gun-boats, secured to buoys, formed the second line of defence. Finally, right inside came the *Askold* and *Bayan*, which swept the whole fairway with their guns. These two cruisers were the third line of defence.

A floating torpedo-net defence for the protection of the guard-ships was being made with the greatest haste. Such a net defence is a boom, from which torpedo-nets are suspended. They were placed right across the shallow entrance, and as the nets reached from the surface of the water to the bottom, they formed a very safe protection against any torpedoes fired from the roads inwards.

We found out that the Japanese intended, after the failures of their "fire-ships," to try and cover the sea with some burning liquid. Their plan was as follows:—when the flood tide was running its strongest, certain steamers were to be made to drift with it up to the entrance. These steamers were to be filled with petroleum, *benzin*, and any other liquid capable of burning on the water, and the Japanese meant to set them on fire after they had commenced drifting, and then to blow them up. We made some trials to that end, which proved that such an attack would constitute a very serious danger for our squadron. This danger was especially great with southerly winds, even very light ones. Our inventive geniuses were well to the front at once. They constructed several booms of non-flammable material, which would stop the burning stream (only the surface had to be barred). All schemes were at once tested and the best adopted. The admiral was true to his maxim: "Everyone makes mistakes. Far rather acknowledge your mistake ten times over, and start afresh, than be permanently inactive and only consider how the thing had best be done. *Le mieux c'est l'ennemi du bien.*"

Amongst others, the following measures were adopted:—the ships which lay in the fairway for the protection of the harbour entrance were placed with their sterns to seaward. They were secured with strong stern hawsers to buoys, securely moored. When the burning stream approached, they were to move their engines full speed ahead. This was bound to produce a powerful surface current outwards. Would it be strong enough to overcome the fiery stream on the surface? That was the question. Nothing but the actual test would prove it. Meanwhile, the admiral would not leave even the most trifling "dodge" untried, if it promised any advantage.

The repairs of our battleships were now taken in hand. The engineers promised to complete the *Tsesarevitch* by the end of May, and the *Retvisan* in June. Some use was even found for the damaged and useless cofferdam of the *Retvisan*. It was repaired, altered in outline, and placed against the *Sebastopol*. By means of this, the damage that battleship had received on March 12 (collision) was made good.

Nearly every night the destroyers were sent to sea. This was done, less with the object of looking for the enemy, who had completely disappeared, than as an exercise. These boats had now to acquire the war training which they ought to have possessed long ago.

The main thing was that no one remained idle.

These were beautiful times. Our new commander-in-chief thought of everything. For instance, all ceremonies were abolished. If a senior officer passed the ship, all work went on calmly. This was even the case if he came on board.

"I haven't come here to hold parades. When God permits the war to come to an end, the old routine can be started again. Now, we have no time for such like." Thus Makaroff spoke, half joking, half in earnest.

The Uniform Regulations were also simplified as much as possible. The monkey-jacket was worn for everything. However, we were all ordered always to carry some arm, for all contingencies. The choice of weapon was left to each individual. According to circumstances, it might be sword, dirk (worn afloat by all commissioned officers), or even pistol. Still better was a good revolver, not worn in a case or belt, but simply in one's pocket.

On April 3 a tragi-comedy was enacted. In broad daylight and in fine weather a merchant steamer, showing no colours, was sighted heading boldly for Port Arthur. We were all delighted, since it was quite clear that she was bringing in supplies of some kind. When the vessel reached the limits of range of our fortress guns she stopped, and evidently had a look round. Then, instead, as we expected, of making recognition signals to Golden Hill, she turned short round and steamed away—showing Japanese colours.

When the cruiser on guard duty steamed out and began to chase her, all that was left of her was a small puff of smoke on the horizon.

The squadron was in such good spirits that this piece of "colossal cheek," carried out with impunity, only evoked hearty laughter. It gave rise to a number of well-meant witticisms with reference to "Beardy." Much in this way the soldiers of Napoleon's Old Guard must have smiled half-respectfully, half-familiarly, when their emperor could not get his foot into the stirrup.

"It seems that 'Little Grandfather' was quite mad with rage. He certainly had been made a fool of and no mistake. It is quite incredible. Every one sees the steamer, she goes everywhere, turns everything topsy-turvy, and then gets clean away before our eyes. There is no fool like an old fool, my 'Little Grandfather.'" Our people mocked away in this style, and chuckled at the thought that their ideal chief had for once in a way been taken in.

Orders were given that between daybreak and dusk the cruiser on guard duty in the inner harbour was to be prepared to go to sea at a moment's notice. All the same, it was the state of the tide which decided, even in case of cruisers, whether they could go out. If low water coincided with daybreak or dusk, the guard-ship was paralysed. The natural solution of this dilemma was to keep the cruiser in the roads and to relieve her as the state of the tide permitted. But this would have meant exposing one of our cruisers to torpedo attack every night, and we only possessed very few of them. The admiral found a very happy solution. As I have already mentioned, the Japanese "fireships," which had grounded at the foot of Golden Hill, formed a kind of breakwater.

Between them and the *Shilka* the steamer *Eduard Barri* was sunk. She thus acted as a kind of breakwater, behind which a number of buoys were securely moored. The cruiser on guard secured head and stern between these buoys. There she was well protected against Whitehead torpedoes by the submerged hull, could not swing, and, irrespective of wind and tide, always had her broadside facing seawards, whilst her bows headed the right way for getting to sea. The cruiser was thus always in a position to meet an attack from seaward with the whole of her armament. On the other hand, she had only to cast off her bow and stern fasts, if required to chase. It was so simple and so obvious, yet no one had hit upon it before.

On April 6, Golden Hill signal station reported the "Greyhounds" in sight. The *Bayan* was the guard-ship outside. All remaining cruisers were ordered to raise steam. There was, however, no occasion for them to go out. The "Greyhounds" only showed themselves and disappeared at once. The weather was now spoiling.

On April 7 it rained nearly twenty-four hours on end, and on the 8th there was a thick fog. We neither saw nor heard anything of the enemy.

On April 9 the *Diana* was on guard. We cruised about the whole day outside Port Arthur, and kept a sharp look-out, but saw and heard nothing.[3]

On April 10 the weather at last improved, and orders were given for the whole squadron to go to sea next day for tactical exercises.

The moving out began at 6.30 a.m. By about 8.30 all ships were out—that is, five battleships, four cruisers, and the destroyers. We proceeded in cruising formation towards Talienwan, and performed evolutions. There was a very light Easterly wind. The sky was cloudless, the horizon clear, and the range of vision in the clear air very great. The signalmen with the best and most experienced "seamen's eyes" sat in the crows' nests, close under the truck (also an institution of Makaroff's), and kept as sharp a look-out as they possibly could. The torpedo officers did not budge from the receivers of the wireless instruments. All was in vain; there was nothing to be intercepted in the air, nothing to be seen afloat. Our sailing had certainly become known, and it was in no one's interest to remain in the neighbourhood of Port Arthur.

We went as far as Talienwan, described a curve to the southward, and returned, getting back at 4 p.m.

On April 12 the *Diana* was again on guard. The day passed without any occurrence of note. That night we inaugurated the new billet behind the sunken steamers.

Towards 10 p.m. Admiral Makaroff and his staff came on board.

Apart from the short apparition of the "Greyhounds" on April 6—and even that was not fully authenticated—two weeks had now passed, during which the enemy had given no sign of life. That was certainly suspicious, and therefore all destroyers ready for sea were sent out in a body during the night of April 12-13. The boats were this time to go a long way. They were given the task of searching the Elliot Islands. These islands are about 60 to 70 miles from Port Arthur, and it seemed very probable that the Japanese occasionally used them as a base. Theoretically, the dark period of one night sufficed completely for the purpose. The destroyers were promised, however, that at daybreak the *Askold* would in any case go out to meet them. The cruiser was to cover the boats if they had been delayed, and were obliged to return by day.

The *Askold* had been chosen so as to obviate any possible mistake.

---

3. We were only an guard by day and had to keep under weigh. The work of placing the buoys, at which the guard-ship was to lie, was not yet completed.

She was the only vessel in the Far East with five funnels, and could therefore be recognised without any signals, even in the dark. The weather now turned wet. It varied between drizzle and light rain. The admiral went through our battery. The men were at their action stations, and he said a few words to them, which means so much in war. Hardly had he completed his tour, when something was sighted. It was difficult to say what it was. Still, we saw in the searchlight beam from Cross Hill what were undoubtedly the outlines of vessels. They bore S. 60° E. Taking into account that our searchlights could not quite reach them, and estimating our distance from Cross Hill, as well as the angle at which its searchlights were trained, we made their distance to be about 2 miles.

The drizzling rain was brightly lit up by the searchlight beams, and rendered the field of view opaque. It seemed as if these shadows sometimes lay motionless, sometimes moved backwards and forwards on the same spot. It was now 10.30 p.m.

"Shall I open fire?" the captain asked. "Oh, who can tell what it is," the admiral replied rather crossly. "They are probably our own destroyers. They know nothing of night work. Some of them probably got separated from the rest and are now pottering about in front of Port Arthur. They can't find the others, and dare not return into harbour from fear of being taken for Japanese. Bad luck to it!" Makaroff mastered his ill-humour at once, and added in a calm voice: "Note the bearing and distance very carefully. If these turn out not to be our boats, we must certainly search the place very carefully tomorrow. Possibly something unpleasant for us has been dropped there."

The vessels now became visible, but only for a moment and then disappeared in the rain.

At 10.50 p.m. we heard to the southward of us, approximately in the direction of White Wolf Hill, the sound of guns. It did not appear to come either from the shore, or from the sub-division of harbour defence destroyers, which were watching the southern boom placed there.

The remainder of the night passed peacefully. We saw nothing; in fact, we could really see nothing on account of the rain.

Just as it was getting light next morning, at 4.15, the admiral and staff returned to the *Petropavlovsk*. Precisely at that moment several columns of smoke showed up on the eastern horizon. These were our destroyers returning from their expedition, which had been carried out successfully, but without result. They had not found anything in the bays of the Elliot Islands. Unhappily, the boats did not all return. The admiral's fears had been only too fully justified. Some of the boats had lost touch with the main body, and had not regained it Suddenly we saw the flashes of guns in the dawn to the southeast—a direction in which we had not looked for anything, (It was 5.25.) The firing could be heard distinctly. Who were fighting there, we were unable to make out, owing to the great distance. It was clear, however, that small vessels, probably destroyers, were fighting together. We (*Diana*) could have got away quickest, but the admiral apparently did not want to employ the *Diana*, which could have been mistaken for the Iwate, as he had promised the boats a cruiser, unlike any Japanese ship. For some reason or other the *Askold* was not ready.

Consequently, the *Bayan* (four funnels), which also did not resemble any Japanese ship, was ordered out. What with orders and counter-orders a good deal of time was lost. When the *Bayan* steamed out, we thought we had been quite forgotten. We therefore set off without orders and followed her. Of course we were soon left behind. When we reached the open, the *Bayan* was already a long way ahead. It turned out that the destroyer *Strashny* had parted company during the night. On looking for her consorts she came across a Japanese destroyer flotilla, which she joined. The Japanese also did not notice that the *Strashny* was an enemy, so they cruised about together before Port Arthur till daybreak. As soon as it was light enough a mutual recognition took place, and at once a desperate fight commenced, of one against six, at quite close quarters.

The *Bayan* hurried as fast as she could to the assistance of her small comrade. All she could do was to scatter the hostile boats, which were steaming round the place where the *Strashny* had sunk. The Japanese destroyers fled to the southward. The remnants of the *Strashny's* heroic crew were swimming about in life-belts, or clinging to pieces of wreckage. They greeted their cruiser with joy; but already the "Greyhounds" were approaching from the south at top speed, in the place of the destroyers, which had fled.

Sceptics will, of course, say that they were only four protected cruisers opposed to our armoured cruiser. Still, it was four to one. The *Bayan*, or her captain—ship and captain are one—did not hesitate a moment. She covered those in the water with her high sides, lowered boats to pick them up, and faced the attack lying still with her engines stopped. At that moment we were still under Golden Hill and could not make out what was going on. Our hearts stood still at the thought that her engines might be disabled. Could we arrive in time to assist her? Great Heavens, how we cursed the St Petersburg works where the *Diana* had been built! Instead of the 20 knots of the contract, we were hardly going 17. The oldest engineer had now to listen to some very bitter truths from the mouth of the youngest sub-lieutenant. The *Novik* came out and ran past us, as if we were at anchor. The *Novik* was followed by the *Askold*.

"Just look at that! It is easy to see that they were built abroad. That is something different from our 'Goddess.'"

The *Bayan* was already returning. The "Greyhounds" did not follow her. Apparently they had no desire to come within reach of our coast batteries. It was 7. 15 a.m. The destroyers back from the Elliot Islands had already got in safely. At 7.15 the *Petropavlovsk* came out. The *Poltava* followed. The *Bayan* reported by semaphore and wireless what she had seen. She was not sure whether in the heat of the action she had saved everybody: possibly there might still be some men on the wreckage. The admiral at once signalled: "Single line ahead on the *Bayan. Bayan* to lead the squadron back to the scene of the disaster. Everyone to keep a good look-out for wreckage."

The line was formed. As we lay there, with engines stopped, to let the other ships pass and then form up astern, the *Petropavlovsk* passed quite close along our starboard side.

A suppressed "Ah!" passed through the ship's company. The admiral came over to the port side of the bridge—that is, the side nearest to the *Diana*. He wore an overcoat with a fur collar. The wind was blowing about his big, fair beard. "Your health, my lads!" came in his mighty voice. Every word was clear and distinct.

"We wish your Excellency good health!" sounded back in specially hearty, cheery voices.

"God grant a happy issue!"

"Respectful thanks your—"; but the regulation reply did not get beyond this. Instead, there burst out a frantic "Hurrah!"

The admiral had already left the bridge and gone into the charthouse. He now came out again, went right out to the end of the bridge and took off his cap, waving it at us with a smile.

"Hurrah!" sounded again and again from the crew. The men clambered on to each other's shoulders to see "Little Grandfather." "Hurrah!" now shouted the officers, forgetting all restraint, and waved their caps amongst the men.

We saw our admiral for the last time.

In my diary is written as follows:

8 a.m.—We are in single line ahead, in the following order: Bayan, Petropavlovsk, Poltava, Askold, Diana, Novik.

The "Greyhounds" reappeared out of the morning mist. We steamed towards them. This time they were led by two armoured cruisers. The enemy advanced boldly towards us, though he saw that we were the stronger. A long range action commenced. At 8.10 the Japanese turned away suddenly and steamed off to the southward. The shortest distance had been 50 cables, (10,000 yards). We had no losses. For a little while longer we cruised about over the spot where the *Strashny* had gone down, and looked about for any one to save, but without any result. We were then about 15 miles from Port Arthur. Anyone with good eyes could see that the rest of our squadron was coming out. At 8.40 a.m. the Japanese battleships appeared out of the mist. They joined the armoured cruisers and "Greyhounds," and altogether headed straight for us. Now the Japanese were again the stronger, nearly twice as strong, in fact.

We followed our admiral, who was turning towards Port Arthur and retiring. The Japanese followed us, with the evident intention of attacking. The *Novik* and the destroyers made good use of their speed. They steamed ahead and a little to port. The *Diana* became rear ship. I confess quite candidly that our position was causing me some anxiety. We were steaming as fast as we could, but the distance steadily decreased. By nine o'clock we were only 38 cables (7,500 yards) from the hostile leader (apparently *Mikasa*). Our stern 6-inch guns had already adjusted their sights. We were waiting for the flagship to order us to open fire; but no signal came. The Japanese also did not fire, just as if there had been an agreement to that effect. At 9. 1 5 we reached the fire zone of our fortress guns (6 to 7 miles). At 9.30 the enemy gave up the chase, without having fired a gun, and shaped course to the westward. The distance between us began to increase.

"Why did they not fire?" we asked ourselves. The *Diana* and *Askold* had been the rear ships at a distance of 38 cables, surely that was tempting enough to send some "portmanteaus" whizzing across.

Towards 9.30 we joined up with the remainder of the squadron. It was complete except for the damaged ships. The Japanese slowly moved behind Liao-ti-shan, as if they intended to commence their usual bombardment. Admiral Makaroff apparently intended to stand backwards and forwards as usual between White Wolf Hill and Cross

Hill. The sinking of the *Strashny*, the hurried exit of single ships which this had caused, the sighting of the hostile fleet, and the forming up of the squadron—all this had somewhat blunted the impressions of last night, which, moreover, appeared quite unimportant. Neither the admiral nor those about him gave any further thought to the suspicious shadows which we had seen so indistinctly when the searchlights were illuminating the rain so brightly. These shadows, however, had been seen precisely on the "figure of eight" we were making, namely, South of Cross Hill and East of White Wolf Hill. Everyone had forgotten that we were to search out this place to see whether they had dropped "something unpleasant for us."

"The gun-layers to remain at their guns; the remainder fall out, but not to separate," I ordered.

The gunnery lieutenant came up to me. "Now for the old story," he said; "now they will chuck 'portmanteaus' from a distance. Let us go and have a smoke."

"By all means," I replied. "Nothing of any importance is likely to happen now. For today we have got everything behind us. We'll start washing decks. They haven't been touched since the hands were called."

We both came down from the upper bridge. The gunnery lieutenant went to the smoking place, where the slow match was kept burning. I went on the forecastle, where I stood at the starboard bow 6-inch gun, and was just giving the boatswain the usual orders, when an explosion, with a dull, rolling sound shook the whole ship, as if a 12-inch gun had gone off quite close. I looked round vaguely. A second explosion, even more violent! What was happening? Suddenly cries of horror arose: "The *Petropavlovsk!* The *Petropavlovsk!*" Dreading the worst, I rushed to the side. I saw a huge cloud of brown smoke. "That is *pyroxiline*, therefore a torpedo," passed through my mind.

In this cloud I saw the ship's foremast. It was slanting, helpless, not as if it was falling, but as if it were suspended in the air. To the left of this cloud I saw the battleship's stern. It looked as always, as if the awful happenings in the forepart were none of its concern. A third explosion! White steam now began to mix with the brown cloud. The boilers had burst! Suddenly the stern of the battleship rose straight in the air. This happened so rapidly that it did not look as if the bow had gone *down*, but as if the ship had broken in half amidships. For a moment I saw the screws whirling round in the air. Was there a further explosion? I don't know. It appeared to me as if the after-part of the

Petropavlovsk (all that was visible of her) suddenly opened out and belched forth fire and flames, like a volcano. It seemed even as if flames came out of the sea, long after it had closed over the wreck.

Never, even at times when the most important orders were being given, had such silence reigned on board our ship, as at this gruesome spectacle. Habit, however, becomes one's second nature. As an old navigator I was in the habit of noting everything. When I saw the explosion, I mechanically looked at my watch, and then wrote in my note-book: "*9.43.*—Explosion on board *Petropavlovsk*; and then: "*9.44.*—All over."

I believe such, almost unconscious, actions save one's nerves at moments that are so awful that one's brain reels. Now, as I am writing these lines and am living through it all again, I am firmly convinced of this. It was by my writing down these events, with their accurate time by watch, that I first managed to grasp them as real facts, and to think them out logically, as well as the other notes in my book. Without this mechanical action, panic might have seized upon me. Naturally, these workings of the mind were quite unconscious.

Outwardly all the officers of the *Diana*, like myself, remained calm. To judge by all one saw, it appeared to me that every one felt instinctively that an incautious word, a hasty movement, might conjure up a panic. We were passing through one of those critical moments, in which an insignificant external cause may incite the masses to the greatest heroism, as well as produce the most contemptible cowardice. The second-in-command. Rear-Admiral Prince Uktomsky, judged the situation quite rightly. Whilst the destroyers and torpedo craft were hurrying to the spot where the *Petropavlovsk* had sunk, and were saving what there was left to save, he hoisted the signal: "Follow me in single line ahead!" Then he placed his *Peresviet* at the head of the squadron, as if nothing had happened, and led it on as Makaroff had done.

The commander-in-chief had fallen, the command devolved on the next in seniority. *Le roi est mort, vive le roi!* That was well done! Everyone grasped that instantly.

As is known, only seven officers (the Grand Duke Cyril amongst these) and seventy-three men were saved out of the whole crew of the battleship.

The squadron steamed in very good order in the wake of its leader, as usual up to White Wolf Hill. Here it reversed its course in succession towards Cross Hill. On board our ship there was a death-like silence. But this was no sign of depression. Every soul was burning with rage against the successful enemy. All were determined to fight to the last man. The ship's company had gone to action stations of their own accord, and stood ready.

At 10.15 a.m. the *Peresviet* had already turned 16 points. Again a mine exploded, and the *Pobieda*, the second in the line, began to heel over slowly. The *Peresviet* stopped engines and turned short to port. The formation was lost: the whole squadron got mixed. Suddenly guns went off everywhere, here and there ships were struck by shell, projectiles whistled over our heads, and splinters struck the ship's side. Our ship now commenced an irregular fire. I was standing on the upper bridge with the gunnery lieutenant. At first we looked at one another, dazed, as if neither of us would believe his own senses and wanted to have his observations corroborated by the other.

"What is the matter?" he asked. "Panic," I said. There was no need to say more. We both dashed down from the bridge. On the lower bridge I saw the captain standing at the door of the conning tower.

"What are they firing for?"

"I don't know who has ordered it, sir."

"Stop it! They are off their heads!"

What was now going on around us was incredible. Mingled with the thunder of the guns came cries such as: "It's all up with us!"—"Submarines !"—"The ships are all sinking!"—"Fire, fire!"—"Save yourselves!"—The men had completely lost their heads. They hauled the hammocks out of the nettings and tore the life-belts out of each other's hands. Some were standing by to jump overboard. "Sound the cease fire!" roared the gunnery lieutenant. His voice was hardly audible in the general din. He seized the bugler, who had hidden in a corner, by the collar of his coat, and dragged him up to the bridge. At last the bugle sounded, but in a very shaky manner. "What's the matter with you?" I cried. "Have you got something sticking in your throat? Sound again! Again! Don't stop! They don't hear it!"

The notes now came better, but no one paid any attention to them.

There was a crash between the funnels. Afterwards we discovered that it was a Russian shell. Luckily, it only cut the launch's purchase and did no other damage. I ran along the batteries. "Officers, please not to allow any firing. Drive the men away from the guns." Spoken words had no effect on the gun-layers. They did not budge from their guns, and fired shell after shell, aimlessly, at an invisible enemy. We had to use force. It is wonderful how brute physical force can bring men to their senses, when they have lost their heads from the terror of imminent death.

Order was soon restored, and the firing ceased. The men recovered their senses, and with guilty faces commenced collecting the scattered hammocks and lifebelts. The guns' crews fell in at their guns. Some attempted to justify themselves, and addressed the officers timidly. They said: "It had all come so suddenly. Someone had called out, and then all the others joined in."

"What on earth did you fire at? Who ordered you to fire?" shouted the gunner furiously at a gun-layer, whom he had just torn away from his gun with all his strength.

"I" stammered the man. "God knows—I don't."

"You nearly hit the *Askold*. If you had, then God help you!"

"Don't be angry, sir, I quite see it now." I don't think I am boasting when I say that the *Diana* was one of the first ships where this aimless firing into the water and into the air, produced by the general panic, ceased. In the other ships it still lasted some minutes longer.

Some ships remained stationary, others steamed off in any direction, regardless of the formation. Others, again, turned with their helms hard over, and threatened to ram another ship any moment.

Why did the Japanese not make use of this moment to attack us? If they had concentrated their fire on the centre of this huddled-up mass of ships, every shot would have told, whilst hardly any reply would have come from us. Happily, they did not take in the situation, or possibly they could not make up their minds to act. Otherwise they would certainly have annihilated us completely. The *Peresviet* signalled: "Proceed into port, battleships leading."

It was now 10.25 a.m.

The first to enter was, of course, the *Pobieda*. She was able to work her engines, and was only heeling 5° to 6°. She had been lucky. The mine had gone off just under one of her largest coal-bunkers, which had been full, and the coal had absorbed the shock.

If only the *Petropavlovsk* had had such luck! Soon after noon we were back at our old berth in the West Basin.

What a day of misfortune! Before the war broke out we possessed seven battleships. Now only three were left: *Peresviet, Sebastopol*, and *Poltava*. However, this was not the loss which weighed on us. As the squadron was steaming up harbour, and in the absence of all official news, every one, from the oldest to the youngest, was anxiously looking out for signals. Every one still had the secret hope that Makaroff might after all have been saved, but dared not say so aloud. Every one was wishing with all his heart that one of the battleships would soon hoist the flag which we had not long ago greeted with such joy on board the *Novik*.—We were not to see it again!

It was a terrible day. Previous to this, and again later, during the war, I passed through bad moments, but never did I experience such a state of awful depression as after this event. My feelings were shared by all.

"Don't go about like a drowned rat," I said to the boatswain; "you must cheer up the men, keep up their good spirits. You don't seem to be doing anything towards this. For shame! War can't be made without losses. A battleship has gone down and the squadron has been weakened. We shall receive reinforcements. A fresh squadron is coming out. None of your hangdog looks and idleness."

"Yes, yes, your honour," said the boatswain; "we can't do without losses." He spoke in a hesitating tone, and did not look me in the face. "It's not that at all, your honour. What is a battleship? They are welcome to sink another one, and even a couple of cruisers. That's not it; but we have lost our head. Oh, why had it to be just him and not any of the others?" His voice broke, and he turned away. Just as my boatswain, thought also the masses. This idea dominated officers as well as the common seaman, only on the lower deck, amongst those simple people, it was more openly discussed than in the officers' messes.

CHAPTER 6

After Makaroff's Death

There is an old tradition, dating from the early days of Christendom, according to which a perfervid follower of the faith took an axe and demolished the statue of Serapis, cutting it into small pieces. But the heavens did not launch forth thunderbolts, and the earth did not open up, to punish the miscreant, and the heathens were much frightened. Yes, they were frightened, and therefore many had themselves baptized. They did not do this because they no longer believed in their old gods, for one does not lose one's old faith quite so quickly, but because they felt that their old gods had deserted them.

I mention this tale, as it represents very well the depressed frame of mind of the squadron after Makaroff's death. If God permitted something so sad, it meant that He had deserted us. Against this frame of mind energetic measures became necessary. Simple natures, containing little that is complex, such as the majority of our sailors, are as susceptible to a few cheering words as they are to despair. This lightened our task. I don't know what went on in the other ships, but with us on board the *Diana* the officers had never before occupied themselves so much with the men as now. Everywhere in the batteries and on the lower deck diagrams and details of the ships composing the Baltic and Black Sea Fleets were to be seen. We had prepared these ourselves, giving the displacement, armament, and armour, etc., of the ships, and had them reproduced on board.

Around these "Proclamations," as they were jokingly called, the men soon crowded. They discussed them with much eagerness, reckoned up in their heads and on their fingers the numbers of the various classes, and formed in their minds the squadron which might be sent out to the Far East. We often heard very sensible remarks. The officers joined the men here and there, and gave them any necessary explanations.

There was one question, however, which was being discussed with still more eagerness than the reinforcements we might receive. That question was: who was to replace the late Admiral Makaroff? I often went from one group to the other, listened, perhaps joined in occasionally, and explained this or that to the men. Every time I was astonished to see how well the men knew their principal leaders. They seemed to be familiar with all the personal qualities of our admirals. On the lower deck the same names were put forward as candidates for the position of *Commander-in-Chief* as in the officers' messes. They were admirals for whom I also should have voted unhesitatingly. In the first place came the names: "Dubassoff," "Tchooknin," "Rojestvensky". When the men were debating as to which had the greatest chances, one could often see from their remarks how rightly they judged all the circumstances.

"Sinovi [1] won't be sent out. He is too junior. That Alight offend the older ones. Dubassoff—that would be fine."—"But isn't he too old?"—"He old? He's as hard as nails and keen at his work."—"They say Grigori [2] has the best chances."—"No, it will be Dubassoff. His age don't count."—"I think so too. He's the best man. All the same, it would be better if he were younger."—"Why, of course, Dubassoiif."—"No, Sinovi."—"No, Grigori."

Sometimes these debates became very heated. The supporters of one or the other of the admirals were often near to deciding the argument with their fists. Then the boatswain or one of his mates interfered very energetically. "What are you shouting for? Do you think they can hear you at St Petersburg?" This would re-establish peace.

I always listened to these debates with great interest. The war had now lasted two months. The first had passed in a kind of lethargy. The real war only began during the second. The second month, under the command of a popular admiral, had shaken up our people. He had aroused their interests and their cooperation in a splendid way. It was hardly to be believed that these were the same men, who throughout the first month had brooded through their days and had looked upon every effort to arouse them as a piece of persecution on the part of their superiors. "To listen to these men," the torpedo lieutenant once

---

1. Sinovi (Zenobius) Petrovitch (son of Peter) Rojëstvensky. Pronounce: "Rab—jesi—nsky"; the accent on "jest," the "o" in the first syllable becomes a broad "ah," and the "ve" is practically swallowed.—Trans.
2. Grigori (Gregory) Paulovitch (son of Paul) Tchooknin.—Trans.

said to me, "one would think that, since Makaroff's death, the entire fleet rests on the three pillars: Dubassoff, Tchooknin, Rojestvensky."

"Well, and what do you say?"

"They are right."

On the morning of April 15 the viceroy arrived in Port Arthur. His flag was hoisted on board the *Sebastopol*, She lay in the East Basin, alongside the north mole, opposite the captain of the port's house. We hardly noticed this incident.

The younger ones could not bridle their tongues, and said that it was all make-believe. "He won't go into action with us."

The first crushing impression of the catastrophe which had robbed us of our admiral with nearly the whole of his staff, gradually faded away. And now the wildest rumours about the appointment of a successor began to circulate in the squadron. Whence their origin, no one could say. Probably they arose in our own impatient imagination. Again and again we heard the three names: Dubassoff, Tchooknin, Rojëstvensky.

At daybreak on April 15 the Japanese hove in sight. Of course we did not move out. Towards 9 a.m. a bombardment commenced. Liao-ti-shan signal station reported that only the *Kasuga* and *Nishin* were firing. The Japanese had only recently bought these two cruisers and added them to their fleet. This was their first appearance off Port Arthur. Probably they merely wanted to try their guns. The battleships were cruising about to the southward of them, without taking any part in the bombardment. Somewhat nearer, and more to the eastward, almost facing the entrance to Port Arthur, were the "Greyhounds" and two armoured cruisers. On our side the fire was replied to by the *Peresviet* and *Poltava*. This time the Japanese fired carelessly. Most of their shots went short, and fell into the southern part of the West Basin.

Our losses were only two men wounded on Tiger's Tail Peninsula. About 12.30 the Japanese steamed away at high speed. Liao-ti-shan reported that they did so, as one of their cruisers (*Kasuga* or *Nishin*) had struck a mine. Upon this all ships had fired aimlessly into the water. Probably they suspected an attack by submarines, just as we did on April 13. Two days later, Chinese spies reported that the third-class cruiser *Miyaka* had foundered in Kerr Bay (east of Talienwan), on our minefield.

These two items of news were not confirmed by the official Japanese reports from the seat of war. Our enemies always managed to keep their losses secret;³ in direct contrast with us, who always, quite candidly, kept the world informed of the state of repairs on our damaged ships. I am therefore inclined to believe the abovementioned reports, and that all the more, as the Japanese afterwards admitted the foundering of the *Miyaka*. They only put the date one month later. They similarly admitted the damage to the *Kasuga*. They explained this by saying that she had rammed the *Yoshino* in a fog—the latter ship having been sunk.

On our side the destroyer *Silny* maintained that she had sunk the *Yoshino*. On April 13 the *Silny* formed a subdivision with the *Strashny*. In themselves these disputes are without any importance. It is, after all, immaterial why the *Yoshino* sank, how the *Kasuga* was damaged, or on what precise day the *Miyaka* went down. I only mention this to show how successful the Japanese were in preserving their war secrets, and how unsuccessful we were. With us the word "secret" is mere office jargon; with the Japanese it is a matter of conscience, a sacred duty towards their country.

Of course, with us the cult of office secrecy was in full swing. Every order issued by superior authority, which differed only in a minute point from the usual form and only possessed momentary importance, was "secret." The terms "secret," "most secret," "confidential," etc., were conspicuous on all reports, but especially on all orders. The result was that all these awful words lost their meaning completely. They might have been replaced by the words "important" or "interesting." Moreover, the number of secret documents was such that it was physically impossible for any one to write them personally, or even to have them written by some confidential person. It therefore became necessary to employ clerks, or even copyists, who were then always ready to communicate interesting bits of news to their friends—of course, in strict confidence. Now it occasionally happened that real secrets found their way into the pile of office secrets. How could one distinguish them? What was "secret" was always known to everyone, except the one person who ought to have known it, and on whose silence one could have relied.

It once happened that one of the captains or commanders (I mean a particular person) asked a friend on the admiral's staff: "Is it known when we sail?"

---

3. The battleship *Yashima* struck a mine on May 15, and sank the following day on her passage to Japan. It was not till October that rumours reached Europe, and even Japan, of this incident. It became only definitely known after Tsu-shima.

"I have no idea."

On board the ship, the servant of this same officer went to his master, on the same day, and said that he ought to go to the washerwoman.

"Why?"

"I want to get your washing, sir, as we are going to sea."

"Going to sea? You are talking rot."

"No, sir, the admiral's valet told me this morning that everything is to be on board by tomorrow evening."

Once upon a time—it was some years before the war—an admiral commanding a squadron was in great tribulation. He wanted to issue an order to his captains, which he was most anxious to keep secret. "It is really maddening," he said; "everything gets known here, and to those especially who ought *not* to know." "Don't mark it 'secret,'" advised one of those present, "then not a soul will look at it." This is exactly what happened. No one took any interest in this order.

I apologise for this digression, and return to my narrative.

About the middle of April we received the official intimation that Vice-Admiral Skridloff had been appointed commander-in-chief of the Pacific Squadron. This appointment was received afloat without enthusiasm, but on the whole it was considered satisfactory. To judge by the remarks one heard, there was a general agreement to suspend judgment. The admiral was not one of the candidates who had been considered, but—we shall see.

If Makaroff had not been delayed at Mukden by his consultation with the viceroy, he would have been here on the fifteenth day from the date of his appointment, as calculated by some of us. Consequently, Skridloff might be expected between April 30 and May 3. This calculation was not confirmed. Solemn receptions, processions, special church services of intercession and for other purposes, dedications of holy images and banners—all these falsified our calculations. Faces at Port Arthur became more and more gloomy.

The Japanese had apparently disappeared from the face of the earth. Nearly three weeks passed without a sign of them. Meanwhile, the squadron slumbered on in the basins of the inner harbour. Even the scheme of guard-ships in the outer anchorage was abolished.

In fact, everything established by Makaroff disappeared. Precisely the same glorious state of affairs as had obtained before the war reappeared. The flag at the *Sebastopol's* main top-mast head seemed to possess the peculiar power of paralysing all initiative, and of stifling every word except the well-beloved "very good, sir."

The "most obedient servants" once more raised their heads and ruled the roost.

"Here we have the results of fool-hardiness," they said. (Not long ago, together with all the rest, they had cheered the commander-in-chief's flag in the *Novik* with enthusiasm.) "One must carefully distinguish between bravery and fool-hardiness. Very often it is true manliness to avoid danger. One must not hunt up danger only for the sake of cheap popularity. Our adventurous enterprises must now cease. In all service concerns there must, above all, be deliberation and broad views. The viceroy may yet have to justify himself before Russia for having been so weak as to hand over the command to the so-called 'Little Grandfather.' *He* would never have risked such a thing. You see what has been the upshot of it all. Now he will have to put everything to rights. All our hopes are centred on him. God grant that his work may succeed! Kuropatkin well knew what he said when he proposed the toast: 'The good genius of this country—Eugene Alexeieff.'"

This sort of thing they said aloud. They wanted to be heard, and, if possible, to be reported.

It was an ugly picture.

The maxim, "*Be careful and risk nothing,*" once more had the upper hand. Under the hypnotic effect which the flag in the *Sebastopol* produced, a new maxim was added: "*Never do anything without orders or without previously asking permission.*"

Makaroff had said: "I rely upon every one of you, each in his own place, devoting his whole strength towards increasing our preparedness for war." This was so simple that every one understood it. This principle had produced great results; it had left to every captain, to every officer down to the youngest and the lowest, the most complete liberty. Personal initiative occupied the first place, the whole service was carried out on grand lines. We had got so far, that of our own accord we set ourselves tasks which were regularly completed in order. Now everything was upset.

Exercising at general quarters, combined with sub-calibre target practice, had become a regular habit in the *Diana*. When we were about to resume these again as formerly, the new regime showed itself clearly.

There was an order in existence that before every general exercise or large evolution the admiral's permission had to be obtained. This order was always adhered to, but with Makaroff this asking permission had merely the character of a communication of one's intentions.

When a ship hoisted the daily signal: "Permission to carry out such and such an exercise," flag D (the affirmative) was "mast-headed" at once on board the *Petropavlovsk*, where it was always kept ready for instant hoisting.

Now things worked differently.

On the *Diana* making her signal, the *Sebastopol* hoisted the affirmative "at the dip," and kept it there.[4] Finally she hoisted the negative (meaning no). She then asked by semaphore: "Was your last signal made correctly? Did you really mean to carry out target practice?" When we replied in the affirmative, the signal was made for the captain to repair on board the flag-ship.

When he came back he was not very communicative. He only said that in future we were to comply carefully with the routine of work as drawn up and about to be issued by the chief of the staff. This sub-calibre practice had been noted as quite worthy of consideration, but in future this practice was to be regulated so as to enable all ships to participate in it equally, etc., etc.

We had to be prepared for a speedy reappearance of the Japanese off Port Arthur. Consequently, the outer anchorage was being swept by steam launches and pinnaces for mines which the enemy might have placed there.

In return we laid out our mines at the places we did not mean to pass over ourselves. All this was done, but lazily, without any sign of self-confidence or energy.

The reader will ask: were there no men of energy at Port Arthur who took matters in hand themselves and carried out the service in the way it ought to be carried out? Of course there were such men—as was well shown later on—but now they were all under the hypnotic influence I have mentioned. Whoever suggested something new was held to condemn the old ideas. But these old ideas had been sanctified by the viceroy, who vigorously resented any doubt of his infallibility. He was no Makaroff, who asked every one for his candid opinion. Makaroff considered even violent criticism better than enforced silence, which regularly leads to inactive subordination or to passive resistance—there is not much difference between them. Makaroff could be very angry and scold fiercely, but he caught up

---

4. In the Russian Navy the affirmative flag, or answering pendant, close up means: "I see your signal and understand it." At half-mast (at the dip): "I cannot make out your signal clearly, and cannot understand it. Is your signal hoisted correctly?"

eagerly any idea, no matter where it had originated, if there was any chance of its being successful.

Times were indeed changed now that all was based on the myth of Minerva springing fully armed from the brains of Jupiter. What can the voice of the ordinary mortal do against Olympic thunder? There were some men amongst us who wanted to play the part of Prometheus, and how did they fare?—There were many who thought thus. Are they to be judged severely? Their thoughts were the outcome of sad experiences. How could an honest or sincere voice, be it civilian or military, have made itself heard in the province of the Satrap of the Far East. It would have seemed quite natural to be ordered to flog the Yellow Sea for allowing its banks to smell so badly at low water that the great Viceroy was no longer able to sit out on the balcony of his palace. No Themistocles could arise and say: "Strike, but hear me." Here we only had men at the helm whose creed was to keep silence and to agree to everything.

A sad event happened on April 21. In the neighbourhood of Liao-ti-shan a line of mines was being laid out by some harbour craft. As this was being done, one of the mines went off, and Lieutenant Pell and nineteen men lost their lives. I had known Pell from the time of the China campaign. During the Seymour expedition he was wounded in both legs. He was carried along for some time on a stretcher without any medical attendance. More than once he was in danger of falling into the hands of the Boxers, who gave no quarter. Still Pell recovered. He again saw active service, and was fated to so sad a death, and that, too, awing to the imperfections of a weapon of which he was a specialist. (Pell was a torpedo lieutenant.)

About this time I was very unexpectedly made member of a commission to examine the Japanese who had been taken prisoners on March 26, on board the steamer *Hayen-Maru*, and the papers found on them. It was rather strange that the executive officer of a man-of-war should be put on such a commission. To the non-seamen amongst my readers I must explain that the captain of a ship is, so to speak, the king, who only appears personally at highly critical moments. The second-in-command, or executive officer, acts in the name of the captain, on his orders or with his approval. He is the prime minister, who bears the immediate responsibility for the internal organisation. One may say (leaving aside exceptional cases) that the captain is the pendulum, which regulates the movement of the clock, the second-in-command the spring which produces the force required to work the mechanism. If the second-in-command is only a few hours out of the ship it has a bad effect on the life on board. This is inevitable; the second-in-command must practically be always on board. In the ward room the fact of his going on shore is quite an event. One can often hear a remark such as: "That was before 'number one' went on shore the last time."

Personally, I had nothing to say against taking part in this commission's labours. To tell the truth, I was rather glad. It was, after all, quite tempting to be sometimes out of the ship on duty and to meet other people. It was rather the captain who took the matter to heart. "It would have been better if they had appointed me," was his view, and he went off at once to the viceroy's naval office. There, however, he was told that it was known that I had some knowledge of the Japanese language and the Japanese and Chinese characters. That was why they had selected me. He had to be satisfied with this. At first I did not quite believe in these motives. It was certainly known to some in the squadron that once upon a time I had studied the Japanese language, as well as the Japanese-Chinese characters, for a year. At that time I had reached the point where I could freely read and translate Japanese newspapers. But that was six years ago. Since then, from want of practice, I had forgotten much. I nowise considered myself justified in playing the interpreter, especially in so important a case. But already at the first meeting I had, willy-nilly, to lay aside my modesty and to try and furbish up my knowledge as well as I could.

It turned out that in this whole enormous staff there was not one person who was a thorough master of the Japanese language and characters. We employed as interpreter a sub-lieutenant of the naval reserve, who had been called out and who at other times was a student of Oriental languages at Vladivostok. It was hard to say which of us two knew least. Fortunately, my colleague possessed a rare quality: he was free from professional conceit. We worked together in friendship and harmony, laughed heartily when we got hopelessly stuck, and then tried to get out again with our united forces.

How would such an examination have been carried out amongst the Japanese? On board every ship, in every regiment or battalion, even in every company, they had people who spoke and wrote Russian fluently. What a hail of cross-questioning in their own language would the members of our commission have been exposed to if they had been in the position of the Japanese whom they examined!

The commission met in the state reception rooms of the casino, which were generally kept locked. On one occasion when, after a meeting, I had to wait for my boat which was to take me back on board, and which was late, I went on board the *Sebastopol* (lying alongside) and looked up my old friend and shipmate B—— (since dead), her second-in-command.

As always happens at a meeting after a long separation, we embraced, and mutually began a whole string of questions. Our conversation was interrupted every moment by the "guard call." Every time B—— had to rush off and meet at the gangway some admiral or general, either coming on board or going away.

"What a lot of 'Big Wigs' you seem to have coming on board here," I said with astonishment.

B—— made a gesture of disgust. "Don't talk of it!" he burst out. "You imagine, perhaps, that I am the commander of this ship? The whole of my work is done by the first lieutenant. I only run backwards and forwards, escort to the gangway, receive at the gangway, receive, escort."

"What is the meaning of this?" I pointed at a crowd of workmen. Carpenters were putting up a number of cabins in the mess with wooden partitions along the bulkhead; they were hanging doors and fitting windows. Painters were pasting wall-papers on the bulkheads of these cabins. Other men were busy screwing in hooks, placing furniture, etc., etc.

"That is all for the viceroy's staff. Up to now I don't even know how many there are and when this great immigration is to cease, notwithstanding all my efforts to find out."

"But when you go to sea—go into action? What then? On board our ship orders were given to remove all woodwork, except what was absolutely indispensable. All furniture and ornamentations have been sent on shore, so as not to provide food for flames in any fire. Our bulkheads are made of steel, but the doors were made of wood, so the latter had to be replaced by canvas screens; and on board here you are actually building up cabins with inflammable material! What will this lead to?"

B—— became quite furious. "Are you mocking at us?" he flared up. "Where will this lead to? In these conditions we shall simply go to the devil."

I was bound to agree with him. The maxim "*Be careful and risk nothing*" was again in force. Judgment had been passed on Makaroff's adventures. They would not be repeated. This was shown clearly in everything around us—in the viceroy's orders, above all, in the attitude of the leading personages since Admiral Alexeieff had hoisted his flag in the *Sebastopol*, and generally in the talk of the "most obedient servants."

During the night of April 30, Japanese destroyers appeared in the outer anchorage. They were certainly going to lay out mines. When they were lit up by our searchlights and fired on by our batteries, they beat a hasty retreat, but their task was probably accomplished.

On May 3, at 1 a.m., I was awakened by the sound of far-off guns.

Where can this be and what can be the meaning of it, I thought, and strained my ears. Was it the right or the left flank which was firing? It would be unpleasant to leave one's warm bunk merely to satisfy one's curiosity, and to go up on the bridge in the wet and cold of a dark night. From our place in the West Basin we could under no circumstances take part in an action.

Suddenly the single guns changed into a continuous, rolling thunder. Even through my screened port I could see repeated flashes, sometimes light red, sometimes golden yellow. It was evident that everyone who could was firing. Sleep was now out of the question.

Little was to be seen from the *Diana's* bridge. The edges of Golden Hill, Lighthouse Hill, and Tiger's Tail Peninsula were like the side-slips of a stage. We were the "supers" waiting behind these for the moment when we were to step on the stage, and, like these, could only guess what was being enacted there.

The Japanese were trying for the third time, and with even more desperate pluck than before, to block the entrance to Port Arthur.

The enemy had doubtless heard from their spies that their previous attempts had miscarried, and similarly what measures we had taken against renewed attempts. They knew that they could no longer reach the entrance on a straight course, but would have to follow an artificially winding fairway. What did they do? Under the furious fire of our batteries and guard-ships they placed destroyers at the turning-points. These showed the "fire-ships" their path.

Eyewitnesses described that the pluck of these boats was simply fabulous. One of these destroyers was blown up by our mines, another was sunk by gun-fire, and probably many were damaged. But they accomplished their task.

The experiences of this war are still too recent and acquired at too great a cost to be made public.

When by and by archives are thrown open, then we shall hear all the details of this attack. For the present I must confine myself to the notes of my diary and the accounts of other eye-witnesses, not more reliable.

The "fire-ships" numbered twelve. Four of these sank, or could not face our fire and fled seawards. Eight held on.

The whole of these eight steamers sank at a distance from the entrance, but two got through all the turns in the fairway and reached the *Chailar*. Fortunately, they did not sink across the fairway. But that was neither their fault nor our merit, but mere chance. In any case it must be admitted that Makaroff's system of defence against "fire-ships," as elaborated by him in detail and laid down in instructions, had been brilliantly vindicated once more. The coast batteries, guard and defence vessels, all worked splendidly.

The Viceroy was present at this affair on board the *Otvajny*. There was nothing for him to do but to listen to the playing of the piece as set to orchestra by the gifted composer, our "Little Grandfather."

A certain class of men afterwards delighted in dilating on the manner in which Admiral Alexeieff had personally directed the repulse of the Japanese block-ships ". . . under the hail of projectiles from the machine guns of these steamers." [5] They are the followers of the admiral, who admire his talents, historians who attempt to embellish his reports, flowery though they already are. In the interest of truth I must, in the first place, state that notwithstanding this hail of projectiles we sustained no losses whatever. If this had really existed, it was assuredly directed against the nearest adversaries. These were the guard-ships at the booms, the guard-boats, and the batteries of quick-firing guns which had only recently been pushed forward as far as possible, and had been built close to the water's edge.

The *Otvajny* was lying abreast of the second line of defence between Golden Hill and the entrance to the East Basin. She could not possibly have been exposed to any hail of projectiles. The viceroy's precious life was never in danger. Outside the *Otvajny* lay the two outer obstructions, the breakwater of sunken vessels, the first line of defence—*Gilyak* and water batteries—and finally a solid boom with torpedo-nets, which reached nearly to the bottom. This last obstruction really closed the actual mouth of the harbour.

Moreover, the *Otvajny* lay in the rear part of the entrance, not the outer part. It was hardly possible to observe the march of events from

---

5. *Ruskaya Starina*, April 1907.

her, let alone to issue orders. That could perhaps at the most have been done from the *Gilyak*; but this vessel lay well forward. To go to her the viceroy did not consider necessary.

Be this as it may, the entrance, thank God! remained free. The newly sunk "fire-ships" only strengthened the breakwater of submerged vessels which Makaroff had constructed. A further attempt at blocking was thus nearly hopeless.

On February 24 and on March 27 it had been calm, and the survivors of the crews on board the Japanese "blocking ships" had turned to account the general confusion (these forty or fifty men were indeed .hardly worth troubling about) and had escaped to sea in small boats. There they were picked up by their cruisers and destroyers. We only picked up some corpses. We buried them with full military honours. (This action was thoroughly appreciated in Japan. Many Japanese realised then that we were, after all, not the Barbarians we had been described as.)

On May 3 the conditions were quite different. A fresh south-easter was blowing, force 3 to 4. In the roads there was a choppy sea, and a swell outside. It was difficult enough to get out the small, mostly damaged boats and to man them. To pull up against wind and sea was simply impossible.

A portion of the Japanese succeeded in getting such of their boats as had remained intact into the water. They eventually had to beach them and surrender as prisoners. The remainder swam about on wreckage, or kept themselves above water by clinging to the masts and funnels of the sunken vessels. These were crying out despairingly for help. I need not say that our steamboats hastened to save the drowning as soon as the action was over. A moment before they had been firing their torpedoes against the enemy; now for the sake of this same enemy, they risked being dashed to pieces in the seas which were breaking over the sunken vessels.

I should not like to pass over in silence an interesting detail connected with this. The Japanese who were saved by our steamboats were evidently much sobered by their cold bath. On the other hand, those who had reached the shore threw themselves with shouts of "*Banzai*," half-naked and quite unarmed as they were, on our men, who were running to their assistance. Naturally, our soldiers and bluejackets never thought of using their arms under such conditions. They threw away their pistols and took on the "mad Japanese" with their fists, laughing and joking. Some of these Japanese had to be secured with ropes; they were not to be subdued. Perhaps there was a good reason for this. When, prompted by curiosity, we went over the former "fire-ships" which had been sunk, we were astonished at the large number of half-empty brandy bottles we found on board. This discovery was all the more extraordinary as the Japanese are a most sober people. Their national beverage, *saké*, is not stronger than our ordinary beer, and is drunk out of tiny cups. This showed that not even Japanese nerves could face the truly hellish situation the "fire-ships" found themselves in when making for their goal. The Japanese were inebriated with patriotism and the joy of victory, but this had evidently to be supplemented with alcohol.

This discovery spread everywhere by unknown means with extraordinary rapidity. It helped considerably to raise the spirits of our crews. The majority of our men consider it to be as great a sin to drink spirits on the eve of battle, as before going to Holy Communion. They often refuse to drink their government spirit ration when they are having their dinners in sight of the enemy.

"That's not the way of doing things," said petty officer Tkatcheff in his mess. "You should face God pure as a candle burning before a shrine. Think of your oath!"[6]

I confess we officers plucked up courage when we heard remarks such as these. We gained fresh hopes. Were we not bound to succeed, if we all were like *"candles before a shrine"*?

At daybreak on May 3 the Japanese Squadron hove in sight. We prepared to be bombarded. The signal went up "to stand by to fight at anchor"—that is, we were to reply in like manner to their high-angle fire. No bombardment, however, took place.

The first confused, but ominous rumours of the Battle of the Yalu now reached Port Arthur. Our losses were reported to have amounted to two thousand men and twenty guns. We could not believe this. Had the Japanese really landed there, and had we kept so bad a look-out? Our guns in their hands? How could this be possible? Should we have to pull down the column of victory (at St Petersburg) cast from captured Turkish guns?

On May 5 the whole Japanese Squadron was again in sight from Port Arthur all day.

At 11.30 a.m. the commander-in-chief's flag was struck on board the *Sebastopol*, and a rear-admiral's flag took its place. Admiral Vityeft took command of the squadron. The viceroy went off to Mukden.

---

6. All Russian soldiers and sailors are sworn in on entering the service.—Trans.

For some days already a special train had been waiting at New Hill. However, we had got quite accustomed to the sight, and thought the train was only there for any emergency. The viceroy left so suddenly that many of our leading personages only heard of his departure after he had gone. Of course His Excellency was not escorted solemnly to the train. It was even said that some of the gentlemen on Alexeieff's staff, who happened to be absent that morning, had not caught the "special," and had to follow on later.

I cannot say that this obvious flight made any strong impression on the squadron. Some of us were even quite pleased. But all saw in this an alarming symptom; one avoided discussing it aloud. All conversations in the mess were quickly spread amongst the men by the servants. But we were living in times when we were bound to pay close attention to the spirits of our people. The more detailed news from the north, from Turentchen—the heroic attack of the 11th Rifle regiment, the high percentage of losses—somewhat softened the effect of the first bad impressions. We were beaten, but had no need to be ashamed.

The historians I have already mentioned state:—

> On May 5, the viceroy, in accordance with the emperor's orders, handed over the command of the squadron to Rear-Admiral Vityeft, and proceeded from Port Arthur to Mukden, accompanied by his staff.

> Events now followed one another in rapid succession. On May 6, it was already known that the Japanese had landed at Pitsevo, N.W. of the Elliot Islands, at the same spot where, in the war with China, they had landed some batteries of mortars.

> In consequence of this the viceroy telegraphed to Vityeft already on May 6, whilst still on his journey, that is, at Van-fan-gou:—

> Destroyer attacks against the enemy's transports very advisable, and very important for the defence of the fortress. The enemy's transports are all now within the radius of action of our destroyers.[7]

How disastrous for Russia that this excellent idea of preventing a Japanese landing had only occurred to the viceroy when he was at Van-fan-gou, where he was out of range of the Japanese guns and no longer able personally to lead a risky undertaking! We at Port Arthur

---
7. *Ruskaya Starina,* April-May 1907.

knew, of course, that "events were following one another in rapid succession"; yet not so rapidly but that the Japanese intention of landing at Pitsevo only reached Port Arthur after the viceroy had departed thence, "in accordance with the emperor's orders." We knew very well that this order of the emperor's was merely an approval of his suggestion. (Telegraph secrets are on oath, but they sometimes leak out.) The Japanese had been preparing quite openly since April 28 to land at Pitsevo, utilising the Elliot and Blonde Islands as bases. They placed booms across the narrow passages and mines in the wider ones—all in the direction of Port Arthur. By May 4 they had advanced with these protective measures within 7 miles of Pitsevo. It was quite clear where they were going to land.

In view of this situation the viceroy asked "most humbly and respectfully" what he was to do. Was he to remain in Port Arthur, which might be cut off any moment, or proceed to Mukden? This was the most favourable moment for preventing the free development of the Japanese operations. The Viceroy was, in the first place, the admiral, and should have been at the head of his fleet. His flight did not take place in consequence of the emperor's orders, but with the emperor's permission, which he had asked for. That is a very different thing.

On May 6 the Japanese effected their landing. The railway was destroyed. We offered no resistance.

A little later it was found that this had only been a flying column of Japanese. Railway communication was re-established. Two more large trains with war material arrived from the north; in truth, they were lucky enough just to slip through. The Japanese Squadron was daily in sight of Port Arthur. The Chinese reported that something like seventy vessels were lying off Pitsevo. The Japanese apparently were still in doubt whether to disembark definitely. They did not know whether they had actually blocked up Port Arthur at their last attempt, or whether our inactivity was only to be explained by our intention to await the most favourable moment and to fall upon them when their disembarkation was in full swing.

Suppressed indignation prevailed throughout the squadron, and grew from day to day. As a matter of fact, we still had available three undamaged battleships,[8] one armoured, three first class, and one second class protected cruisers, four gun-boats, and over twenty destroyers. With this force we could unquestionably have undertaken

---

8. The *Sebastopol's* damages had not prevented her from getting out on March 18 and April 10 (that is, under Makaroff).

something against the disembarkation which was taking place only 60 miles from us. In the officers' messes a plan to that effect was being eagerly discussed. The spring weather frequently brought fogs. This might have been turned to account. We should have gone out as far as possible without being seen, destroyed the fleet of transports, and at once returned to Port Arthur. Of course we should not have got off without fighting. The Japanese would have made every possible effort to prevent our safe return. We should have had to break out through the blockade of our own port. It was a matter of course that we should have suffered severely. But damages from gun-fire are always less serious than those from mines or torpedoes. We should have made good the former in greater part without dock or cofferdam.

As soon as the *Tsesarevitch*, *Retvisan*, and *Pobieda* were repaired, we could therefore have been up to our full numbers once more. If the battle were to end in our being decisively defeated and our main forces annihilated, it would cost the Japanese dearly. They would have been forced to stay away for a considerable time and get their ships thoroughly repaired. Meanwhile, their disembarked army would have been in a sorry plight. From the number of transports we estimated the force to consist of thirty thousand men. These would have been left without provisions or land transport. The Japanese would have been obliged to fall back on the Yalu to join hands with their army operating in these regions.

So as to calm the general excitement, the "higher circles" started the rumour that our inactivity was part of General Kuropatkin's plan of operations. It was even said that the general had asked the viceroy not to interfere with the landing of the Japanese to the eastward of Port Arthur, as he feared a landing at Niutchwan. Of course no one could doubt our being victorious on land. The statement of a great general was cited to the effect that he knew of twelve different methods of landing an army, but not one of re-embarking it after a repulse. It was maintained that it would be better not to risk our ships just now. The squadron must be saved up for the moment when the Japanese were not to be allowed to return. The well-known maxim of "*be careful and risk nothing*" somewhat discredited these rumours. Still, no other explanation was forthcoming.

We all knew that the day before his departure the Viceroy had held a conference with the principal commanders. Its decisions were kept secret. One point, however, soon became known: the arming of the new batteries on the land front with ships' guns. A little later an order to that effect appeared. Our excitement was to be calmed by the explanation that only the guns of the damaged battleships were to be used. Moreover, this was only to be a temporary measure, whilst the ships concerned were under repair. It was not quite easy to believe all this.

On May 7 or 8 (I don't know the exact date, as I did not note it down) a meeting of the principal naval and military commanders, under the presidency of Stoessel, took place on board the *Sebastopol*. When our captain returned on board he told us nothing about the meeting. (This is why my diary does not contain the day and hour of this wretched event.) But on the morning of the 9th it all came out, as the orderly brought off the minutes of the proceedings, signed by all participants. This fateful document had not even been put into an envelope. Any and everybody, down to the writers and orderlies, could become acquainted with its contents. On the morning of the 9th it was brought on board the *Diana*. The captain being still asleep, I received the document. When I had opened it, I had the misfortune to read what was afterwards known in the squadron as the "Great Edict of Renunciation by the Navy." The following is a verbatim quotation from my diary:

> *May 9.*—I have accidentally read the minutes of the famous meeting. We have destroyed ourselves. What a disgrace! Thank God! two have not signed this infamy.

The minutes commenced with a statement to the effect that the squadron was momentarily in such a situation that active enterprises had no chance of success. On these grounds, therefore, all its means must be utilised for the defence of Port Arthur until better times came round again. The spirits of all afloat were extremely depressed. They were not much better than on the day of Makaroff's death. Our last hopes vanished.

No doubt it was presumptuous, but I could not help it. I asked the captain for an explanation. How was it possible? How could any one sign such a resolution? The captain was not in a very talkative mood. None the less, he did not hesitate to enlighten me. He said that the meeting was a mere matter of form. The viceroy had ordered everything himself at a council of war the day before his departure. The minutes had only been drafted as a matter of form. The instructions left behind by the viceroy were clear enough. They prescribed the programme of our future activity. Adventures *à la* Makaroff must cease, in all service matters, etc., etc. (see above).

"But why does it not appear anywhere that all this was simply *ordered* by the viceroy? Why this comedy of the council of war? On these minutes of the proceedings the most important signature, the viceroy's, is missing: his name is not even mentioned. Such as it now stands this paper will in the end be your 'charge sheet.'" The captain's reply was not very clear. His contention was that when things were ordered, discussions were superfluous. A protest would anyhow not have produced any effect.

There were some who did not believe that the decision of the council of war had been laid down beforehand by the viceroy. I can only say that all those who were present at these meetings had only one idea—how to guess aright "His Excellency's" views. That was the fault of the moral atmosphere created by Alexeieff. He who interpreted them aright was fortunate. He who tried his best but did not succeed, was treated with indulgence. But if anyone dared to have an opinion of his own, it was best to put a cross before his name.[9] When the fortress and the squadron had been taken so completely by surprise by the events of the first days of the war, all our leaders were in a state of uncertainty and fear. They were in fear, not as to the fate of the fortress or the squadron, but as to their own fate, which absolutely and solely depended on "his" views of these events and "his" manner of twisting things. One of the principal reasons for the enthusiasm with which Makaroff was received, was that from that moment the various commanders had no more need to break their heads over the question: "What is the viceroy thinking?"

From December 1899, the moment at which Admiral Alexeieff arrived at Port Arthur, the defeat of our squadron was being prepared. Alexeieff turned our ships into floating barracks, and stifled in the crews every particle of enterprise, of initiative. The power which this man yielded was great, and subject to no control whatever. He used it to force upon men, who in action later on proved themselves to be both brave and able, the conviction that it was quite useless even to attempt to influence any of his decisions—nay, more: that to hold views differing from his was a crime.

This hypnotic state lasted for many years. The feeling of repression under which the squadron lived during the Viceroy's presence was so great that it eventually crept into our flesh and blood. We felt it for a long time, long after Admiral Alexeieff had fled, long after Port Arthur had been besieged and cut off from the rest of the world.

---

9. The usual abbreviation for the defunct.—Trans.

CHAPTER 7

Battle of Kintchao

The organisation of the Japanese intelligence service, especially as regarded spies, was simply ideal. They knew our most secret orders—if possible, before our own ships. Need I say that they knew the contents of the "Great Edict," which had been only carried about in the town and port on the very day of its appearance? Henceforth they no longer dreaded any interference on our part. They disembarked their army with guns, transport, provisions, etc., etc., just as at peace manoeuvres. The enemy became careless in a manner which was simply exasperating. From May 3 to 10, the Japanese had kept their transports behind their protective booms and a ring of guard-ships. Then they still dreaded possible attacks from us, and dared not begin operations on a large scale. During that time their squadron blockaded Port Arthur during daylight, so as to be able to frustrate at once any offensive attempt on our side. But it remained on the horizon and dared not approach within range of the guns of the coast batteries and of the battleships.

After May 10 the hostile squadron invariably approached quite close, in marked contrast to its former caution. It was as if the enemy knew the order we had received: "Don't fire for fear of provoking a bombardment."

The executive officer of a ship is the senior of her officers. An enormous difference exists between his position and that of the captain, although he is the captain's first assistant. This is the reason why my diary contains not only my personal views and impressions, but the reflex of what went on in the minds of all officers not in independent command. I once wrote in it (I am quoting textually, without any "editing"):—

It must be confessed that the fleet is a luxury for Russia. Why a fleet if we have no seamen? Possibly there are many who are glad that Makaroff is dead, for now we no longer rush into senseless adventures. We spare ourselves and our ships. But what will be the effect of this? A ship rotting away in port is worse than one which sinks in battle. In the latter case she has at least done something, has had some object.

Many others thought like I did.

During this time of general apathy and inactivity (if one does not count the construction of land batteries) the captain of the *Amur* performed a plucky action. This officer had apparently been annoyed at the very free and easy behaviour of the Japanese. Consequently, he was only awaiting a favourable opportunity to run out and sow a few mines, where the enemy generally cruised with so much impunity.

This favourable opportunity presented itself on May 14. A light fog came on, and the Japanese disappeared from view. The *Amur* went out and also disappeared in the fog. After a little more than two hours she returned, safe and sound. On her return journey to Port Arthur the *Amur* took in very clearly some Japanese wireless messages. However she saw nothing. It was to be hoped that she also had not been seen. A very important point was the fact that it had not been possible to make sure from the shore where the *Amur* had gone.

I have already mentioned the extraordinary assurance with which the Japanese cruised amongst the mines we had laid out for them. Somehow they never came upon them. They certainly kept in their pay amongst the Chinese inhabitants of Kwantung not only ordinary spies, but experienced pilots, who were able to note all the movements of our ships on a chart. Besides which there was another way. They had only to obtain a copy of our secret instructions. This was perhaps the simpler plan of the two.

We were at breakfast on May 15, when the officer of the watch sent down to report that the Japanese squadron was in sight. No one paid any attention to this. This was strictly in accordance with our latest orders. Suddenly we heard the sound of people running about on deck, some loud exclamations, and then what sounded like distant shouting, which penetrated to all decks below. "The Japanese are on top of our mines!" the quartermaster at me, instead of making a proper report.

There was great excitement on deck. The men went aloft. Every one tried to get up as high as possible, in hopes of getting a view of something over Golden Hill, Lighthouse Hill, and Tiger Hill. The gunnery lieutenant forgot his rheumatism and went into the foretop. The sub-lieutenants climbed higher still.

Loud cheering was suddenly heard from Golden Hill and the adjoining batteries.

"Another one! Another one! She has sunk!" shouted our people from aloft.

At first we could not believe this. Then semaphores began to work everywhere, and the signal station on Golden Hill hoisted the signal: "A hostile battleship sunk." The fact could no longer be doubted.

"Out! Let us go out and destroy all the rest!" people were shouting everywhere.

I still believe today, as I believed then, that we could have destroyed them. But how were we, without steam, to get out into the roads? The brilliant, the only favourable opportunity of the whole war was missed.

The official reports of this scene, described by me with such minute accuracy, say that it was easy for the senseless crowd on board the *Diana* to shout: "Let us destroy the rest!" As a matter of fact, it would have been impossible to do so—they maintained.

Well, let us see.

According to the Japanese reports the battleships *Hatsuse*, *Yashima*, and *Shikishima*, as well as the light cruisers *Kasagi* and *Tatsuta*, steamed past Port Arthur that day in single line ahead, at a distance of 10 miles. The *Hatsuse* sank fifty seconds after she had struck a mine. The *Yashima* also hit a mine. She was kept afloat with difficulty. (The ship never reached Japan. She sank on the way there.) One battleship and two small cruisers were left. They rendered every assistance to the badly damaged *Yashima*.

At this time we had at our disposal the perfectly intact battleships *Peresviet*, *Poltava*, and also the *Sebastopol*. The latter had been damaged during the evolutions on March 12. (She had a crack in her outer skin and one of her propeller blades was bent.) None the less she could have gone out just as well as she did on March 18 and April 10. Besides, we had our cruisers, *viz.*, the armoured cruiser *Bayan*, the protected cruisers *Askold*, *Pallada*, *Diana*, and *Novik*, as well as four gun-boats and two destroyer flotillas.

I maintain that this force of ships could have destroyed the remainder of the Japanese ships, provided they had been ready for sea at 11 a.m. on May 15, and had gone out at once.

Those in command at Port Arthur had, however, already lost all faith in the possibility of such a success. Perhaps also they were too much penetrated with the idea, which had been industriously circulated, that we were unable to make a move of any kind until the, as yet highly problematical, reinforcements from Russia had arrived out. At any rate the squadron was not ready for sea, nor was the order given to raise steam at the moment of this occurrence. And yet one battleship (*Peresviet*) and all the cruisers had water-tube boilers; they might have been ready in half an hour.

Only just before 1 p.m. the destroyers were sent out. They were to harass the enemy, and if possible to attack him. At the same time the cruisers were ordered to raise steam. It was too late. The enemy's armoured cruisers had already arrived for the protection of the damaged battleships. They chased away our destroyers with ease, and when we were ready to go out, all that was left of the Japanese were some small puffs of smoke on the horizon.

This failure to act was worse in its effects than actual losses.

"We can never do anything. Where is this to end?" was the cry of the more excitable amongst us. "It was decreed by Providence," replied the philosophically minded ones. But all were now of a sudden agreed that we had nothing further to hope for from the future. There remained nothing more for us to do but to bow to the truth of the "Great Edict." Never have I seen spirits fall so rapidly. By and by, it is true, they went up again, but only because every one had resolved to fight to the finish as in duty bound, in any case and under any circumstances.

It was precisely on this day that the Japanese army of invasion finally cut off Port Arthur. What would have been its fate if we had, I don't say destroyed, but merely scattered the hostile squadron, in its then state of confusion and discouragement? We could have sunk the fleet of transports and, under the protection of our guns, destroyed the provisions which had been stored up at Pitsevo.

It is awful to think of all this now!

On May 16 we had rumours of some insignificant fighting north of Kintchao. Our side had merely delayed the enemy, and then retired to their "impregnable" position on the narrow neck of land.

On May 17 the signal to raise steam was made twice, and twice we had to put out fires again. Eventually only the *Novik* and the destroyers went out. They returned very soon. What they did I could not find out.

The success of May 15, of course, produced a lively interest in mines. Talienwan Bay had already been completely blocked with mines at the commencement of the war. On May 18 the *Amur* was sent out to place mines also between Talienwan and Port Arthur, opposite the small bay called the "Kurort," near Dalny. The *Novik* and the destroyers were sent out to protect the *Amur*. When the "Greyhounds" appeared, the *Askold* went out in support. The ships indulged in a long range action, without, however, producing any effect. Of course, this particular enterprise could not possibly have any results later on; the Japanese had seen everything.

About the middle of May we started sweeping for the mines laid out by the Japanese in the outer roads with redoubled energy. On their side the Japanese worked with all their might to lay out double as many mines as we had fished out.

For instance, during the night of May 20, three small steamers appeared in the roads and busied themselves there. They were lit up by the searchlights from the forts and fired at by the batteries and the guard-boats at the entrance for about half an hour. Our people maintained that one steamer had been blown up. When next morning our boats set out to sweep for mines, they found forty peculiar wooden frames floating about on the water.[1] This number, of course, corresponded with the number of mines thrown out by the steamers. But we only found five mines—not a very comforting result.

In view of the enemy's great boldness, orders were issued for the guard-boats hitherto stationed in the mouth of the harbour to be replaced by a cruiser.[2] We were the first to be employed thus. On the evening of May 21 we secured the ship to the buoys in the entrance itself, near the shores of Tiger's Tail Peninsula.

From our inactivity at the time of the catastrophe of May 15, and during the succeeding days, the Japanese had evidently drawn the conclusion that we were quite harmless. For nearly a week they, at any rate, never came in sight.

Meanwhile, the effects of the "Great Edict" began to spread to such ships as were perfectly ready for sea and for action. From the *Diana* a searchlight was removed and put up at our position at Kintchao. With the searchlight we had to detach to the shore a sub-lieutenant, two leading torpedo-men, two torpedo-men, and two stokers.

---
1. A species of sledge on which the Japanese launched their mines overboard.
2. To place a cruiser as guard-ship in the roads, as in Makaroff's time, was not risked. But then the viceroy had himself abolished the arrangement.

On May 24 the *Diana's* wardroom was in a state bordering on open mutiny. The officers were swearing in their choicest terms.

The younger members were the most violent: "We won't allow it; we'll stop it by force; we'll never agree to such a thing," was heard on all sides.

The following was the cause. Naturally, the assurance that the guns which had been removed from the battleships under repair to the forts were only lent for a short time was merely to sugar the bitter pill. That was only to be expected. These guns remained away permanently, as the Defence Scheme of Port Arthur only existed on paper. The constructors promised to complete the *Retvisan's* repairs by June 2. Now the rumour was being circulated that the secondary and light Q.F. armament which the *Retvisan* had supplied to the forts was to be replaced by those of the *Diana* or *Pallada*—the ship thus disarmed being laid up.

On May 21 we received a new captain, (Prince Lieven). Our old one got a better command. He went to the *Tsesarevitch* (this battleship was completed soon after the *Retvisan*). I thought it my duty to inform the new captain what the general feeling was on board; I did not conceal from him the fact that I shared the views of my messmates, although, of course, I would carry out any order received from my superiors. My satisfaction was great indeed when I found the captain was in no way astonished at my report; he quietly stroked his pointed beard, and said: "Why all this excitement? I should like to see them start on this disarming of the *Diana*. Just let them come along." This was said with so much assurance that I went into the mess and said: "Gentlemen, it is all nonsense; we are not going to be disarmed."

They all believed me, and peace reigned once more.

On May 25 the Japanese began their attack on Kintchao, the key to the Kwantung peninsula. On that day from the early morning we had constant requests for men to transport guns and war material by rail to these positions; more and more men were thus employed. Out of our (reduced) complement of 456 men we eventually had 283 on shore. They only returned after midnight. Towards 9 p.m. on May 25 a thunderstorm made its appearance; it was still far off, and we mistook the thunder for the firing of distant guns. By midnight it had reached us; it was accompanied by an almost tropical downpour.

On the morning of May 26 we heard that this thunderstorm had done great damage at our land front; the greater part of the shell which had been stacked in readiness had exploded or become useless. Lightning conductors were now to be erected: this had not been thought of before. At daybreak signal was made to the *Poltava*, *Peresviet*, and all cruisers, the *Amur* and the destroyers to get up steam. Presumably we were to go out in support of our troops who were defending the neck of land; at least that is how we understood this order. The evening before (May 25) the gun-boats had received orders to go to Talienwan: however, only one of these, the *Bobr*, had sailed. The remainder, no doubt in accordance with the spirit of the "Great Edict," were calmly making good defects in engines and boilers, and were therefore not ready for sea; their captains were superseded. It was too late; this unjust severity could not put things right.

The *Bobr* got out safely through the mines and appeared on the morning of the 26th in the north-east portion of Talienwan Bay. From there she fired at the Japanese, who were attacking our right flank. The enemy was repulsed with heavy losses. At 11 a.m. the signal station on Golden Hill made the general semaphore—"The fleet is informed that the enemy's attack has been repulsed. The *Bobr* fought brilliantly."

To many it appeared strange that the *Bobr* returned to Port Arthur the same day having (of course by "superior orders") left the position where she had been of such service. We received her with cheers, but involuntarily we felt bitter doubts.

Why was the *Bobr* withdrawn? Why, on the contrary, were the *Gremyashtchy*, *Otvajny* and *Gilyak* not sent out to support her? These vessels had got their engines into working order again and were ready for sea. Why was the sailing of the cruisers and destroyers which already had steam up countermanded? From information which reached the squadron a fierce battle was raging at Kintchao. Our army was fighting brilliantly; on the other hand, eye-witnesses told of much that was praiseworthy on the Japanese side. The prowess of our adversaries was universally admitted.

Later on I received some details from a military officer, who had been decorated with the Cross of St George [3] for an act of bravery witnessed by hundreds. He said:—

> Do you know there was a moment when I was thoroughly frightened. The enemy came on like a savage horde. I was posted with my battery behind the left flank, with orders to prevent it being turned at low water. The battle begins: we can't join

---

3. In Russia the commander-in-chief has power to confer decorations on the spot.—Trans.

in, but get hit and suffer losses, very considerable ones, in fact. An ugly situation—but never mind, we keep still, but boiling with rage. Just you wait, we think; when our turn comes we'll give it these fellows; we are in splendid spirits. At last we get our chance: the tide had fallen and the enemy is trying to turn our flank. What their strength was at the beginning I can't say. Probably they had already suffered losses on our front. What we had before our guns appeared to be a battalion, but they had colours, and had therefore once been a regiment. The enemy wheels towards the beach and straight at us: the men only advance with difficulty, wading in water up to the chest. The bottom is slippery clay; we open fire: nearly every shot is a hit; whoever is hit in the leg falls and is drowned, none of them rise again.

They become fewer and fewer, but on they come. The colours move about, they pass from one hand to the other: still they are advancing. 'Load with shrapnel!' I shout. 'Faster! Faster!' I no longer know what I order. Then I myself worked a gun—our losses were heavy. The wounded drag themselves along and help to pass shell; even the dead horses seem to come to life again. Only with the last man did the colours sink into the water; only then did I realise what we had felt at the thought—'The enemy will be on top of us at once.' When everything was over and we only had the smooth surface of the sea before us, there were many volunteers to look for the colours. We thought that the flag might float up: it did not. The last bearer did not let go his grasp. The flag lies buried with him in the deep mud. We could not find a trace of it. Soon after the enemy's gun-boats arrived and commenced to fire at our left flank. They worked well; our traverses, which had been strengthened, were simply blown away by them.

As is known. General Fock gave orders during the night to evacuate the position. The evacuation had not been prepared for. We had intended to maintain ourselves on the isthmus several weeks longer. The result was utter confusion; the same troops which had only just repulsed the attack of the enemy's best forces like heroes, retired in complete disorder as after a defeat.

"If we retire, we are being pursued; if we are being pursued, the enemy is at our heels"—thus argued the rank and file. The result was that we fired on our own supply columns. Once it was still worse: two regiments skirmished against one another and nearly had a battle by themselves.

The same night the first destroyer flotilla was got ready in a great hurry and sent out into Society Bay (Society Bay lies to the west of the isthmus of Kintchao). They were to attack the Japanese gun-boats, which had fired at our left flank and thus supported the attack of the right wing of the Japanese army.

This expedition of our destroyers ended disastrously. The gun-boats were, naturally, not found (as a matter of course they had gone to sea for the night). When the *Vnushitelny* was looking for them amongst the islands she grounded on a rocky patch. She had to be blown up so as not to fall into the hands of the enemy.

All these days passed like a fever. Our painful uncertainty was only intensified by the wildest rumours, which told now of victories, now of defeats.

I have promised my readers to do my best to reproduce all our impressions and feelings during these awful days with photographic accuracy. But how difficult this is! We had lots of work, and work which was both heavy and hateful. We had to surrender our guns and mount them in the battery on the land front. For these days my diary only contains single short sentences (sometimes several entries in the twenty-four hours). Between the lines of these one can read my bitter indignation. I nearly went so far as to curse everything. I will reproduce them without comment.

May 29.—I feel wretched: I don't feel inclined to write any more. We are giving up the fleet. The squadron and the fortress, lost beyond hope, are to be saved, and for this purpose we are disarming the ships. How senseless! It is flying in the face of all reason. Yes, with a ship her whole crew goes down; on shore not so—that is where the shoe pinches. Kuropatkin is to drive the Japanese into the water: that sounds fine, but what do the results of Turentchen and Kintchao promise? We ought to go out and fight, not sit here in idleness. A battle is said to be impossible because the forces are unequal: are they so in reality? And if they were? Then we must force our way through to Vladivostok. They say this would be like flight; that we must not desert; our comrades here. All very fine—what heroes we are! not in the least conceited! Kutusoff sacrificed Moscow, and thus saved the army and Russia; we are sacrificing the squadron, go on shore and try to save Port Arthur.

It looks like self-sacrifice on our part. In reality we thus have greater chances of saving our lives: one can't be drowned on shore. The Diana surrenders two 6-inch and four 12-pounder Q.F. guns, but that is nothing, much worse is in store.

11.30 p.m.—The moon is shining; out in the roads a Japanese destroyer flotilla is passing from east to west. Probably they are laying out mines.

11.52.—*Gilyak* and the other vessels in the entrance open fire. The distance is from 40 to so cables (8,000 to 10,000 yards). The batteries are also firing.

12.8.—The Japanese have gone. Probably they have completed their task. They came notwithstanding the moonlight night, just as if to mock at us; we never tried to chase them, we are suffering from hydrophobia.

June 2.—The cruisers and destroyers are being prepared for an expedition. It came on foggy, and only the destroyers sailed for the Gulf of Petchili. It is quite incomprehensible. In a fog we can't go out—one can't see anything; in clear weather we also can't go out—the enemy would see us before we saw him. Our nerves are so unstrung that we see a bad omen in everything. Today, for instance, we had, towards 11 p.m., a regular tropical thunderstorm, combined with a curious phenomenon. The clouds were mostly high up, but a single white cloud which looked as if it possessed its own means of illumination was lying quite low over Golden Hill. It covered the hill half-way down, and its white colour contrasted sharply with the dark background. During the flashes of lightning it turned purple. Does this forebode anything? How stupid!

June 3.—Our destroyers returned at 8 a.m. in safety. They saw nothing and did nothing, but at least they are unhurt, and we must be thankful for that much; besides, it is a good omen; they have at least risked something.

These were weary times also as regards physical labour, especially for us cruisers. When we were on guard at night in the entrance, we always had to exchange shots with the Japanese who were bent on laying out mines in the roads. Our men were then only allowed to sleep fully dressed, half the guns' crews at the guns, the other half somewhere near. Moreover, we worked night and day in the land batteries. Of our four divisions [4] we always had one at that work, one on watch, a third just off watch and getting ready for work, the fourth just relieved from work and resting in readiness for the next watch; added to that was the coaling and the boatwork in sweeping for mines. There were days when the men dropped from sheer fatigue or went to sleep all standing.

Yes, it was sad; and all because we had lost our "head," as the men said.

That Admiral Vityeft had got the command of the squadron was pure chance. It was only in consequence of Admiral Alexeieff having fled and Admiral Skridloff not having arrived. That Vityeft was personally brave admits of no doubt; he has proved it. For the rest, he had the reputation of being a scrupulously honest man and a diligent worker, but he had served almost the whole of his time on shore. A seaman he was not; he confessed it quite openly. When Vityeft assumed command of the squadron, he said at the first meeting of flag-officers and captains: "Gentlemen, I expect you to assist me with words and deeds; I am no leader of a fleet." Vityeft said this quite honestly and openly. In my opinion he had better have held his tongue.

In war there can only be *one* leader; this is the fundamental condition of any success. An army without a leader *may* perish in consequence, a leaderless fleet *must* perish. The laws of war are based on the teachings of history. It is not for nothing that they lay such stress on the powers of a single leader. For the one supreme leader even a council of war, which he may call together at critical moments, is only advisory. According to our laws the commander-in-chief may join his vote to that of the minority in the council of war, or even to a single vote, which he may consider the best, and thus make it decisive. The decision thus arrived at cannot be questioned.

At the famous council of war at Filach (1812) the majority recoiled at the thought of giving up the capital without fighting; what may have passed in Kutusoff's mind? Was he firmly convinced of the infallibility of his personal opinion? Who can tell? But he certainly did not renounce his right as leader of finally deciding, and said: "*We will sacrifice Moscow, so as to save the army, to save Russia*," and all obeyed.

By his declaration Vityeft renounced his unlimited powers as dictator and left it to the majority. What does majority mean? It seems to me that in every council of war there will always be one man whose

---

4. The crew of a ship is divided into two watches, and each watch into two divisions, (called "parts" in the British Navy—Trans).

courage and determination make him conspicuous (for both these attributes are rare). Then there are a few who approach him. Amongst the remainder there will be a certain number of pusillanimous souls. That is why our law governing councils of war says that the leader is to support the most courageous opinion, without reference to the number of votes recorded for it.

With us things were different.

On thinking these events over again, which already belong to history, I cannot say that today I would write down in my diary the harsh words cited above. There were extenuating circumstances; there was a factor which weighed heavily on the council of war of our admirals and captains. In 1812 the generals did not want to abandon Moscow, so as to become a prey to the enemy, as they dreaded the reproaches of all Russia. True, Port Arthur was not Moscow, but our admirals did not want to desert it at a critical moment, as they dreaded the reproaches of their comrades in the army. This reproach was already in the air; anonymous writings already began to reach the ships. I will mention one of these: it was a parody on the well-known tale of *Grandfather Masai and the Hares*. In this parody the relations between fleet and army was described very transparently. Unfortunately I no longer possess the text, I lost it in the battle; I can only give the contents from memory.

> In a big courtyard there lived some white rabbits, and grey-haired dogs watched over them.[5] Once there was great danger; the wolves were coming. The dogs prepared for defence, but the rabbits said: 'Don't alarm yourselves, we know a dodge to keep out the wolves.' But when the fight began and the dogs were getting worsted, the rabbits got nervous, and one fine day they decamped to the north (read 'Vladivostok') under the leadership of the 'oldest and biggest coward.' They left nothing behind but a mighty stink, which took away the breath of the poor dogs. The dogs were fighting for their lives with the wolves, when Grandfather Masai (read 'Kuropatkin') came to their assistance and drove off the enemy. When he had done this he called back the rabbits and asked them: ' Why did you desert your faithful friends and make off?' The rabbits replied: 'Forgive us, Grandfather, we merely took our furs to a place of safety; our furs are surely more valuable than the skin of a mere dog.'

---

5. Naval officers possess white tunics, whilst military officers have grey overcoats.

Then spoke Grandfather Masai, and said: 'You have soiled your furs and they are no longer worth anything'; and he took up his stick and chastised them.

This lampoon was produced on a typewriter; it was sent by post to all admirals, captains, and executive officers, and officers' messes—that is, a considerable number of copies appeared at the same time. It was clear that some one took a great interest in spreading it.

The relations between army and navy (at Port Arthur) had never been particularly friendly; with the outbreak of war they became very bad.

I believe I am already able to consider the past with comparative calm and impartiality; but I cannot rid myself of the idea that someone had his hand in this from personal interests. Someone suggested to the army that our failures at sea were not the fault of the commanders in the fleet, but of the bad elements under their orders (officers and men). The same thing was whispered to the navy about the army.

The army violently accused the squadron of having been caught unprepared by the enemy's attack. The navy, on the other hand, maintained that the fortress had been taken by surprise by the war. On February 9, only two hastily prepared batteries had been able to support the squadron. The remainder had not been manned, and the guns were still swaddled up for the winter.

It was the case of *the kettle and the pot*: still, someone had an interest in furthering this squabble. How otherwise can the following be explained?

In the officers' messes on board the ships whose guns had been landed to strengthen the land front scenes were enacted which were not far removed from mutiny. It went so far that some officers threatened to get up steam, go to sea, and if the fortress tried to prevent them, to fire at the forts. At the same time the people in the forts abused the navy for not wanting to fight and for landing their guns. The irritation against us became so great, that in all seriousness the proposal was made for the fortress artillery to fire on the squadron to force it to put to sea and fight.

A singular misunderstanding. Was it not purposely disseminated amongst the two most important defenders of the Russian cause, of Russian honour in the Far East?

Later on this misunderstanding was cleared up. The instinct of the masses realised that they were not enemies. But did this do any good?

Did the army and navy henceforth look upon the Japanese as their common enemy? No; they looked upon their superiors as the common enemy.

However, I must not anticipate; I propose to describe the successive feelings in the beleaguered fortress, as noted in my diary in the same chronological order as the events.

For what are we to blame the late Admiral Vityeft? Was it his fault that he was' not born a Kutusoff? Is he guilty, because at the council of war he did not join the two votes who demanded that we should go to sea and plunge into the deadly battle without fear of the reproach of having deserted our comrades of the army? History will decide.

One must be just to Vityeft; he was consistent. In the council of war of the senior commanders he joined the majority. He was equally ready later on to listen to the voices of the other majority—the entire personnel of the squadron. This majority was young, perhaps also inexperienced and silly, but it was full of enthusiasm. It was indignant at the part which it had been forced to play, and often nearly mutinied.

Of course I cannot say whether it was due to orders from above or to the pressure of public opinion in the squadron—anyhow, the news soon spread in the ships that the old orders were cancelled and that we were to go to sea as soon as the battleships were repaired. It was received with enthusiasm.

We (*Diana*) had surrendered all our 3-pounder Q.F. guns and rifle calibre machine guns, in addition to the previously mentioned guns and searchlights. The other ships had landed as much or even more, for, generally speaking, nearly the whole of the light Q.F. armament (including the 6-pounders which we did not carry) had been disembarked. In the general rejoicing no one bothered about them.

"God be with our guns ! let us hope they will be of some use. We shall do very well with what we have left," was said in our mess.

The outer anchorage was now diligently swept for mines so as to clear a channel through the hostile minefield out to sea. Many people now came forward who combined the spirit of enterprise with a genius for inventions. Beside the yard craft, the steam-hoppers attached to the dredgers were fitted up as mine-sweepers. These craft were really intended to take the mud, which was dredged up, out to sea. They were clumsy, but strong, and drew but little water, and therefore highly suitable for this new service. They answered their helm even in a seaway or in a swell, and towed hundreds of fathoms of sweeps along. The destroyers also had to learn the art of mine-sweeping. They took the place of the other mine-sweepers outside the range of the coast batteries, and cleared the channel where these hoppers could not be employed.

The Japanese, of course, noticed our renewed activity. They came nearly every night and dropped new mines in the place of those we had fished up. As soon as the moon had gone down or was hidden by clouds they appeared here and there, and the firing from the batteries and guard vessels began. It was a pity that no cruiser was kept out in the roads as guard-ship; that would have been a much more serious threat for the enemy. Port Arthur was cut off, but Alexeieff had abolished Makaroff's measures. That was why no one dared to reintroduce them. The viceroy was a long way off, but to do anything against his orders seemed highly dangerous. War or no war—what would he think of it?

Henceforth a subdivision of destroyers was sent out on guard. That was always something.

During the night of June 6-7 our searchlights discovered three small steamers in the roads. Doubtless they were mine-layers; one of them was sunk. The battery on Cross Hill and the destroyers on guard disputed the honour of having destroyed her.

On June 9, Japanese warships appeared again off Port Arthur after a long pause.

On June 11, it was foggy; under cover of the fog some destroyers were sent out that morning: six to Pigeon Bay, three to Tache Bay (to the eastward), two others were on guard in the roads. All returned safe and sound the following morning; but they had seen nothing and done nothing.

Work on the damaged battleships was progressing apace; on the other hand, the party which was opposed to going to sea displayed increased zeal. Thus a very positive report was spread on June 13 that the *Pobieda* was only to get back half the 6-inch guns she had landed, also that it was proposed to sacrifice a cruiser—probably *Diana* or *Pallada*—to complete her armament. Need I say what impression this news created on board us? Actually on the eve of battle we were to be disarmed! Happily, things turned out differently.

At this time our troops had already retired up to the Green Mountains. Dalny was in the hands of the enemy. From Chinese sources we heard that they were busily employed in clearing Talienwan Bay of our mines, and in putting to rights the docks, workshops, quays, etc. I forgot to mention that we had been firmly convinced that our position on the Isthmus of Kintchao was impregnable. Consequently, until this position was captured by the enemy we had not taken any measures at Dalny for transferring to Port Arthur the immense quantities of stores at that commercial port and its depot of railway plant. The powerful dynamos, the plant of the workshops and the stores of all kinds in Dalny were treasures for the besieged fortress and the squadron blocked up there.

Even after May 27 there was a week of hesitation. Apparently it was the intention to fortify the heights near Nangalin and to delay the enemy here for a considerable time. When this plan was definitely abandoned and our troops began to retire on the Green Mountains, orders were given to remove as much as possible from Dalny and to destroy the rest. A portion was got away, everything else was burnt, blown up, thrown into the sea, or rendered useless in some other way; but owing to the great hurry we were in, this was not done thoroughly enough. The Japanese were soon able, without special exertions, to get everything at the port into working order again.[6]

On June 14 the enemy attacked the Green Mountains with determination. A flanking column was sent along the beach (in the neighbourhood of Sikou Bay), covered by the fire of thirteen destroyers. From Port Arthur the *Novik* and a destroyer flotilla were sent out. The parts were reversed and the Japanese had to retire.

On June 15 the Japanese again came in sight. This time it was not single ships, but a squadron consisting of two battleships, two protected cruisers, and twelve destroyers. We expected the entire Japanese Fleet.

Some said:—

> No wonder the Japanese are, after all, no children. They make their dispositions in time. We inform the world how the work is progressing on board our damaged battleships, that the port is not blocked up, and that we mean to attack the Japanese soon. With all that we are still sitting here and dare not show our nose outside! I suppose we are waiting for the Japanese Fleet to assemble here!

On the evening of June 15 a mysterious event happened which was never cleared up. (The Japanese know how to keep their losses dark.) The day had been very hot (77° F. in the shade). In the evening I was on the upper bridge with the gunnery lieutenant; we were enjoy-

---

[6]. We heard later that the cruiser *Tchiyoda*, which had struck a mine in July, was repaired in the dock at Dalny with the assistance of the local workshops.

ing a breath of the cool night air, and at the same time peering attentively into the darkness in which the fortress searchlights were moving backwards and forwards. *Diana* was guard-ship in the entrance; signalmen and specially picked look-out men were stationed everywhere on the bridges, on the upper deck, and at the gangways close to the water.[7] The sky was overcast, and neither moon nor stars were visible. It was absolutely calm, there was no swell, and there was no sound of the sea breaking on the beach or over the banks near it.

Suddenly—or were we mistaken?—there was a flash far away to the south. No, there was no mistake, we heard the muffled sound of a very distant explosion. In an instant all searchlights were trained in that direction. Their white beams were eagerly searching about in the dark like giant antennae of some fabulous monster. There, in the same direction, we saw the characteristic greenish-golden flashes. We heard the brisk but intermittent fire of guns.

This lasted perhaps ten to fifteen minutes; then everything was still and dark. I looked at my watch: it was 10.50 p.m. I need not say that at the first sound the crew of the *Diana* rushed to their general quarter-stations; everyone with bated breath followed this unexpected night action.

"Surely there can't be any of us out there?" asked the gunnery lieutenant.

"No," I replied decidedly. "We are the guard-ship, and nothing could get out without our knowledge. They are certainly not ships belonging to our side."

"Then the Japanese are fighting each other."

We estimated the distance to be about 10 miles. It was just where the Japanese generally cruised about. But what had happened? There were only two possible answers to the question, and equally likely. Either a Japanese had struck one of our mines and had fired aimlessly into the water, or a Japanese destroyer had attacked a ship of its own side in error: both were equally agreeable to us.

On the following day, June 16, nothing was to be seen of the Japanese; the *Amur* seized this opportunity and went to lay out mines to the westward of Kwantung. On her way back she struck something, and tore open her side; the damage was not serious. Some thought it was a good sign; they maintained that if the *Amur* had sprung a leak in deep water something must have been lying there; as no rock could

---

7. At night one often sees better when placed low down close to the surface of the water than when high up.

have got there suddenly it must be a Japanese wreck.[8]

On June 17 the destroyer *Lieutenant Burakoff* returned safely. She had been sent to Inkau: she narrowly escaped falling into the hands of the Japanese cruisers. Thanks to the haziness of the weather, and especially to her speed, she got through.

What bitter irony! Our best, that is, our most reliable and speedy destroyer, was the *Lieutenant Burakoff*. This vessel we had taken from the Chinese [9] at the capture of Taku, and the Chinese had had her built in Germany ten years previously; she was the only one of the whole flotilla which was suitable for a task such as running a blockade.

During this time our troops were gradually falling back on Port Arthur. At several points they had delayed the enemy's advance for a short time.

On June 18 the *Otvajny*, *Gremyasktchi*, *Novik*, and four destroyers went out. They were to prevent an attack on our left flank by their fire.

---

8. Later we realised that these rumours were only circulated to quiet the minds of our people. In reality the *Amur* had struck the wreck of the *Shilka*, which had been sunk by us; it was her own fault.

9. That is, the British destroyers, under Captain Keyes, had captured her and handed her over to the Russians.—Trans

CHAPTER 8

The Beginning of the End

On the afternoon of June 18 the greatest activity prevailed throughout the harbour and the basins of Port Arthur. The men-of-war hauled their bows round towards the channel leading out, tugs were taking our transports into the corners of the basins, so as not to block the fairway; here coals were being taken in, there stores or provisions. Floating cranes were lifting the buoys and moorings which had been laid out temporarily; yard craft were removing the second and third booms. The fact that our squadron was to go to sea was an official secret, but all this animated scene proclaimed it aloud. Even a landsman was bound to notice it. It was enough to make one lose courage; I should have liked to cry out aloud: "My friends, why all this to do?"

On June 20 high water was at 2 p.m. All preparations for going to sea could have been completed by then if commenced at daylight. Did "they" not know what was common knowledge in the squadron, in the port, in the town, in the fortress? Did "they" not know that the Japanese were accurately and immediately informed of our every step, every movement? Did "they" not know that the Japanese invariably had knowledge of the plans and intentions of our leaders, thanks to our "bureaucratic" methods in treating secrets? Why, the Japanese were often better informed than we officers, who were reduced to guessing.

Since that strange midnight encounter of June 15 the Japanese had completely disappeared. Our mine-sweeping flotilla cleared a channel to the S.S.E. and buoyed it without any interference on the part of the enemy. The searchlights were diligently worked but could not discover anything suspicious during those nights. When the channel was searched once more to make doubly sure, no new mines were to be seen. The Japanese minelayers had quite given up operations in our roads. It looked as if we really might hope to surprise the enemy, if we went out unexpectedly. Perhaps their main body was off Vladivostok; perhaps they were so firmly convinced that we would undertake nothing, that their ships were taking in supplies, making good defects, or simply resting in Japanese ports. Such Japanese vessels as had been left behind to keep up the blockade might have gone into some bay (their flying base) to coal. Who could know?

In any case it appeared to me to be perfectly incomprehensible that our very obvious preparations had been begun several days before the date of sailing. But worse was to follow. At 5 a.m. on June 20 the *Sebastopol* and *Poltava* received orders by signal to raise steam; these two ships had cylindrical boilers; at 7.30 a.m. the same order was signalled to all other ships. Then came the general signal: "Prepare to sail at noon."

Soon after 8 a.m. a hectographed order reached us; in it the admiral communicated the happy intelligence that the repairs on the damaged battleships were completed and that the entire squadron was once more ready for sea. He then called upon God and the Heavenly Hosts, and declared that we would now go to sea and once more start active operations.[1] At the same time was published a special number of the *Novy Krai*, a newspaper which appeared regularly in Port Arthur. In this number the above-mentioned orders were printed as a sensational piece of news. It was clear the editor had certain connections which permitted him to obtain a copy of the order the evening before.

At 10 a.m. the admirals and captains were suddenly summoned to the *Tsesarevitch* (flagship). At 10.20 she hoisted the general signal: "Let fires die out."

"What is it?"—"What has happened?" the officers asked me, surprised and scared.

"I don't know; wait till the captain is back, he will be able to tell us."

Meanwhile, steam-boats were going from ship to ship calling in again the above-mentioned order; we were ordered not to register it. At the same time a perfect army of orderlies rushed through the town and all over the harbour to confiscate that fatal number of the *Novy Krai*.

The torpedo lieutenant was beside himself with rage. "Quite use-

---

1. Is it not remarkable how closely this order resembles the solemn Army Order, in which General Kuropatkin announced the beginning of offensive operations?

less," he mocked; "the Japanese have already read the order—probably they had a proof sheet."—"Much ado about nothing," grumbled the paymaster; he had always taken a pessimistic view of things.

Our spirits could not have been at a lower level than they were.

The captain returned; we gathered that "they" had thought better of it at the last moment. The day had been an unfortunate choice, it was said, as high water was in the afternoon. No sooner had the squadron got out, than night would have been upon us, and with it the risk of torpedo attacks. It had been decided to wait two or three days until high water came at daylight; then in God's name we should make an early start.

"Oh, is that it?" I could not help saying; "but why had all this to be 'piped at the main hatchway'? What capital chances we should have had if we had gone out suddenly."

The captain tried to be jocular: "It is easy to be wise after the event," he said; but somehow it did not sound very convincing.

In my diary I wrote:

We are waiting for the Japanese to inform us that they are aware of our intentions; why, we are simply provoking them. At 9 p.m. on June 21 we get a circular to the effect that ships are to be ready to sail at 2.30 a.m. on the 22nd; towards midnight, the signal—'Sailing postponed.'

At 2 a.m. on the 22nd Japanese destroyers appeared in the roads; we could congratulate ourselves: they had been waiting for us. Everything that could, fired at them. Now we could recommence our mine-sweeping.

Towards 2 p.m. Liao-ti-shan reported a squadron of cruisers and destroyers in sight. Very disagreeable. The buoyed channel to seaward was swept for mines—it was clear. Curious!

The *Vsadnik, Gaidamak,* and eight destroyers were sent out for the night to guard the roads; why wasn't a cruiser sent out as guard-ship? Why? Towards 10 p.m. we heard guns outside. The Japanese had again appeared, but our destroyers had attacked and driven them away. Our losses and damages were insignificant, only the *Boyevoi* had a biggish hole. We are definitely to go out tomorrow. 'God grant a happy issue!' as Makaroff used to say.

At 4 a.m. on June 23 we started moving out; it was just beginning to get light; orders were given for all ships to anchor outside until the whole squadron was out and the mine-sweeping flotilla ready to precede us. The order for anchoring prescribed the following:—We were to pass the sunken ships, the booms and mines, then turn sharp to port (east) and anchor in order of fleet numbers in two columns close outside our line of mine defences. The Japanese mine-layers had hitherto not risked coming as near as that to the water batteries—at least no Japanese mines had been found there up to date. The *Diana* was lying in the entrance; she was the first to go out, the *Novik* at the same time. Then followed the battleships and cruisers just as they lay nearest the entrance.

When we had reached our billet (the furthest east) we dropped an anchor. The assembling of the squadron was bound to take two or three hours. We therefore sent our men to breakfast, and gave them free time to rest and gather strength for the heavy day before them. Far away, bearing S.S.E., hostile torpedo craft hove in sight from time to time. We—that is, the officers—were on the point of going down to the mess when we heard a shout from the bridge—"Mine astern!" "In fact, less than 100 *sachen* (about 200 yards) astern of the *Diana* a Japanese mine could be seen just under the surface, distinguished by the chain slings on the lid. A section of the small-arm men were ordered up to destroy it.[2]

"Just as well we did not keep a little more to port in taking up our billet," said the captain, and stroked his beard as was his custom. "That might have been a nice business."

"Yes; and lucky, too, that the mine came to the surface," I replied in the same tone. "Swinging whilst weighing we might easily have struck it."

The *Tsesarevitch* was just coming out of harbour; she suddenly turned short and stopped. "Mine just floated up under the flagship's bow!" shouted a signalman.

The *Peresviet* had already anchored. We suddenly heard rifle-fire from her direction. She, like ourselves, was evidently firing at mines.

The ships came out one by one with the greatest caution. Each one tried to follow exactly in the wake of ships which had already come out. Everyone anchored as soon as possible. Whoever chanced to get a few yards too much to the right or the left might hit a mine. There were sure to be some which had not come up, but still floated

---

2. A rifle bullet or small shell only produces a slight shock; consequently the mine does not explode, but a hole is made in its shell. Through this hole water pours in and the mine sinks, that is, lies on the bottom, where it is harmless.

at the right depth. Naturally, there was no question of adhering to the plan of anchorage.

Towards 9 a.m. we had counted five mines awash.

"How lucky for us that the Japanese had moored them so badly," the captain said laughingly. "They are all coming up."

"Five have come up, but how many more are there? "said the torpedo lieutenant.

The flagship signalled: "Hoist out steamboats and search the water between ships."

The mine-searching flotilla came out and swept the water further seaward (that is, from the squadron). They found nothing; but amongst the ships a rich haul was made. By noon ten or eleven mines had either been exploded on being hooked or floated up and destroyed by gun-fire. One exploded thus quite close to our stern; it was 20 to 30 yards off. When the water which had been thrown up by it came down again, all who were standing on our poop got a cold shower bath.

On each side of us the water was free. The squadron had anchored exactly on top of the mine-field.

"How is it possible for us to have run along all those mines and never to have touched one?" was the general question.

The men said "God has helped us"; many took off their caps and crossed themselves.

Today nothing was heard in the mess in the way of a joke at the Japanese failure. Everyone was silent: some looked as if they had something on their minds which they dared not speak of aloud. I believe that we were all depressed by the same thought. These mines must have been laid yesterday or last night, for everything hereabouts was clear of mines until then. It was quite possible our people had not kept a sharp look-out, and had never noticed anything, but why were the mines placed just here? Why precisely at the place where the squadron was to anchor? Did the Japanese by any chance know our most secret "plan of anchorage" ? Surely this could not be—yet the fact remained.

"A very stupid business," said my neighbour, the gunnery lieutenant, quite suddenly; nothing more.

All were silent; no one asked why it was such a stupid business.

Noon.—The mine-searching flotilla is still steaming backwards and forwards, sweeping the channel seaward. Far away on the horizon we can make out some Japanese destroyers. Time passes quickly.

The officers had already begun to make sarcastic remarks about our exit: "No doubt we are only waiting for the next high water to go in again. We are certainly not going to sea just before dark."

Officers as well as men in our ship had hardly got any sleep the previous night, and since 3 a.m. everyone had been on his legs. Yet no one used this pause to get some rest. Everyone was moving about furious and impatient. "Of course we are going back again—we are to be locked up again for a month"; that was the kind of talk one heard amongst the various groups about the deck.

Suddenly, at one o'clock, the flagship began reorganising the squadron by flags. This acted like a warm sunbeam. Every one cheered up and plucked up courage. The younger officers became so enthusiastic that they called for champagne. One of the youngest members held up his glass and began to recite a passage from *Borodino* (poet Lermontoff): "*What are we to do? Go into winter quarters? Are our leaders afraid of tearing the enemy's coats with our bayonets?*"

At 1.40 p.m. a *Te Deum* commenced, but I was unable to attend, as at 1.50 our signal went up to weigh. *Diana* was the first ship to do this. We were to get to sea and avoid as far as possible the Japanese mines. Therefore the following procedure was ordered. The mine-sweeping flotilla was to lead out, steaming by subdivisions. Then followed three subdivisions of the second destroyer flotilla, also towing sweeps; then in single line ahead *Diana*, *Askold*, all the battleships, *Bayan* and *Pallada*. The *Novik* and first destroyer flotilla, which were attached to the squadron, received orders to proceed out independently. We moved ahead very slowly, that is, at 6 knots. At higher speeds the sweeps floated up.

We were all in excellent spirits. At last we had resolved upon something. If we are now to go down, it will at least not have been in vain. It is merely a question of getting at the enemy and sticking to him.

"We shall burst up in any case," the torpedo lieutenant observed in an argumentative tone. When we all went for him, he continued: "*Diana* leads the line; she will therefore be the first in action; we shall also hit the first mine which has escaped the sweeps. But if we *don't* hit a mine, then the *Diana* will burst from mere pride at the great honour of leading the squadron."

The torpedo lieutenant was evidently rather pleased with his *bon mot*, at which we all laughed heartily.

At 2.35 the Japanese destroyers were cheeky enough to fire at our mine sweepers. The *Novik* and her destroyers were sent after them. The *Diana* also opened fire on them with her 6-inch guns over the heads of our own vessels. Firing went on for about a quarter of an hour. When the Japanese realised the uselessness of their performance they steamed away at full speed to the south-east.

Our chaplain, Hieronomach (monk and priest) Gavril (Gabriel), had continued the *Te Deum* in spite of our clearing for action. He walked along the decks with the Cross and Holy Water, and reached the upper deck when the engagement was in full swing. He paced along slowly and solemnly in his green and gold-embroidered cassock. It made a strange, indelible impression in the midst of an engagement, when the sound of the guns mingled with the voices of the choir singing the anthem: "*O Lord, save thy servants.*" The guns were dealing out death and destruction, and amongst them went the priest who was blessing them. All heads were bared to receive the blessing of the Lord—perhaps for the last time. Only one moment each gun-layer moved aside from his sights, to kiss the Cross with which the priest had blessed him.

"A brave man, our father," the captain said *sotto voce*.

We changed our course to starboard and to port so as to follow the windings of the channel which our minesweepers were clearing through the mines (they buoyed the channel as they went along.) We generally proceeded in a south-easterly direction.

At 3 p.m. we sighted a new enemy in place of the Japanese destroyers which had fled. At first the "Greyhounds" appeared, then one of the older cruisers (apparently *Matsushima*), and finally two armoured cruisers. They made no attempt to disturb our solemn procession, and thus provoked a good deal of witticism on the part of our jesters. They said the enemy had better attack us while we were "burying the cat," instead of idling about.

By 4.30 p.m. we assumed that we were in clear water. The squadron stopped, the mine-sweepers hauled in their lines (a wearisome business) and started back to Port Arthur, convoyed by the second destroyer flotilla. For the present the squadron remained stopped so as to cover their retreat. At five o'clock we began taking up battle formation. This was single line ahead. The battleships, led by the flagship, came first, then followed the cruisers led by the *Askold*.

We shaped course S. 20° E.—in other words, for Shantung.

At 6.40 the Japanese main body hove in sight on the port bow. Its course lay across ours. The Japanese were nearly complete. They had four battleships, with which the *Kasuga* and *Nishin* evidently formed one division, and four armoured cruisers. Besides this we made out the Chin Yuen leading three of the older cruisers, the "Greyhounds," a second squadron of protected cruisers, and the destroyers. In the divisions of the latter, which were nearest to us, we counted eighteen boats. But behind them were yet a considerable number of columns of smoke.

"They are all there; even the old *Chin Yuen* had to turn out," the officers were remarking to each other. "This is the result of the way in which we keep our secrets. During the last four days the Japanese have even been able to recall the ships off Vladivostok. Now the fun will begin."

However, I repeat we were in excellent spirits. We were looking forward to the battle bravely and cheerfully.

"There will be no turning-in tonight, old chap," the sailors joked. "Tonight it will be a case of a shake-down at the gun. Mind you save up something from your supper." Laughingly they tucked away some sugar in their blue frocks and distributed the tea-kettles and tea at the guns.

"Tonight soda-water and sandwiches are to be ready for the officers of the different quarters," was the mess president's order.

At 7 p.m. we went to "Action" stations.

The hostile fleet was getting nearer.

Suddenly our flagship turned to port with full helm, nearly 16 points. The other ships followed in her wake. The Japanese did not follow us, but continued their course. (Perhaps they did not believe that we really meant to go back, and suspected some *ruse de guerre* in our movements.)

At 7.50 we lost sight of the Japanese Fleet in the dusk. Its last course had been about west.

We also at first did not believe in the intentions of our leader. But the longer we stood on, the clearer it became. The squadron was returning to Port Arthur—it was flying, although it had merely sighted the enemy. What was up? What had happened? Everyone asked himself these questions, full of annoyance and astonishment.

We had no time for much guessing, for we had to act. The hostile fleet had disappeared to the westward, but his destroyers were deploying on the horizon, out of range of our guns; we had already counted thirty. They were evidently trying to draw ahead of us on both sides—obviously with the view of attacking us.

When the squadron turned, it was 23 miles from Port Arthur. It grew dark very fast: the larger part of the destroyers worked round us to the eastward, that is, our starboard side, the smaller portion on our port side. Our cruisers (*Askold*, *Bayan*, *Pallada* and *Diana*) increased speed and took station on the starboard bow of the battleships; the *Novik* and destroyers were similarly placed to port. I do not know whether we received the orders for this by flag signal, semaphore, or any other means (I did not note this). What we had to do was clear. We were to draw the torpedo attack on us and thus to cover the battleships. The weather was favourable: the night clear and calm, with the moon in its first quarter. It was not very light, but one could see well.

The attack began as soon as the after-glow had died away in the western sky. It is difficult to analyse and write down one's feelings during a torpedo attack, especially when it is one's first experience of the kind. By and by one gets accustomed to anything. My diary only says:—

> For half an hour we fired like mad. Brave fellows these Japanese. They all attacked with great pluck and dash; they probably got some hits. They are gone, and we are unhurt. 9.35 p.m.—We have just anchored.

During this night's run the hostile destroyers were not the principal danger; we could head off these boats; but this time we returned without having our mine-sweepers in front, and not even by the same channel by which we had gone out by day: we might strike a mine any moment.

God helped us this time as well. Only the *Sebastopol* fouled and exploded a mine; happily, she was able to stop the leak and continue with her consorts.

We all anchored in the roads at Port Arthur without signal, without any orders whatever, as if by inspiration, but we somehow did it well.

The ships of the squadron were anchored in two lines. These formed a semi-circle, one end of which was near the shore between Golden and Cross Hills, the other below White Wolf Hill.

As soon as we had anchored we got out the torpedo-nets and went to "man-and-arm ship" stations. The attacks commenced soon after.

Curiously enough, the Japanese never once attempted an attack *en masse*; each time they only sent a group of four or five boats: the same mistake as on February 8.

Meanwhile, the powerful searchlights of the fortress formed a wall of light across the ends of our line, which nothing could pass without being seen. Every group of hostile destroyers which tried to do this came under the concentrated fire of the entire squadron; even at great distances (5 to 6 miles). The theory which prescribes the use of only the secondary and light armament against torpedo attack was completely upset. The big turret guns of the battleships fired away their expensive segment shell just as the 6-inch. How heavy this fire was, and what went on in the zone through which the Japanese destroyers had to pass, not even those who were on board could, I take it, describe. Eye-witnesses who observed this spectacle from the shore in perfect security, could not find words which were strong enough to describe what they saw.

A captain of the garrison artillery, whom I met two or three days later, was still quite excited: "It is impossible to describe it," he said; "the squadron was brightly-lit up by the flashes of its own guns, but around the destroyers the bursting shell were brighter than our searchlights."

Even Japanese nerves could not stand that. In this hell seconds seemed minutes. One lost all measure of time and space. According to the fortress rangefinders, not a single destroyer got nearer than 3 miles from the squadron (that is, of course, too great a distance at which to fire a torpedo). But doubtless they were firmly convinced that they had got quite close up, and had fired their torpedoes at the usual distance of a few cables. The attacks became especially fierce when the moon had set at about 2. 10 a.m. In my diary I find:—

2.30.—A hellish fire. 3. 10.—The attack beaten off, the enemy gone.

The last attack took place at about 3.30 a.m.; after that the dawn put an end to the terrors of the night.

What were the Japanese losses? We don't know: they always knew how to keep their secrets.[3]

Another interesting note (from my diary).

> When we were firing with the guns of one side only during these torpedo attacks, the guns' crews at the disengaged side lay round their guns and snored.

---

3. Next morning we found five or six "Schwartzkopf" torpedoes in the roads. How many had sunk, or drifted away with the tide?

Were they so dead-tired, or had they in truth got accustomed to everything?

During the engagement we never had time to reflect upon what we were doing. We had to exert our bodily and mental powers to their fullest capacity. When day dawned and the enemy disappeared we had leisure to think over our situation.

Many of us still had a faint hope that our retreat did not mean the end of our operations. It was thought that we had only placed ourselves under the protection of the shore searchlights for the night.

"That was all for the best," said our optimists. "Thanks to these powerful beams we were able to beat off the attack. The Japanese must assuredly have suffered losses in their flotillas, besides which they have burnt their coal and fired away their torpedoes. The boats will first of all have to replenish their store of both. Consequently, we may count upon one or two peaceful nights at sea."

"Quite so, if only it really were our plan," replied the sceptics. "But suppose we have simply bolted."

However, no one would concede this. In fact, those who had hinted at this were overwhelmed with reproaches. We were so anxious to believe that the "Great Edict" stood condemned, and that we were really bent on fighting it out.

On June 24 (next day), at 5 a.m., the flagship made the general signal—"Proceed into port." This shattered our last illusions.

The shadow of death seemed to lie on our ship. Only a few minutes before the officers had looked almost cheerful, notwithstanding thirty hours without rest or peace, and had kept the men in good spirits with jokes and kindly words. Now, at one blow, all life seemed to have gone out of them; their faces all became dark and dejected.

The *Pallada* relieved the *Diana* as guard-ship; she went straight to the latter's buoys and we secured to buoys in the West Basin. We made a good evolution of it, but every one worked automatically and from sheer force of habit, without the slightest "go," and that desire to outdo the other ships in smartness.

We went in to remain there. Was it not a matter of perfect indifference how it was done?

By 11 a.m. the whole movement was finished. Little was eaten at breakfast, and of talk there was still less. After breakfast every one at once went to his cabin.

"And now for a little sleep," I thought, as I threw myself on my bed.

But no sleep came. Perhaps I was overtired—perhaps there was some other cause.

My thoughts began to wander. Single words passed through my half-dreaming memory:—"We half fled—fled without fighting. Yesterday morning God helped us—last night we remained unharmed by the Grace of God—and what have we done ourselves?"

I believe that the fate of the Port Arthur Squadron was finally sealed on that day.

On shore the Japanese continued their attacks against the fortress.

On June 26 they were already as far as Lunwantung. They were supported by a destroyer flotilla, which fired into the flank of our positions from seaward. We sent out the *Novik*, *Otvajny*, *Bobr*, and the destroyers to drive the former away, and in return to bring the enemy's flank under fire.

The Japanese destroyers retired at first, but in a short time three small cruisers appeared in support. Against these we on our side sent out the *Pallada* and *Diana*. The enemy at once retired without fighting.

In the evening we re-entered the harbour.

During the night there was a brisk fire against Japanese boats. They were there evidently to drop mines. This was how they intended to prevent our ships from going out to the support of the Russian troops.

On June 27 we had a repetition of the previous day's doings.

At daylight the *Gilyak*, *Otvajny*, *Gremyashtcky*, and the destroyers went out and bombarded the enemy's entrenched positions on the heights east of Lunwantung; the *Diana* went as well in support, in case the Japanese cruisers should appear. We received orders to anchor in the roads, and to stand by to weigh at any moment in support of the destroyers. We counted fifteen wooden frames floating about. They were of the kind the Japanese used for dropping their mines overboard.

This was the result of their midnight visit. The minesweeping flotilla did not go out today. We had to clear a channel ourselves with the ships' steam-boats. We succeeded in fishing out two mines.

From early morning that day we had the outlines or hostile ships in sight on the horizon. At nine o'clock we were able to make out the *Akashi*, *Suma*, *Akitsushio*, and a flotilla of ten destroyers. Soon after eleven heavy rain set in; it was no longer possible to see further than a mile or two. We got out our torpedo-nets and stood by to repulse a torpedo attack as at night or in a fog. At 3 p.m. we received orders not to come in, but to remain out the night. Our berth was to be where Makaroff had placed the cruisers on guard behind the sunken vessels. So they had at last made up their minds to this. For two months and a half this berth, which was right in the entrance and protected the roads at least against any too bold attacks, had been kept empty.

In the evening the rain ceased, but the sky remained overcast, and after sundown it became pitch dark. The Japanese had, of course, noticed that the cruisers had not gone in, and at once tried their luck.

At 9 p.m. two Japanese destroyers crept along the shore from Liao-ti-shan. They had hoisted some of the very characteristic square sails of the Chinese *junks* on their masts, and had thus very successfully eluded the watchfulness of our shore searchlights. The Japanese safely got up to us, but when we turned our searchlights on them [4] we discovered their disguise. When the *Diana* opened fire on them they lowered away their sails and rushed to the attack. It was a wonderful moment when these boats, brightly lit up by our searchlights, put their helms over to fire their torpedoes. One of them came up to less than 15 cables (1½ miles); I saw quite plainly when two of our 6-inch shell hit her: the one abaft the funnels, the other at the waterline under the bridge. This latter must have caused serious damage. We could see with our naked eyes how her bow went down and her speed dropped.

A signalman near me could not suppress his delight, "Splendid! Off he goes with his tail between his legs!"

Some on board us maintained that when the other destroyer turned off to fire, one of her torpedoes had been exploded by our shell. The boat they said had foundered. The same thing was said to have been seen from Golden Hill.

In the middle of this engagement one of the only two 6-inch guns we were able to use against the enemy ceased firing. What was up? One really hardly likes to write it down. During the loading the string with which the bag of smokeless powder flakes in the cartridge case was tied up, came undone. The flakes had fallen out of the bag and had piled up behind the base of the projectile. In consequence the cartridge case would not go home, and the breech could not be closed. The attempts to clear the powder chamber from the rear with the hand, a stick, or a hook, had failed. The gun had to be unloaded—that

---

4. With her own searchlights a ship can only make out a torpedo-boat or destroyer at 1½ or 2 miles, according to the state of the weather.

is, the projectile which had got jammed in the grooves of the rifling had to be pushed out from the muzzle with the cleaning rod.

"What splendid quick-firers," I said unconsciously. I really did not want to hurt the feelings of the gunnery lieutenant, who was perfectly innocent in this.

He shrugged his shoulders. "The system according to which our cartridges are loaded, their hermetically closing lid, which is only removed immediately before the cartridge is placed in the gun—all this is not my invention. Our 'Technical Committee' has elaborated and then approved all this. Am I expected to open each cartridge case and examine it before loading, when in action? In future we shall, of course, have to do this, but it will be done at the expense of rapid shooting."

The following was now to be the routine of the cruiser guard-ships:—Three times twenty-four hours in the roads, three times twenty-four hours in the entrance, three times twenty-four hours' rest in the basin. Of course the word "rest" was an elastic term. All we could claim was to have a little more rest than the others. When the cruiser division had to undertake any job the cruiser whose turn it was to "rest" sailed with the remainder.

The weather got bad. Rain and fogs were frequent. We had southeast winds. They were not very strong, but always raised a heavy swell, which interfered a great deal with the work of our mine-sweeping flotilla.

The Japanese did not come in sight for several days. But on July 3 they attacked the *Pallada*. It was the last night of her guard (she had relieved us on June 30). Again, on July 4, they attacked the *Bayan*, which had relieved the *Pallada*, but in both cases unsuccessfully.

On the morning of June 3 the destroyer *Lieutenant Burakoff* returned in safety. She had been sent to Inkau with despatches. Doubtless she had brought back orders from the commander-in-chief, as she had been absent four days. With her speed she could have gone there and back in one night.

I should not like to omit an incident which is connected with this episode. Perhaps it is of no importance, yet it appears to me to be quite characteristic.

The destroyer *Lieutenant Burakoff* had now run the blockade a second time, and thus enabled the besieged fortress to get into direct communication a second time with the commander-in-chief of our army.

In the Statutes of the Order of St George it is quite clearly stated that whoever breaks through the enemy's lines and brings the commander-in-chief important news will be rewarded with the Order. Was the news which the *Lieutenant Burakoff* brought not important? Was he playing at postman for some private correspondence between two friends, which possessed no value whatever? Twice she fulfilled the conditions laid down by the Statutes of the Order of St George. None the less her captain only received the Order of St Vladimir at the hands of Admiral Vityeft, who, moreover, pointed out how high this reward was, which the officer should try to earn by further exertions. From the local official *Gazette* we, however, knew full well what a shower of rewards for war services descended even on persons whose participation in any operations against the enemy was more than doubtful.

On July 3, 4, and 5, the *Novik*, gun-boats, and destroyers, headed by the mine-sweeping flotilla, went out daily and bombarded the coast between Lunwantung and Sikou Bay. All the cruisers were kept under steam at a moment's notice, in case Japanese cruisers showed any intention of interfering with our vessels. Our services were not required once. The hostile fleet, for some reason or other, did not consider it necessary to make even an attempt at chasing away our few ships. Meanwhile, these same ships caused the enemy's army heavy losses and contributed largely toward forcing them to retire, if only for a short time.

When the *Novik*, gun-boats, and destroyers returned on the evening of July 5, they were received by the coast batteries with the playing of bands and cheers.

Three days of rainy weather now made all active operations impossible. Then we once more bestirred ourselves. On July 8 a new attack by the gun-boats and destroyers against the Japanese left flank took place. The *Askold* was guard-ship outside, but the *Diana* was also sent out to meet any eventuality.

On the horizon, about 10 miles off, we could dimly see the outlines of three ships, apparently the *Matsushima*, *Itsukushima*, and *Hashidate*. They attempted nothing against our boats. But towards 3 p.m. a division of Japanese destroyers approached. They retired after a short artillery duel, when the gun-boats began to fire on them. Meanwhile, the steamer *Bogatyr* laid out mines in Tache Bay. The *Bogatyr* had been converted into a mine-layer. The *Amur* was still in dock repairing her under-water damage.

We of the *Diana* viewed these doings of the *Bogatyr* with some suspicion. "If Tache Bay is being blocked up with mines, it means that the retreat from Lunwantung heights is being prepared, also the retreat from Green Hill and the Wolf Hills. Bad business. The investment of the fortress is complete." This was whispered about amongst the officers.

On July 9 a "big operation" was begun. The *Novik*, the destroyers, all first-class cruisers, and even the *Poltava* went out. At 9.30 this solemn procession, headed by the mine-sweeping flotilla, set off towards Lunwantung. Some large ships were in sight on the horizon, but so far off that we could hardly make them out. Several divisions of hostile destroyers were somewhat nearer. These latter once attempted to attack the mine-sweeping flotilla, but when the cruisers opened fire on them, they retreated hastily, and disappeared. When we had reached our destination, the *Poltava* anchored in the eastern portion of Tache Bay. The cruisers went on as far as Lunwantung, but no further, for here both the Japanese and we had been laying out mines at night with equal energy. The destroyers went ahead nearly up to Sikou. Towards 2 p.m. we began to shell the flank of the Japanese position. Our fire was improved by Morse signals from the shore, which told us where our shell were pitching.

The enemy became restless. His ships, which had been in sight a long time, now approached us up to 55 cables (11,000 yards) and opened fire on us at that long range. They were the *Matsushima, Itsukushima, Hashidate*, a division of gun-boats, and some destroyers.

They did not dare come any nearer. It afterwards turned out that the *Bayan* had, by a lucky shot, hit one of the Japanese cruisers in the stern with one of her 8-inch guns. We must, I feel sure, have scored other hits as well. At least the Japanese retreated very rapidly to a distance of 7 to 8 miles. The *Bogatyr* again dropped mines in Tache Bay.

We could not help suspecting that the entire "big operation" was only intended to cover this latter enterprise.

That was a bad sign. But there were others which were worse. The arsenal of the fortress commenced serving out small arms for the entire ships' companies,[5] and every soul on board, including even stokers and the "daymen," were drilled as small-arm men and put through a

---

5. According to rule, only the seamen and a few petty officers of the crew were armed with small arms. The specialists, that is, gun-layers, electricians, torpedomen, signalmen, and helmsmen, were only aimed with revolvers. The engine-room personnel possessed no arms at all.

course of musketry at the butts. Up to now the landing parties were ordered to be only of such strength that, without them, the ship could still develop her full engine power and man the guns of one side. Consequently we had kept the whole of the engine-room personnel, the specialists of all branches, and half the seamen on board. The Port Arthur Squadron was evidently to prepare for a long and close siege together with the garrison of the fortress.

The following rules were now established:—On the signal being made to land small-arm companies, the whole crew, except the abovementioned specialists, and half the officers were sent. The further signal to land the "Reserve Companies" meant all the remainder. We were only to retain on board the senior specialists amongst the officers and petty officers. In our case these amounted to forty all told, and these were so far as possible to work the guns in case of need. At critical moments they were to destroy the ship to prevent her from falling into the hands of the victorious enemy—a sad prospect.

CHAPTER 9

The Fleet Fights on Land

It was on July 9 that our turn came round for guard-ship. The *Diana* therefore remained outside after the "big operation."

We had the hot and rainy weather typical of the tropical zone. The sky was overcast. It was not very hot, but close; the air was thick with moist steam. Through this kind of haze our searchlight beams had a milky appearance and did not light up distant objects well, whilst they blinded one's eyes, so that one could not see anything. Our 24-inch projectors hardly reached 12 cables (2,400 yards), and even the big 36-inch lights of the fortress only 2½ miles.

Our time on guard was a busy one. The Japanese were evidently furious at our frequent excursions. They turned the favourable weather to good account, and appeared every night in the roads to drop mines and attack the guard-ship.

On July 10 the Japanese only reconnoitred and did not come inside of 30 cables (6,000 yards) from us. The *Diana*, *Gilyak*, and the coast batteries concentrated their fire on them and had no difficulty in chasing them away. To make up for this, two destroyers made a plucky attack on us the following night. They were already discovered at a distance of 3 miles, but did not fire their torpedoes until they had got to 15 cables (3,000 yards). The next morning we fished up two Whitehead torpedoes which had not sunk.[1] They had evidently been intended for us. On the other hand, we had distinctly seen some of our shell make hits. The hostile boats succeeded in effecting their escape, but they certainly suffered losses in men and damages to their vessels.

During the night of the 12th the attack was renewed. Again it had no results, but apparently we were in luck. We observed one destroyer

---

1. The Whitehead torpedo possesses an arrangement which sinks it automatically, when it has missed its object, so as to avoid it falling into the enemy's hands.

at about 22 cables (4,400 yards) suddenly stop, and then slowly turn round 16 points, evidently with her engines only. All round her the sea was literally boiling with our shell. Then we saw a mass of thick black smoke, such as is caused by the explosion of a torpedo head loaded with melinite. When this had cleared away, our searchlights could not discover anything of the destroyer. Possibly she had sunk. The others escaped.

I say "possibly," and dare not state it categorically. My experience of war has taught me that in a night action things often look as one would like them to look. Moreover, not one person, but many together see these things. How is this? Is it a case of self-hypnotism or hallucination *en masse?* Let experts decide. Of this fact there can be no doubt. There were examples not only on our side, but also on that of the adversary. In Port Arthur we often got copies of the *Chefoo Press,* Chinese who ran the blockade in their junks brought them. In this paper, during June and July, we read three times:

> The *Diana* has been sunk in consequence of a successful torpedo attack.

One picture of our foundering was described with much detail. I am sure that the commanders of the Japanese destroyers did not render their superiors any reports which were intentionally false. They certainly did not do so for the simple reason that their superiors were able to verify the reports by their spies, if not the next day, certainly in three days. It is certain that not only the captains, but many men of the crews of these destroyers, firmly believed that they had three times been eye-witnesses of the foundering of the *Diana.*

However, I have digressed from the course of events.

On July 12 the *Pallada* took up our billet in the roads. We went to that of the guard-ship in the entrance.

On July 13 the Japanese tried for the first time to interfere with the work of our mine-sweeping flotilla. Towards 1 p.m., at a distance of 4 miles from the shore, it was fired upon by five hostile destroyers. These helpless steamers had, of course, to cast off their lines and return to the protection of the coast batteries and guard-ships. A few rounds from the *Pallada* and *Bobr* sufficed to cool the ardour of the Japanese destroyers and to drive them to a considerable distance.

During the night of July 14 the Japanese attacked the *Pallada* with destroyers, but without success. This was their last attempt to sink the cruiser on guard. They had satisfied themselves that these attempts were useless, and costly to themselves, and in future only appeared in the roads at night to lay mines.

Of course we also learnt something from our bitter experiences and adopted Japanese methods. We fitted our destroyers for the purpose, and then sent them out at night to strew mines where the blockading ships were in the habit of cruising about by day. This, naturally, did not remain unknown to our energetic and alert opponents. They at once commenced a systematic search of the waters where we had laid our mines outside the range of our coast batteries and guard-ships.

Such cases as occurred on July 13, when our minesweeping craft were attacked by the enemy with impunity, had to be prevented. In future this flotilla was only sent out under a convoy of two or three gun-boats and a destroyer flotilla. The Japanese did the same. Consequently, during the whole of July, people on shore were daily able to witness a strange, almost ludicrous spectacle. Our mine-sweeping flotilla searched for the mines which had been laid by the Japanese. In their wake, where everything had been cleared, came the gun-boats. To seaward of this procession were our destroyers. Then came an empty space of 15 or 20 cables (3,000 to 4,000 yards), and beyond this the Japanese destroyers, out of range of the batteries and guard-ships. Still further out the Japanese mine-sweeping craft were looking for the mines we had placed, and with them were the gun-boats and small cruisers protecting them.

Sometimes the destroyers got bored and approached one another somewhat nearer. Then they commenced firing at one another at long range (for their guns). But it never developed into a regular fight. They soon separated again. Sometimes the Japanese destroyers showed "cheek." Under the belief that either the *Askold*, *Pallada*, or *Diana* were in the roads, they would carelessly approach the guard-ship up to 55 or 60 cables (11,000 to 12,000 yards). Suddenly they discovered that it was the *Bayan*, which was sending them a few segment shell from her 8-inch guns. Then all was confusion and hasty retreat. On board the guard-ship people laughed and joked, for this was always a little change.

The order in which the ships went on guard was now suddenly changed. On July 15 the *Pallada* was to have relieved us in the entrance. But she had urgent defects and went into the West Basin. We remained out. On the 18th we again for some reason could not get a relief. On the 22nd we took over the guard duties in the road, where we remained, not three times, but four times twenty-four hours.

During these days (especially between July 19 and 25) we had almost incessant rain, fog, and thunderstorms. It was only during rare and short intervals that the weather became tolerable.

On July 21 our destroyers, fourteen in number, went out on some night enterprise. Why and whither remained unknown to us.

On July 22, at 10.45 p.m., our searchlights discovered a Chinese *junk*. She was coming from seaward, and making straight for the roads and the entrance with great boldness. We opened fire. The *junk* obstinately continued her course for some time. Then she turned off and ran on a rocky reef projecting from Golden Hill (Lutin Rock). Towards 2 a.m. several destroyers appeared for a moment. They disappeared as quickly when our batteries opened fire on them.

On July 23 the admiral commanding the cruisers came on board the *Diana*. He swore at us, and rated us roundly. He said we had fired on the junk which was bringing us a mail from Chefoo. It was quite clear that if this junk had been expected she should have been furnished with recognition signals. Moreover, our superiors ought to have informed us, the cruiser on guard, that such a craft was expected. Without this we were fully justified in not allowing the junk to approach us within torpedo range, or to enter the harbour. Might this not be a Japanese *ruse de guerre?* Might not the junk have carried some apparatus for launching a torpedo? Possibly she was herself a gigantic mine laden with hundredweights of melinite or *shimose*. Naturally every officer could listen to our admiral and say to himself: "*Jupiter, thou art angry, therefore thou art in the wrong.*"

There was no need for anyone to take his thunder to heart, I might even have omitted this episode, as it does not offer the reader anything of special interest. But there was another point in connection with this. I was aghast at the indifference, not merely calm but contemptuous, with which this unmerited censure of our superior was met. He was, as it were, talking into space, without reaching any one.

At breakfast one of the sub-lieutenants referred to the injustice of the treatment we had received, and said that the man who was censuring us had been in the wrong himself. He was at once silenced by a sharp remark of his neighbour. The latter merely said: "Be quiet! it is not worth talking about. What else can we expect?" There was silence all round, and I suddenly realised that the second-in-command had a far more important and difficult duty to perform here than the mere outward one of maintaining order on board with all means at his disposal. I suddenly remembered a number of incidents to which, absorbed by the multitude of my duties, I had at the time not attached any significance. Once, for instance, being anxious to raise the spirits of the men, I began mentioning the rumours that it was intended taking the squadron to sea to fight a decisive battle. These rumours, which were just then going their rounds in the squadron, had originated with the chief of the staff. It was said that we had only returned on June 24 on account of the *Sebastopol's* leak, that the repairs were going on apace, and that as soon as they were completed we were to offer battle to the enemy. No one had contradicted me.

But when I had finished, my neighbour said quite softly, as if it were to himself: "What is the good of talking about it? Do you really believe this yourself?"—Another time I had come into the mess unexpectedly and overheard a fragment of conversation. Someone was just saying: "Why should we ask him? Of course he will talk us over. His views on the service and on our duty demand this. He himself..." On my appearance the conversation was suddenly broken off. Now I understood everything. It was I who was meant. I remembered many another thing, all trivialities, but symptomatic.

Yes, there was no longer any doubt possible. My messmates avoided discussing the events of the war with me, as they thought that I was not open with them. And that on board the *Diana*, in our mess, hitherto so harmonious and united! The war had made us friends, but this friendship was not proof in the case of a "superior." And I was one of their "superiors."

Should I try and speak quite openly with my messmates? Might I forget my duty to maintain the prestige of leadership by all possible means? I should have done this, had I spoken of all that lay heavy on my heart. If I wanted to maintain my popularity I should have to begin by criticising all orders received. But that would have been useless. I should only have demoralised people still more without effecting any change in the orders. Beside which I should anyhow not have gained my object—their "superior" I remained. Instead, I should have lost their esteem, and this was what I valued most, and which could be of some service to us in action.

I saw before my eyes a picture of utter demoralisation. Of discipline there only remained the outer forms. Its real basis, belief in the superiors, was gone. But it was this belief alone which could guarantee obedience, self-denial, self-sacrifice—in a word, success. The tone amongst the officers was bound to influence to some extent that of the men. What did all this mean for the future?—History has answered.

During the last days of the siege about 9,000 men fit for work were counted in our positions. When the fortress was surrendered the Japanese made 23,000 prisoners, not counting sick and wounded. They were all soldiers, and were in good health.

I was no prophet, and could not predict all this. But now that I was oppressed by all these sad thoughts, I could not help recalling a conversation of the early days of the war. We were speaking of the surprise attack by the Japanese.

"We have been betrayed," said the gentleman with whom I was talking."

"Indeed? And what is your idea of the matter?" I replied. "Do you believe that the Japanese have bribed someone?"

"It is all one," he urged. "Perhaps the cause is bribery, perhaps personal guilt, malice, our imagination, or simple stupidity."

It may be that I was wrong, but I was under the belief that this line of reasoning—though not so bluntly put—was gaining more and more ground. This reticence, this taciturnity, this reserve of the officers when in the presence of their superiors, was only too eloquent.

On July 24, at 3 a.m., we in the *Diana*—she was on guard—heard guns to the eastward. It appeared to come from Tache Bay, where the destroyers *Boyevoy*, *Grosovoy*, and *Lieutenant Burakoff* were patrolling. On account of the weather—fog and drizzle—we could see nothing. At daylight everything was cleared up. This night action had ended very sadly for us. Japanese destroyers, torpedoboats, or more probably steam launches armed with torpedoes, had made use of the favourable weather and had penetrated into Tache Bay at low water. Our land patrol had not noticed anything. The Japanese then attacked our vessels from the shore side, from where they had not expected any attack. The *Grosovoy* was not hurt, but the *Boyevoy* was much damaged. Her foremost stokehold was blown up. But the worst was that the *Burakof*, our only fast boat, was blown nearly in two and sunk. With her we lost the only halfway reliable means of getting into communication with the commander-in-chief *via* Niu-chwang.

In the morning of July 24 everything which could be procured in Port Arthur in the shape of salvage appliances was sent to Tache Bay, escorted by the *Novik*, the gunboats, and destroyers. Towards eight o'clock the *Boyevoy* was towed past us stern first, her injured parts, as it were, "done up in plasters." The salving of the *Burakoff* was quite hopeless. No sooner was the procession in the harbour than a fog came on as thick as milk. On July 25 we were at last relieved. When we reached the West Basin we looked forward to our time there as to paradise. The deck hands who had been all the time in "watch and watch" wanted a thorough rest. The engine-room staff had also had strenuous times, as the ship had to be kept under steam all the time. Besides, all the machinery and boilers required a good overhaul. But all this came to nought. Early on July 26 the signal was made: "*Retvisan*, all cruisers, and destroyers raise steam."

The engineers had just commenced opening up the machinery. They were taken unawares, but one must do them the justice to say that they were equal to the occasion. We were only half an hour behindhand in getting to sea. When we reached the roads at 1.30 p.m. the *Askold*, *Bayan*, and *Pallada* were already at anchor with nets out. The weather was hardly promising for an expedition. From time to time it rained so hard that our range of vision was reduced to 1 or 2 miles. The senior officer of these ships apparently thought the same. Before we had time to take up our berth he signalled to us: "Proceed into port." We turned round, and as we steamed in the other ships were taking in their nets. We had just secured to our buoys in the West Basin when it cleared up. The cruisers, which had just weighed to come in, were ordered by signal from Golden Hill to proceed to Lunwantung and bombard the hostile positions.

For us this appeared to be an insult. We were despised, and were not to join in this. Our captain at once went to see the admiral and to ask for an explanation. He came back quite satisfied, and said that our going out at all was due to a misunderstanding. We were to have two days of complete rest and overhaul our machinery and boilers. It was a fact that by force of circumstances throughout the last month the *Diana* had hardly had a day's peace. We had either been out in the roads or in the entrance. We had hardly gone up harbour when the despatch of all the cruisers had been decided upon. We were so weary that we looked upon the new order as an act of grace, and did not at all envy our comrades the laurels they might pluck meanwhile.

These were hard times indeed.

On July 26, the Japanese attacked our positions along the whole line. Their gun-boats and light cruisers supported them from seaward on both flanks. Our troops fell back before the enemy's first attack. It was said that owing to some misunderstanding, some of our positions had been evacuated almost without fighting. When the *Askold*, *Bayan*, and *Palladia* appeared and had chased away the small Japanese vessels which had been harassing our right wing, the situation changed. Fortune had apparently favoured us again. The *Bayan* succeeded during the long range engagement in hitting the *Itsukushima* with an 8-inch shell. One of the Japanese destroyers was apparently also hit, and beat a hasty retreat. The cruiser *Tchiyoda* struck a mine. She did not sink, but was towed back to Talienwan in a dangerous condition. (She was repaired in the dock at Dalny.)

Our cruisers returned about 7.30 p.m. Semi-officially we were informed that all positions which had at first been evacuated were again in our hands.

All night long we heard the dull roar of guns from the land front. At daylight it increased in intensity. The rain had ceased and the fog lifted. At six o'clock on the morning of July 27 our gun-boats, the cruisers, and the *Retvisan* went out in support of our army. The Japanese attacked with fresh troops, but our people were so encouraged by yesterday's successes that they did not give way. Towards 11 a.m. the *Retvisan*'s 12-inch guns began to speak. Their mighty roar drowned the whole din of battle. How glad we were to hear them! Our most fervid vows accompanied each round fired by the *Retvisan*. On our right wing, which was supported from seaward, the situation was not so bad. On the other hand, the accounts from the left wing were not good. Opposite to Itchenza, where we had twenty-four field guns, the Japanese had got eighty into position. Moreover, the enemy was supported from seaward by his gun-boats.

All ships landed their doctors and stretcher parties. Soon after noon the firing ceased. Towards three o'clock our ships returned to the roads and came up harbour in the evening. At seven o'clock our neighbour, the *Bayan*, came to her berth in the West Basin. Our experienced eyes noticed that she was down by the bows, and had evidently been damaged. Later we heard that just as the *Bayan* had reached the roads, she had struck a mine. Her watertight bulkheads had stood, only the foremost stokehold was flooded. All the same, our only armoured cruiser was *hors-de-combat*.

"This is a further reason for our not going to sea. We must now wait until the *Bayan* is repaired."

I turned round to face the speaker, and had difficulty in restraining myself.

"You seem pleased at our misfortunes. Do you still dare to mock?"

He looked at me steadily with his grey eyes, half-respectfully, half-mockingly.

"By no means. I am only trying to discover at once the motive which will probably influence our leaders in their orders."

On July 27 the *Diana* suffered a severe loss in the person of Korosteleff, the constructor attached to the ship.

Korosteleff was an indefatigable worker and a first-rate engineer. He possessed thorough scientific training and a rich practical experience. Whilst the cruiser was being built he was employed in the dockyard. In the mess the standing joke about him was that he was "personally acquainted" with every rivet in the ship. For the captain and executive officer he was more than the right hand. Korosteleff had a fine presence, and at first sight he looked healthy. But the doctors said that he suffered from the heart and the nerves. The six months of war had had a bad effect on his health.

Latterly he had suffered more and more from choking fits.

"What ails him?" I asked our young, sympathetic disciple of Æsculapius.

"Weak heart," he answered sadly.

"Can't you help him? You only seem to treat him after an attack. Can't you cure him? Are there no means? Can't his complaint be radically cured?"

"If he goes ashore, rests, and once more has a peaceful occupation, he can live to be a hundred.—Not much of a warrior! When some poisonous vermin comes off with the provisions, in the coal, etc., and he discovers it, he does not kill it, but he packs it into a box and takes it ashore.—What trouble I had with him after the *Petropavlovsk* went down! He can't stand or get over anything so awful as that was."

"Well, then, order him back to Russia."

"Easier said than done. Just you go and suggest such a thing to him. I have already tried it. If he goes he will only get worse. He is so sensitive that he believes he could never stand the disgrace and would shoot himself. Wait and see! His obstinacy will avenge itself!" With these angry words the doctor departed.

During these few days of rest in the West Basin every one had only one desire: as soon as possible to have a bath and then a good sleep. Life in the mess ceased uncommonly early.

On July 26, towards 10 p.m., I was just getting into my bed, when I heard some one groaning. I quickly dressed and went out. Korosteleff was sitting in the mess in semi-darkness. His head had sunk on his arms, which were stretched across the table, and he was rocking from side to side. Behind him stood a pale servant, who had quite lost his head, and kept saying: "Your honour! your honour! What is up? What is the matter with you?"

"Call the doctor, and don't behave like a fool," I called out, and hastened to assist my good old messmate.

"The doctor can do nothing more—shall I fetch the priest?—He is dying."

"Don't talk. Run, in the devil's name, and do what you are told!"

The servant disappeared. Korosteleff changed his position. He leant back in the armchair and, half-lying, half-sitting, tugged away at his jacket. I quickly unbuttoned his collar, poured a decanter of water over his head, and turned an electric fan straight at his face. I had often done this before. It required neither time nor reflection. Korosteleff ceased groaning. In his eyes, wide open, consciousness seemed to return.

"Now, my friend! Courage! The doctor will be here in a moment. He will bring you round again with his stuff."

Korosteleff began to stammer. His convulsive fingers snatched at his throat one moment, the next they seized my hand. "No, no—tell the people—that is the wrong valve—not that spindle—it won't fit—I am choking—I won't...."

The doctor hurried in with the sick berth steward and some assistants. The sick man was carried to his cabin.

The next morning the doctor declared that life on board was so depressing for the patient (that was really his whole complaint) that he must be landed at once. If this were not done, he could not guarantee his life for an hour.

"A steamboat at the starboard gangway!" I called out to the quartermaster, who had answered my bell. Then I went to the captain and reported the sad case.

The officers were just at breakfast. As I passed the door I looked in and said: "Gentlemen, help Korosteleff to pack; he has to go to hospital." All understood what was the matter, and at once went to the sick man.

"Is it as bad as that?" said the captain. "Send him away at once. I'll sign the necessary papers later. What a pitiful thing! This splendid fellow, and a good workman! He was so clever and shrewd! Let us hope that he'll pull through."

I told the captain that I had anticipated his orders and had made all arrangements in his name.

"Of course, of course—quite right. Any loss of time might have been fatal."

I have had to see many who were severely wounded and dying. The agonies through which Korosteleff had to pass have indelibly impressed themselves on my memory.

Our young doctor (our only one, though by the complement we were allowed two) had sat up all night with the patient. Now Korosteleff was again conscious, but from time to time his mind was wandering, though his eyes were open. He spoke to those around him, calling them by name, and then suddenly uttered a number of wholly disconnected words.

"Well, well—you are all such dear fellows—tell me, is this really necessary?—Must I go ashore?—Into the green country?—Well, well,—I am in want of rest. It is beautiful in the green country—I'm so accustomed to my small cabin—I thought it might become my coffin." (At that moment the sound of guns came across from Lunwantung.) "Do you hear that?—They're nailing down the lid. I won't! I won't! Help!—Oh, it's gone, is it?—How glad I am!—God knows what I thought."

It was particularly terrible to see how perfectly healthy this doomed man appeared to be every now and then. He dressed himself (assisted by those near), went up on deck and down the ladder into the boat quite unsupported. We all accompanied him. All those who worked immediately under Korosteleff, mostly from the engine-room staff, came on deck.

"Goodbye—goodbye!" he said, and struggled painfully with his feelings.

"Get well quickly and come back!"—"Come back soon!"—"We want you on board. Without you we are like people without hands." Cries such as these, intermingled with "*Au revoir!*" came from all sides.

The sick man forced himself to remain standing. He bowed repeatedly and smiled pleasantly, but looked utterly tired and hopeless, as much as to say that he did not believe our assurances, but that he did not want to contradict us in the hour of separation. Suddenly he became restless and began to protest. Korosteleff had, of course, been placed on the cushions in the stern-sheets aft, the most comfortable place. No, he did not want that. He dragged himself forward in the boat.

"But you will be more comfortable aft."

"No, no; I won't sit with my back to the *Diana*.—I built her myself.—I know every rivet of her.—This is the last time I shall see her.—I want to be able to look at her to the last."

We then all felt that there was no sense in talking to him in this tone of artificial hope. It was not we who cheered him up, but he us. We all remained silent and took off our caps. The boat shoved off and steamed towards the north shore of the West Basin. Once more we saw a white handkerchief fluttering, and waved back with our caps. Someone shouted "Hurrah!" but hardly anyone joined in this. The sick man was already too far away, he could not have heard it anyhow,

"Well, how goes it with him?" we all asked the doctor when he returned on board from the hospital, where he had taken the sick man.

"Bad—very bad. He'll hardly pull through."

There was general commotion.

"Then why did you send him on shore? Surely he might have been allowed to die here amongst his friends?—Are you afraid of corpses? No—these doctors! For them a patient is only a numbered object."

The doctor got angry.

"If your ship is hopelessly damaged, then you are bound to destroy her with everything on board, so that she may not fall into the enemy's hands. But by your oath you are bound to defend the ship as long as there is the faintest glimmer of hope.—Korosteleff wanted the green country. His cabin was his grave, he said. When they were firing he thought they were nailing down his coffin. He is out of all this now! It may be that his life will be spared. Such cases have been known."

Korosteleff died in hospital at 1.30 a.m. on July 28. His end was so calm and peaceful that the nursing sister on duty did not at once notice it.

Next day was the solemn funeral.

"My God!" thought I, "yet another bloodless victim of the war! How many fall thus without our knowing it?"

During the night of July 28 our troops fell back all along the line.

In the morning an immediate attack by the enemy was evidently expected. All ships were ordered to disembark landing parties. During the afternoon they were re-embarked.

Arrangements had been made "from above" to ensure that no news of the operations of the army could reach the garrison. Notwithstanding this, the news penetrated everywhere, into the town, into the fortress, into the squadron—by means of Chinese. We had quite accurate details about our failure at Van-fan-gou, and already on July 15 the rear-guard action of Haitchen was spoken of. Then came Tashichao, that is, the evacuation of Niu-chwang.

Hopes of any success on land became mere pious aspirations. On the other hand, a very decided rumour gained ground to the effect that a second squadron was being fitted out at Cronstadt, and that it might start any day. We did not quite believe this rumour. The sceptics said that we did not possess another "squadron," that it was possible to get together in a relatively short time a number of ships, both new ones and old ones reconstructed, but much time would be required to turn them into a "squadron." Only a homogeneous, well-drilled, well-organised squadron should be sent out. If any one imagined that a badly organised "*armada*" would do as well—why, it would hardly get as far as Port Arthur!

A small number of optimists tried to represent the situation more favourably: "It will take two or three months to collect the new squadron in the home ports," they said. "During that time something can be learnt; the remainder can be acquired on the way out."—"Indeed," was the reply. "A retriever cannot be trained on the way to a shoot. No; the Japanese have been training their squadron for eight years, without stinting the cost of keeping it in full commission. We have seen the results. Do you remember what Makaroff says in one of his books?—'*One cannot hope to carry out in war anything which has not been learnt in peace.*'"

I believe (I may be wrong) that there was no faith in our administration. The majority was of opinion that these rumours of a prospective arrival of a second squadron were chiefly intended as an excuse for our inactivity. They were to make us believe that we were saving up the ships against the arrival of the expected reinforcements. All this was not put forward openly, but one "read it between the lines "during all conversations.

"As soon as they begin to bombard us from the land side it will be all up with our squadron. The second squadron cannot arrive in any case before this happens. We must not shut our eyes to this danger. The fate of Port Arthur is sealed. If we want to save the squadron we must go to Vladivostok. If not we must risk annihilation in action and at the same time cause the enemy as much damage as possible. It is criminal to leave the ships here to be pounded to pieces by the shore guns."

Many thought thus.

On July 29, or during the night of the 30th (I can't say for certain, for in these times we simply lived on rumours), our troops evacuated the Green Hills, Takushan, and the Wolf Hills. The latter were given up almost without a struggle. All the same we had some losses. It was said that they were caused by the Japanese firing into our flank during our retreat, causing much confusion in our ranks.

The real siege of the fortress may be counted as commencing on July 30. From morning until 2 p.m. of that day the *Retvisan, Peresviet,* and *Pobieda* bombarded by indirect fire the valley of Lun-ho, in which the enemy was specially active.

The night of July 31 was disturbed. In the evening we got the signal:

"Keep cleared for action during the night.—Landing parties to be kept ready.—The battleships will open fire at daybreak.—*Novik*, gunboats, and .destroyers are to go out at 6 a.m.," etc.

The Japanese, however, did not attack, perhaps on account of the weather. We had almost incessant rain and fog.

On August 1 we were again guard ship in the roads.

When the weather was particularly bad, one could hear strange remarks in the mess. The officers did not address me directly, but they "sounded," so to speak, by expressing their ideas in my presence. It was thus said that we should clear out of this place. That we should seize the opportunity when we could not be seen either from the shore or the sea, to cast off from the buoys and break out to Vladivostok. If we are then annihilated, said some of them, well then we are annihilated. If, on the other hand, we do get through to Vladivostok, we can get new guns for the old ones, and then we shall still be good for something. Here we should simply be made prizes of.

Sometimes I pretended not to hear any of this, but occasionally I had to cry halt. I declared that if we did this, we should be deserting our post like a sentry. The admiral commanding the squadron was in a better position to judge of all the circumstances than we. If he did not go out he had his reasons. At a given moment the admiral required all our forces for the decisive battle, every gun would then be of great value. No one contradicted me, but I felt and saw that the officers did not believe my words as to a decisive battle. As regarded the "great value of every gun," I received the laconic reply: "Except, of course, those we have sent on shore."

Yes, demoralisation was in full swing.

In these days a quite new and very sad defect showed itself in connection with our gun armament.

On one occasion when we were firing as usual at Japanese destroyers one of our 6-inch guns suddenly ceased firing. "What's the matter?" the captain shouted furiously, when he saw that the gun was being unloaded from the muzzle. "Has the cartridge again not been examined and fallen to pieces?"

"No, sir, it is not the cartridge," reported the officer in charge excitedly from the upper deck. "It is much worse! We can't get the projectile far enough in."

The following facts were then elicited. Ammunition had been sent out to Port Arthur in great haste, as it seemed likely that the communications of the fortress with the north might be cut off. In consequence of this a large batch of shell had not been examined at all, or only in part.

Of course the department making the issue could quote paragraph 527 of the instructions. These provide that the gunnery lieutenant is to stop the issue and report to the captain if any articles are found not to correspond exactly with the sealed pattern. With equal force the gunnery lieutenant could point out that he was unable to do this; that he was without any means, and, above all, lacked the requisite time for careful examination of all stores we drew from the local depots to fill up our deficiencies. The storekeepers at Port Arthur, again, were quite in their right when they maintained that they had received these shell from the factory and the central department at home, and that they also lacked means and time for gauging. In short, as usual, every one, that is, no one, was to blame, but the fact remained.

Our gunnery lieutenant was in great trouble over this discovery. We had always filled up our allowance of shell as they were expended. In the shell rooms the new shell had been stowed in the empty racks. It was impossible now to say which were the shell received before the war, and which were not. It was equally impossible now, in time of war, to make a careful examination of the whole of our projectiles. We could only do this by degrees, by unstowing a small number of shell at a time. We required time—but did we know how much time we still had at our disposal? That all depended on the enemy.

A further defect was discovered. I don't know whether it was in consequence of bad gauging or simply of bad metal. Our cast-iron shell (the cheapest and therefore the most numerous in our outfit) often burst on leaving the muzzle. When the *Gilyak* was firing at Japanese destroyers and her projectiles passed close to us (when guard-ship), we afterwards frequently picked up splinters of the cast-iron shell on our decks in the morning. In the first instance, the neighbouring ships were endangered, but the gun itself could be disabled if a shell burst in the bore. Orders were therefore given to fire cast-iron shell only with practice charges (that is, half charges).

That was a sad order. We were no longer able to develop the full power of our guns. But, alas, it had to be!

On August 2 we were directed to leave it free to such of our servants as had voluntarily enlisted to have their engagements cancelled with a view to getting away to Cheefoo by the next Chinese *junk*.

A sad premonitory symptom!

The Japanese were now not very active. They were probably busy building heavy siege batteries. The ships of the squadron fired at them from the basins indirectly, and tried to interfere with their work. In this way the fleet defended the fortress towards the land.

What irony!—The fleet was fighting on land!

On August 4 we were relieved in the roads and took up our berth in the entrance.

CHAPTER 10

Our Last Days in Port Arthur

It was quite curious to note the revulsion that took place in the general feeling afloat during the next few days. I have repeatedly noticed such changes during the war, but cannot explain them. At first the masses do not believe in the intentions their leaders have openly avowed. And this notwithstanding that the latter have never given the slightest cause for suspecting the honesty of their intentions. The men ought therefore to believe them. Then there is a sudden revulsion. These same people are now as firmly persuaded that their leaders have this or that honest intention, although it has never been expressed and only presumed. How is this? It is a psychological riddle. Savants may solve it—or perhaps the spiritists? Who can tell?

No more grandiloquent orders were issued announcing the resumption of the offensive, with simultaneous appeals to the Heavenly Hosts. No sensational rumours were spread in the town. The clerks who were sent to the sdmiral's office did not bring back bits of news confided to them by some "very reliable people"; yet there was something in the air.

In the mess I was once more treated as a messmate. No one held aloof from me, but all were ready to hear my advice or my views on this or that. "On deck," that is, on duty, my orders were no longer merely formally executed, but in the manner I was always anxious to see—that is, with zeal and intelligence.

Whence came this change in our relations? The fact that I was their superior had only quite recently separated me from my messmates like a solid wall. Why did this no longer interfere with our familiar intercourse? Who had pulled down this wall?

It is true, some of the battleships had got back a portion of their 6-inch guns, which they had lent to the land forts. But it had always been promised that these guns would only remain on shore so long as their ships were laid up for repairs, and that they would be returned for certain. That was not the whole reason. No; I repeat, there was something in the air.

What now followed proved that my deductions were correct. About this time Admiral Vityeft received orders to proceed to Vladivostok with the squadron. This categorical order came direct from His Majesty. It left absolutely no doubt as to its meaning. How unlike the orders we generally received from the viceroy! In these there was always some saving clause to cover their author in the event of the enterprise failing. The gentlemen who admire Admiral Alexeieff and who defend his actions before the war and during the war, pretend that he had repeatedly "categorically" demanded from Admiral Vityeft "decisive" steps.

I should like to submit this to the reader's judgment.

The most "definite, categorical" order from the viceroy was brought to Port Arthur on July 3 by the destroyer *Lieutenant Burakoff* (even his defenders admit that). It ended textually thus:

> Keep before your eyes the fact that the squadron can only remain in Port Arthur as long as it is safe there. In the other eventuality, go to sea in good time *and proceed, without engaging in battle, if this be possible, to Vladivostok.* [1]

Can these "directions" be called a categorical demand for decisive steps? There was not a word in this of the possibility of defeat, and this was both a safeguard for the viceroy, who issued the order, and a trap for the one who was to execute it. The manner in which the phrase "if this be possible" is introduced is particularly clever. What does it refer to?—the battle which is to be avoided or the voyage to Vladivostok?

On August 7 one could well say: "*This is the beginning of the end.*" On that day Port Arthur itself was bombarded for the first time from the land side. The bombardment commenced at 11.35 a.m. From the shell which did not burst we made out that a battery of 4.7-inch guns was at work. The Japanese had apparently profited by the experience of the Boer War. Until the regular siege artillery arrived, they took ships' guns of that calibre and mounted them for field service.[2]

---

1. *Ruskaya Starina*, April and May 1907—*The Squadron of Port Arthur before Its End*, by Biélomor.
2. It would be interesting to find out whether these mountings were extemporised or had already been prepared before the war.

The Japanese fire was not continuous, but in series of seven or eight rounds. Between these they paused. The first series fell altogether in the main street of the old city, near the Port Hospital; the second fell more to the westward, that is, on the quay of the commercial port. It destroyed the coal which was stacked there.

The third series fell on the open place in front of the admiral's landing-steps, a little to the westward of the place where the *Tsesarevitch* lay alongside. We saw that she had been hit. Luckily, only one of the shells was well placed. It destroyed the wireless office on board. The operator, a torpedo-machinist, was killed as he was sending a message. The admiral commanding, Rear-Admiral Vityeft, was slightly wounded in the leg by a splinter. About 1 p.m. the fire was directed towards the entrance. As before, the Japanese fired series of seven or eight guns. These series were apparently laid for successive points from south to north.

I say it quite frankly, when I saw from our bridge that the Japanese shell, by the way they pitched, followed a regular course moving from the southward of us towards the berths of the cruisers, my heart felt heavy. Heavy, with anxiety, not with fear, for the chances of war decree that not every mine hits a ship, nor every splinter a forehead. A bombardment is a game of chance, in which one stakes one's life. The chances of losing one's life at a bombardment are much less than those of a particular number turning up at roulette. But the novice at this game is excited at the idea that he might possibly win enough on one stake to set him up for life. Similarly in war, everybody in his first battle believes himself to be the predestined victim of the first shot. Later on this passes away. The game becomes a real game.

On August 7 our officers, as well as the men, watched this game with equal eagerness, although it was forbidden to come on deck to look on at the bombardment.

"They fire well and, above all, systematically," the gunnery lieutenant declared in a dogmatising manner and directed his binoculars at the spot where the shells pitched.

"Oh, this series is evidently passing over us! Look! Do you see?"

One shot had gone wide and struck far on our right. Another hit somewhat nearer; a third off the starboard beam.

"The devil! Where will the next one pitch?"

For some seconds there was the silence of death (just as round the roulette table whilst the little ball is skipping over the ribs on the revolving disc). The shell strikes the water and bursts. It was on the port beam, and splinters rained against the ship side and over the deck.

"No hit, but nearly! Good luck this time!" people were calling out all round. This was said with an air of utter indifference. It even sounded a little like mockery at the enemy's failure, at the fate which somehow had not reached us. Everyone felt relieved, like a man who has been pitched overboard, head first, and who suddenly comes to the surface and draws a deep breath.

The following shots of this series fell to the left at increasing distances.

The captain came up to me and mentioned, in an irritated voice, that the flagship had now made the signal for the second time— "Don't keep more men on deck than necessary," and that we seemed to be having a regular bazaar going on on the upper deck. He knows well enough what drives the men up from below. These men, who have been "proved in the fire" long ago, can stand this game easier in the open. They want to be able to see and hear the shell, they can't stand remaining between decks without any occupation and waiting for the next shell to knock them over,

"Can't you devise something? "the captain asked in a more gracious tone. "Don't you know of some occupation for the men?"

A happy thought strikes me. The cable deck is just now the best protected space. A lecture might be held there for the ship's company. Sub-lieutenant Sh—— is a talented lecturer, he has already procured the crew many a happy half hour during the monotony of the siege by his talent. He must sit down there and read them *The Fair of Sorotchnisk* (humorous tale by Gogol).

The news of this spread all over the ship. The upper deck quickly became empty. Salvoes of laughter soon came up the forecastle hatch. They sound strange alongside the metallic buzzing of the enemy's shell and the dull roar of our guns replying to them.

I went down two or three times. Upon my word, it was really very jolly there.

Whilst watching this bombardment I observed something which was very satisfactory for us. The Japanese made very good practice, but their fuses were bad. I carefully watched ten series, and noted the shell which did not burst. The shell all struck on land, that is, on solid ground. None the less thirty-two out of seventy-six did not burst.[3]

The bombardment lasted all day. The guns of our land forts and of

---

3. The Japanese removed this defect during the course of the war. Their shell burst brilliantly afterwards.

the battleships replied, but this infernal little Japanese battery was so well hidden that we never managed to destroy it.

At seven in the evening it came on to rain. Soon it was coming down hard; this lasted till 11 p.m., with few interruptions.

Just before sunset the Japanese concentrated their fire on the right centre of our land front and then delivered a very determined attack. They probably thought they could turn the bad weather to account. At first we only heard single rifle shots. Soon it turned into a continuous rattle. The forts worked their searchlights at the same time and fired star shell.

The same evening, as we were lying on guard in the entrance, we observed a mysterious event, which was never cleared up subsequently.

About 11.25 p.m. we noticed out to sea to the south-east, about 8 or 10 miles off, a faint light, which rapidly grew to a big flame surmounted by clouds of smoke. It was evidently a ship on fire. We were keeping a sharp lookout all round, in hopes of getting some clue as to what was going on. Suddenly a bright light flashed up, a good way to the right of the fire, bearing almost south, and a few seconds later we heard a dull detonation as of an explosion. The whole thing was enacted in a few moments, but was observed simultaneously by several people. Later we could see nothing in that direction. Darkness and silence reigned there. On the other hand, the fire raging to the south-east increased rapidly. The unknown vessel burnt so mightily that even the clouds above it turned blood-red. Perhaps it was still moving by its own means, perhaps the tide was taking it along, but the distance became less and less.

Shortly before midnight we saw a new explosion, this time much nearer to the burning ship.

About 12.30 the brilliantly illuminated foremast of the ship was taken by our Barr and Stroud rangefinder. The distance was 50 cables (5 miles). With the glass one could distinctly make out the ship's side glowing red. Along it a row of intensely bright spots were visible. These were evidently the scuttles out of which the flames were bursting from the interior.

The burning ship did not keep on a straight course, but turned sometimes to starboard and sometimes to port. Sometimes we saw her broadside on, sometimes she turned her bow or her stern towards us. For the seaman this was a sign that invisible friends were surrounding the ship trying to take her in tow. Soon after 1 a.m. their efforts seemed to have succeeded. The ship slowly moved away to port, that is, to the northward. We lost sight of her in the direction of Talienwan at about 1.45. Neither our batteries nor the guard-ship fired.

There were great speculations on the *Diana's* bridge. What might this drama be which we had just witnessed? Quite lately the Chinese had repeatedly reported to us that the Japanese were preparing a new desperate attempt to block up our squadron in Port Arthur. The fireships and block-ships were not to come singly this time, but in groups of four abreast, secured together with chains.

Had the Japanese, in such an attempt, come upon the mines which our destroyers had laid out during the preceding nights? But then what started the fire? Was it caused by an accident or through carelessness? It was, anyhow, clear that the Japanese had been unlucky that night.

During the night the batteries on our land front only fired occasionally. On August 8 the bombardment of the town and harbour by the land batteries was continued at 7.45 a.m. Our gun-boats and destroyers were all sent out into the roads. Here our mine-sweeping flotilla was working with might and main.

At 9 a.m. a lucky shot of the enemy's set fire to a shed in which was stored a quantity of lubricating oil in tanks (the shed was close to the south-west corner of the East Basin). It was just as well that the main oil depot close by had not been hit. A bright flame at once shot up and a gigantic cloud of thick black smoke rolled up into the air—for the Japanese an admirable mark. The enemy now directed his whole fire on the spot. However, on that day they were not successful. The Japanese knew the direction very accurately, but they were somewhat out in distance. Consequently they poured an incessant stream of fire for several hours on the bare northern slope of Golden Hill, on which there was not a soul.

The parties sent from the ships and port establishments to put out the fire suffered no losses.

The main depot was successfully cleared. The burning oil, flowing out of the tanks, which had burst, was diverted by a trench into a natural hollow in rear. Here it partly burned itself out, partly was put out, that is, smothered with earth.

Towards noon the fire was out, and at one o'clock the bombardment suddenly ceased.

The admiral expressed his "special satisfaction" by signal to the *Peresviet*. We heard that she had been successful in hitting the "infernal little battery" and silencing it.

During the afternoon, and especially in the evening, a fierce battle was raging at our right centre. The light northerly wind occasionally brought us the rattling sound of machine gun and infantry fire, which penetrated the thunder of the larger guns. There was a pause between lo and 10.30 p.m., then the fight broke out afresh, and continued with great violence until midnight. Occasionally short messages from the front told us that the fight was for Takushan Hill, which passed several times from one hand into the other. Finally, the hill remained neutral for a while. We had evacuated it, but the Japanese were unable to maintain themselves on it. The mortar battery on Golden Hill threw its ii-inch shell on those heights throughout the night at regular half-hour intervals. In these circumstances it was quite out of the question for men to stay there, leave alone to entrench themselves.

At 8 a.m. on August 9 we noticed that the Japanese had got their "infernal little battery" into working order again, but had moved it. They started bombarding us once more. Their fire was mainly directed against the battleships in the West Basin, There were a few hits, but they did no damage. Again the *Retvisan* was specially unlucky. She had a lighter lying alongside, containing two 6-inch guns brought back from the land front. A projectile hit this lighter and it sank with the guns. The battleship was hit below the water-line. The damage was not serious, but the hole admitted about 400 tons of water. This was a quite superfluous cargo, which was peculiarly disagreeable in view of the prospect of having to fight the decisive battle.

Besides this, the turrets and casemates of the *Retvisan* were hit. The ship had three killed and several wounded, the captain amongst the latter (a slight wound only). The bombardment and our reply to it lasted all day. Later in the evening there was a short but fierce fight on our right wing. The ships of the squadron hastily filled up with coal and stores. The Japanese had not been in sight to seaward these last two days, and during that time they had not laid out any mines in the roads.

The night of August 9-10 was calm and hot (80° F.), but not close, thanks to a light breeze from the north. We had completed all our preparations for going to sea, and every one was now sleeping soundly, so as to gather strength for the coming day.

I will not indulge in speculations as to the feelings with which the squadron greeted the sun on August 10. During these last days there had hardly been any communication between the ships. I will merely endeavour to describe the general feeling on board the *Diana*. There was nowhere anything like the enthusiasm which had marked the short time under Makaroff. Neither were we filled with that craving for revenge, as was the case during the first moment after the foundering of the *Petropavlovsk*, nor were we in the state of elation as after the unexpected success of May 15;[4] yes, not even in that state of cheerful determination with which we had greeted the signal to weigh on June 23.

All that was a thing of the past. These events had left deep marks on every heart, but the feelings they aroused could not be reproduced. Our people, who had long since received their baptism of fire, and who had now so often looked death in the face, prepared for this battle as for a serious task, full of responsibility. "The thing is settled. Tomorrow morning we go out into the deadly fight. Thank God !—Apparently no one is thinking of himself One's duty has to be carried out." These few lines I scribbled in my diary, as I was going to bed on the eve of sailing.

There was yet something in the minds of all which I should not like to pass over in silence. There was a certain sense of satisfaction. We felt that at last there was an end to the divergence between the intentions of the leaders and the hopes and aspirations of the masses.

During these last three days of land bombardment one had often heard the remark, with a ring of malice in it: "Perhaps 'they' will now realise that the Basins of Port Arthur are the graves of our squadron."

The pessimists had then replied: "The grave? That would not be so bad. But this kind of death would not last long, and then would come the resurrection under the Japanese flag, and that is much worse."

The news that our sailing was imminent did not produce any enthusiasm, but only a general sense of relief. It was clear to all that we were bound to go out. The masses saw that so clearly that the reluctance of our leaders had already inspired the most terrible suspicions in the more excitable heads. Sometimes it seemed as if we were again in the frame of mind which obtained in the early days after the surprise attack of February 8. Just as then, so now, we nearly heard the cry of "Treason! Our leaders have betrayed us!" Could there be anything worse than that?

As soon as the day began to break the squadron commenced moving out of harbour. The *Diana* allowed all ships to pass her at her berth as guard-ship, and then moved out as the last at 8.30.

---
4. The blowing up by mines of two Japanese battleships.—Trans.

"Everything all right. Weather calm and everyone at his station," is noted in my diary.

To the eastward, lightly veiled by the morning mist, the *Shikishma*, *Kasuga*, *Nishin*, and a squadron of old cruisers (*Matsushima*, *Itsukushima*, and *Hashidate*), were in sight. The latter set off at high speed to the north-east.

At 8.50 a.m. the *Tsesarevitch* made the general signal "Clear for action." At nine o'clock came a further signal:

The fleet is informed that His Majesty has ordered us to proceed to Vladivostok.

This latter signal was received by us with undisguised approval. "At last! A good man this Vityeft! No going back now!"

Our mine-sweeping flotilla had cleared a channel for us during the preceding days, and, so as to put the enemy on a false scent as far as possible, this channel lay in a different direction from the course we steered on June 23. This time we steamed from the anchorage almost exactly parallel with the eastern shore of Liao-ti-shan. We passed out into the open sea between our mine defences, which surrounded the cape on which stands the lighthouse.

At 10.30 the mine-sweeping flotilla was dismissed. It returned to Port Arthur, escorted by the gun-boats and the second destroyer flotilla. Their senior officer hoisted a signal, which I unfortunately did not note down. So far as I recollect it ran: "God be with you! Goodbye!"

When the *Otvajny* steamed past us with this signal at her masthead all hands came on deck and waved their caps. Every one mentally said: "Goodbye"—*au revoir* would surely have been presumptuous.

We were steaming in battle formation. The *Novik* and the first destroyer flotilla were ahead of the battleships, which, led by the flagship, were in single line ahead, and finally the cruiser division, from which, unhappily, the *Bayan* was missing. Just as the mine-sweepers had been sent home, something seemed to have gone wrong with the flagship's engines. She signalled: "Speed 8 knots."[5]

That! When breaking a blockade and in sight of the enemy!

The weather began to favour us. A light, low-lying fog came on

---

5. The *Tsesarevitch* had constant trouble with her engines. The "*Forges et Chantiers de la Mediterranée* "themselves admitted that an error had been made in the building of the engines. The company made new excentrics for the battleship, and despatched them to Port Arthur. Most unfortunately the war broke out just then, and the consignment never got beyond Shanghai.

from the east and north-east. Port Arthur disappeared from our view altogether; the nearest coastline was only faintly visible through the fog.

At 11.5 a.m. the *Diana* turned to S. 50° E. in the wake of her next ahead.

As we were the rear ship, the whole squadron was now on the new course.

The fog hugged the shore; to seaward it was fairly clear.

At 11.30 we made out the outlines of an armoured cruiser and three light cruisers on the starboard bow; a little more to starboard of these a number of big ships, preceded by destroyers.

At 11.35 the vessels to the starboard of us steamed to south-west. Those to port of us appeared to be trying to join hands with the former. Our squadron increased speed, so that we had to go on 10 knots to keep up.

At 11.50 the flagship hoisted flag "K," This meant "Ship not under control." Again something wrong! We all stopped engines, and waited for the defect to be put to rights. Meanwhile the Japanese were quickly effecting their junction.

At last, at noon the signal was made to proceed at 15 knots. We did not keep up this speed for long. At 12.20 the *Pobieda* hoisted flag "K" and hauled out of the line. Again a delay! The enemy had already joined hands and formed line. At 12.22 our leading ships opened fire. We were steaming dead slow.

"This is our battle fleet—the flower of the Russian Navy!" an officer near me on the bridge was exclaiming in a voice choking with rage. I had not the heart to reprove him, and say: "Hold your tongue, and do your duty." Might he not have replied: "Have the men who created this squadron done their duty?"

No, I could not find anything to say which would really have answered him. My own throat felt as if it were being choked by impotent rage.

At 12.30 the *Tsesarevitch*, which had for some time been gradually turning towards East, suddenly turned 4 points to starboard. The hostile destroyers had been moving about ahead of us, but a long way off. The admiral had therefore become suspicious, and, as we found later, not without cause. Nothing was too insignificant for the Japanese, provided it offered the smallest chance of success. They had thrown out drift mines (without anchors) in the direction of our line of advance. The flagship's alteration of course saved the squadron from the danger of having to steam through this drifting minefield. All the same, we passed very close to some of them. The *Novik* (evidently by order of the admiral) stopped dead, and allowed the whole squadron to pass her, signalling: "Attention—floating mines." Two of these drifted past us on the port side, at no great distance. (To be accurate, we steamed past them.)

After we had passed this minefield, we resumed our previous course.

The enemy's main body, *Mikasa, Shikishima, Fuji, Asaki, Kasuga,* and *Nishin,* had been steering almost on a parallel course to ours for twenty minutes, and had fired at long range, 40 to 50 cables (8,000 to 10,000 yards), with long pauses between. At 12.50 the enemy turned about 16 points, approached us up to 30 cables (6,000 yards), and then steamed away.

It was an exciting moment, especially when the Japanese squadron turned short across our rear and concentrated its whole fire on our three cruisers at the end of the line, without our battleships being able to reply to it. Our regulations do not lay down any definite station in action for the second-in-command. The spirit of the instructions indicates that he is always to be where his presence appears desirable. On board the *Diana* it had been arranged, as most suitable to local conditions, that I should remain on the fore upper bridge. Here I could be seen from any part of the upper deck, and could also be called quickly if necessary. Moreover, I was myself in a position to overlook almost the whole ship. I could not help seeing if any projectile hit us, and could, without waiting to be sent for, run to the place where damage had been done. It will be conceded that the upper bridge was a capital post of observation. I saw everything.

The sea was boiling all round our rear ships. Of course we were also firing like mad. Our guns were roaring incessantly. To this was added the noise of the bursting shell. Clouds of smoke and gigantic columns of water arose all round us. What chaos! And yet this picture of the raging of elements let loose was beautiful.—I heard the call for stretcher parties, saw that blood was streaming on the deck; but this was unable to break the spell. These things seemed trivialities which could not be helped. How tremendously sharp and quick is the working of one's thoughts at such moments! A short cry, a gesture, Suffice to explain all that requires to be told.

The *Askold* (cruiser flagship) only hoisted flags "B" and "L" [6]. Immediately the cruisers went full speed ahead and spread fan-shape to

---

6. "B"—Increase speed. "L"—Steer to port.

port. In this way they got out of their unpleasant situation, and were at the same time enabled to bring their whole broadside to bear.

I should just like to have seen how many elaborate signals would have been necessary to carry out this movement during peace evolutions. How long it would have taken, and what confusion there would have been in the end all the same.

Either fortune favoured us or the Japanese fired badly. On the whole, at least, we got off cheaply. The rear ship (*Diana*) got no direct hits. Our sides, boats, superstructures, ventilators, funnels, and masts, were riddled by small splinters; yet we had only two men wounded. True, I had seen the *Askold's* foremost funnel and the *Pallada's* starboard cutter each struck by a shell. But these ships suffered no losses in men, and had no serious damage. The first encounter had ended in our favour. When they had crossed our tail the Japanese turned again to southward. They steamed along on our starboard quarter and kept up a slow fire at long range, which only our battleships could reply to.

At 1.30 p.m. we (on board *Diana*) allowed the men to "stand easy" and drink their afternoon tea, but not to leave their guns.

Groups were formed on the upper deck, chatting with much animation. Laughter and jokes were heard on all sides. But there was nothing specially characteristic in all this.

"How about forty winks until the enemy hits us over the head?" a young sailor was asking jocularly, and settled down snugly in a tarpaulin, with part of which he kept off the fierce rays of the sun.

"Don't talk nonsense! "came in a rough tone from an older man. "God hears everything."

Yet another small, but characteristic episode. As I was passing along the battery I congratulated the gun-layer of No. 15 gun—Malakow—on his Cross of St George. Malakow, having been wounded, had himself hastily bandaged, and at once returned to his gun, to serve it as before.

It was strange to see how the eyes of this man, who had only quite a short while ago cheerfully looked death in the face, suddenly looked troubled. He stammered, half-confused, half-doubting: "Well, sir, if it is ordered—"

I felt annoyed.

"Who is going to order anything? Take it, you dunderhead; you have earned it by the statutes. Neither the captain nor I have anything to say to it. Your superiors don't make you a present of it. You can demand it; you can go right up to the *Tsar* with your demand. The law gives you the right to demand it."

All those around had become silent, and looked on, some with curiosity, some with unbelief, expressed in their faces. Apparently they were now hearing for the first time that the law stood above the will of their superiors. I walked on rapidly, and did not quite realise what I had done. Had I assisted discipline by my words, or harmed it?

Towards 3 p.m. we altered course to S. 62° E. The cruisers were keeping on the port beam of the battleships at a distance of about 15 to 20 cables (1½ to 2 miles). They were thus outside the range of "overs." We were steaming at a moderate speed, but had to slow down every now and then, so as not to draw too much ahead.

Soon after three o'clock fire ceased altogether. The enemy's main body, which bore abaft our beam, were now nearly hull down, that is, we only saw their funnels and superstructure above the horizon. What was the meaning of this? Perhaps the Japanese were making good their damages. Anyhow, with our 12 to 13 knots we were advancing very markedly. Our road was clear. If only our battleships had been able to go the speed they possessed on paper!

In compliance with the flagship's signal we sent our men to supper.

Our column now approached those of the battleships. Semaphore messages were exchanged. Friends asked one another how they were. The answers we received from the battleships were reassuring.

One of our younger officers could not hold his tongue. "We seem to be in luck," he said.

He was silenced at once. Seamen are more superstitious than sportsmen. They dread above all such boasts as the above.

Meanwhile, the Japanese had put themselves to rights again, and had carried out what they had intended. What could it have been? Who knows the Japanese? They were once more chasing us.

At 4.15 p.m. the distance was 51 cables (10,200 yards), at 4.40, 47 cables (9,400 yards), and at 4.45, the battle began afresh.

As the cruisers were again within reach of "overs," they were ordered to resume their former station—20 cables (4,000 yards)—from the battleships. We turned 4 points to port, and when we had reached the distance ordered, resumed the fleet course. For an hour and a half we were now mere spectators of an action in which we could not in any way participate.

The Japanese cruisers,[7] and not only the old ones, but even the three "Greyhounds," and two armoured cruisers, also kept on the off-

---

7. The *Yoshino* no longer existed at that time.

side of their main body. They, as it were, awaited the issue of the duel between the two main forces. The old Japanese ships, led by the *Chin Yen*, we could make out distinctly to the north, all the rest to the south-west.

For me, this was the hardest moment of the whole day. We had to look on whilst the others were fighting, without being able to lift a finger in aid.

I must here note that the Japanese shell, on bursting, produced thick, greenish brown or black smoke. In the first place, every one of their hits could thus be seen distinctly; secondly, it gave one in the first moment the impression that it had produced some catastrophe. On the other hand, we could only make out the light, transparent smoke of the Russian bursting shell with binoculars, and even then only with difficulty. Our shell were loaded with Pyroxyline, or smokeless powder.

This fact was especially demoralising to the common sailor, who, of course, knows little of the technical part of gunnery.

"Look! How our ships are catching it! The Japanese are hardly getting anything. It is as if they were charmed. The Holy Virgin has deserted us!" Remarks such as these I heard here and there amongst the men.

All binoculars and telescopes were turned on the enemy. All observers were asked to call out loud enough for all to hear, every time there was a Russian hit.

"There is no object in straining one's eyes. War can't be made without losses. There is no object whatever in looking at it. If anyone is hit, it is the will of God," I said, as I walked along the battery.

But the spirits got worse and worse. I don't say that we were threatened with a panic. By no means. We were a long way yet from that. Our men had stood fire, and were determined to fight to the last. I only felt that everyone was devoured by the terrible thought: "Will our battleships be able to stand this fire?" They doubted this, and in battle doubt does no good.

Meanwhile, I was carefully watching the course of the action with my binoculars, and trying to judge of the value of our fire by estimating the "shorts" and "overs." I was bound to own that our gun-layers were not shooting worse than the Japanese. It even appeared to me as if in the long run our fire was more steady and was corrected better. I thought of the possibility of the battle being renewed on the morrow. If it continued like this, we should have the advantage inasmuch as we were saving up our ammunition.

In the proportion in which, in the course of the battle, the distance decreased, a certain very important advantage on the enemy's side was bound to tell more and more. The enemy possessed an abundance of secondary and light armaments, whilst a good third of all our 6-inch and 12-pounder guns and the whole of the lighter Q.F. guns had remained behind at the land front of Port Arthur's defences.

Moreover, it was incontestable that luck was on the side of the Japanese.

Of course the enemy concentrated his fire mainly on our flagships.

The funnels of the *Tsesarevitch* were hit by a large number of shell. (These hits were particularly easy to see.)

At 5.5 p.m. the *Peresviet* (flag of second-in-command) had her main-topmast cut in half, and at 5.8 p.m. the head of her foretopmast went.[8] These damages were of no importance in themselves, but everyone could see them. The shell which hit the head of one of the topmasts was really a bad "over," quite a bad shot in fact—bad, but lucky.

About this time the lashings of the main derrick on board the *Poltava*, which had been secured up and down between the funnels, were shot through. It came down to port with a loud crash. That also was of no importance. It could not even be called damage, as the derrick had to be got into this position whenever boats had to be hoisted in. But everyone who saw this accident from abeam was greatly impressed.

At 5.50 p.m. the *Tsesarevitch* suddenly turned sharp to port. In doing so, she heeled over so much that cries of terror were heard on board us, which reminded one of the foundering of the *Petropavlovsk*. It looked as if the ship was going to capsize.[9]

Happily, it had only the appearance. For a few moments every soul on board the *Diana*, myself included, forgot all about himself and his ship. Every eye was strained to watch what was now going on in our battle squadron.

At first the *Retvisan* (No. 2) followed in the flagship's wake. But her captain quickly noticed that the latter was only hauling out of the line

---

8. The reader will see later what a momentous part these lost topmasts played. The *Peresviet* could no longer hoist any signals.

9. A Japanese (12-inch) shell had hit the conning tower of the *Tsesarevitch*, had destroyed everything inside, and killed every soul. The helm went hard over to starboard of itself when all connections were being smashed. This it was which made the ship heel over so much. She used to heel up to 12° if the helm was put hard over suddenly.

on account of some damage. The *Retvisan*, therefore, not only turned back to the old course, but towards the Japanese. It looked as if she meant to ram the enemy.

The *Pobieda* (No. 3) continued on the old course. The *Tsesarevitch* turned a complete circle to port and broke through the line between the *Peresviet* (No. 4 rear flag), and the *Sebastopol* (No. 5), exactly as if she also intended ramming the Japanese. Like the *Retvisan*, the *Sebastopol* also turned to the south, to avoid the *Tsesarevitch*, and the *Peresviet* did the same. The latter had apparently not made out yet what the flagship's intentions were and did not know whether her movements were intentional or were due to the ship not being under control. The *Poltava* (No. 6) continued on the old course.

For a while it looked as if we were on the point of delivering the decisive blow. In my diary I find noted:

6.5 p.m.—Our battleships are rushing at the enemy in single line abreast.

This note is struck out and the diary continues:—

No, it looks as if they intended to resume the old course and the old formation. Present order of ships: *Retvisan, Pobieda, Peresviet, Sebastopol, Tsesarevitch, Poltava.*

This is also struck out, and across the top is written:—

An error. No formation whatever. They are steaming without any order.

The first note refers to the conditions which were the result of the *Tsesarevitch* sheering out of the line. The second I must have written at the moment when the flagship, steering with her engines, tried to get into the line between the *Sebastopol* and the *Poltava*. The latter was the rear ship and had dropped astern a good deal. The third note represents the state of utter confusion, when no one knew any more who was leading the squadron or what course to steer.

The battleships then commenced to turn independently about 16 points.

I wrote:—

6.10 p.m.—Our battleships are steering N.W. *6.20.*—We are steaming without any formation, course about W. We have made out the signal in the *Tsesarevitch*: 'The admiral hands over command.'

We saw no other signals.[10]

There was no longer any doubt that Admiral Vityeft and his immediate successor and Chief of the Staff, Rear-Admiral Matussevitch, had dropped out. Was the next senior, Rear-Admiral Prince Uktomsky, still alive? The *Peresviet's* topmasts, it is true, were shot away, but could not the admiral's flag have been displayed on their stumps, on the tops, the funnels or any other point clearly visible? If the *Peresviet* flew no flag, it meant that she no longer had an admiral on board. Consequently Rear-Admiral von Reitzenstein, commanding the cruisers, became commander-in-chief. The battleships had either to steam without a leader, or the senior captain would have to take charge until they had formed up with the cruisers.[11]

When the *Tsesarevitch* turned so suddenly to port, the *Askold*, the cruiser flagship, had also turned to the north. Admiral Reitzenstein, however, noticed very soon that the flagship was not carrying out a manoeuvre, but simply hauling out of the line. As soon as he saw that our battleships were getting "clubbed" and that the enemy might take advantage of this, he resolutely led the cruisers to join the battleships. We at once understood his intentions. He wanted to join in the action with our forces, which, though weak, were fresh, and support the battleships, so as to give them time to reform.

Our battleships were steering about N.W. They were a mere rabble, one ship overtaking the other. Their fire was so wild, that some of their projectiles fell very close to us, as we hurried to their assistance.

The enemy's main body were crossing over in rear of our battleships, heading about N.E. His six armoured ships, in single line ahead, were keeping such good station, the intervals between the ships were so small and so regular, that it looked more like peace manoeuvres than war.

But why was the enemy going away? Did the distance deceive us? Had he suffered as much as we? Perhaps it would only have required two or three lucky hits to throw him also into confusion. Why did he not come after us and try to destroy us? We were fleeing. Could he not, or dared he not?

---

10. Because the topmasts of his flagship were shot away, Rear-Admiral Prince Uktomsky was obliged to display the signal for single line ahead on the rails of his upper bridge. Even the ships nearest to him did not notice it once. This was the reason for our long hesitation.

11. I beg the reader's pardon if my narrative is somewhat disconnected. I am endeavouring, for reasons already given, to keep as closely as possible to the short notes I entered in my diary every time something worth noting happened.

I drove all these questions out of my mind by force. I felt as if a veil was before my eyes and I had only one desire: Let us get at the enemy quickly, so that we can fire ourselves and deaden that dreadful feeling that we are beaten, that we are flying.

I find it very hard to have to think this over once again.—I will now proceed with my narrative in the sequence of events. I have noted the exact time by watch against all that now follows.

At 7 p.m. we closed up on the battleships on their starboard side. They were apparently trying to form line ahead. The *Retvisan* was the headmost ship. Again the question arose: Who is leading the squadron? Who is in command?

The *Askold* had the signal flying: "Single line ahead," but no distinguishing signal superior.

To whom was this signal addressed? Was it only meant for the cruisers, or was our admiral assuming the chief command, because he saw no admiral's flag flying anywhere, and did he mean the signal to be "general," that is, addressed to all ships?

The *Askold* was not waiting for the other cruisers to come up astern. She was going at her utmost speed and over-hauling the battleships, just as if she meant to place herself ahead of the *Retvisan* as leader of the squadron. The latter assumption seemed likely. Presumably the captain of the *Pallada* thought so too. He did not increase speed so as to follow the *Askold*, but even reduced speed, with the evident intention of allowing the squadron to draw ahead and then to take up his proper station astern of the last battleship. Our place in the battle formation was astern of the *Pallada*. We were waiting impatiently for further orders.

When the *Askold* had got ahead of the *Retvisan*, she hoisted the signal: "Keep in my wake," but again without a distinguishing signal, and turned to port. In this signal and in this manoeuvre we read the determination to lead the squadron to seaward again, and against the enemy, who appeared no longer anxious to fight.

On the *Diana's* bridge exclamations of joy were heard. We were delighted at Reitzenstein's bold decision, but our joy was premature. Uncertainty and terror soon took its place. The *Retvisan* continued her course. The battleships did not follow the *Askold*, and the latter, with her signal still flying, steamed past us at top speed, like the *Flying Dutchman*. She steamed away to the southward, on an opposite course to the rest of the squadron.

"So he is not in command of the squadron," the captain called out.

"Yet we must follow him."

To overhaul the battleships and like the *Askold* to cross over ahead of them would have taken too long with our poor speed. The captain therefore unhesitatingly decided to break through the rabble of battleships.

Notwithstanding the sadness of the moment I could not help admiring the coolness and assurance with which our captain carried out this dangerous manoeuvre.

All the same, we had waited a little to see whether the battleships would follow the *Askold*. This, and our getting clear of the battleships, took a good ten to fifteen minutes. When we had reached open water, we saw our admiral already far to the southward in action with the enemy's cruisers, and getting out of sight. The captain was outwardly calm, but he stroked his beard nervously.

"How can I follow him with my 17 knots?" he was muttering through his teeth. Suddenly he shrugged his shoulders despairingly and ordered: "Hard a-starboard."

The *Diana* turned to port and formed in the wake of the *Pallada*, which had never tried to follow the *Askold*.[12]

At 7.20 p.m. we were attacked from the northward by the *Chin-Yen*, *Matsushima*, *Itsukushima*, and *Hashidate*. The *Kasuga* and *Nishin*, which had separated from the main body, were approaching from the eastward, and from the south came the "Greyhounds."

Well, for this company at least we were strong enough. They did not succeed in doing us any material damage and were obliged to beat a hasty retreat after a short but hot fight at no more than 20 cables (4,000 yards).

In this engagement the *Diana* was unlucky.

From my post of observation on the fore-bridge I saw a mighty column of black smoke rise up suddenly from the starboard side of the flying deck. I at once hurried to the spot. A shell had struck our Temperley transporter, which was lying on one of the funnel casings, and smashed it. The nearest ventilators, the funnel casings, and the funnel itself as well as the deck were riddled with small splinters, besides which the shell had destroyed a rising main of the steam fire service (this was really an advantage at the moment) and disabled seventeen men; five of these were killed outright (amongst them Sub-lieutenant

---

12. When Admiral von Reitzenstein reached Shanghai, he reported by telegraph that he had hoisted the signal: "Keep in my wake," and gone on 20 and then 22 knots. Since then he had seen nothing of the *Pallada* or *Diana*—no wonder!

Kondratyeff) and twelve wounded. [13]

I cannot help mentioning with much pride how very well the service was carried out on board our cruiser. I ran down as fast as I could from the upper bridge to the upper deck, but by the time I had arrived everything needful had been done. I only saw the last stretcher disappearing down the officer's hatchway. The numbers of the gun, which had fallen out, had already been replaced from the corresponding gun on the opposite (disengaged) side. The gun had happily not been injured and was firing away energetically. Sub-Lieutenant Sh—— had taken over command of the midship group after Kondratyeff's death. He had a dirty broom in his hand, which had been used to clear up the deck, and with this dreadful weapon he was chasing back under cover all those who had rushed over from the port side asking to be allowed to replace the killed and wounded, so as to have a chance of fighting themselves.

"All hands not told off, out of it!" I ordered, and came to his assistance. And those brave lads who had been fighting for the right of being able to get face to face with death, ran back to their places quickly and obediently at the order of "Number one."

There was no need for me to make any further dispositions, and I could only approve what had been done. Then I went to the conning tower to report the effect of the hit to the captain. As I reached the lower bridge, on which the conning tower stood, I heard someone inside making a report to the captain. I heard the words: "Under water, just under the sick-bay," and the captain's sharp voice: "Report to the commander, quick."

"Aye! aye! sir, I hear!" I shouted as loud as I could through the slit between the sides and the roof of the tower. Then I bounded off the bridge and ran aft. "The boatswain's party to follow me." [14]

"Here, sir," replied the boatswain. "All present and everything

---

13. Next day we found amongst the wreckage, the base of this shell stamped 18 cm. It must have been fired by either the *Kasuga* or *Nishin*, the only ships to carry guns of this calibre.

14. The boatswain's party consisted of a number of men under the boatswain who were at the executive officer's disposal for putting out small fires and making small repairs in action. These parties had been considerably strengthened by Makaroff at Port Arthur, and equipped with every kind of appliance for stopping leaks. They were, moreover, specially trained in all manner of leak stopping. These parties were made up of the most experienced and able men. They included the best seamen, petty officers, boatswain's mates, and even specialists and engine-room ratings, such as divers, carpenters, sailmakers, blacksmiths, plumbers, etc.

ready."

It was only when the *Diana* went into dock to be repaired that we were able to ascertain the exact nature and extent of the underwater damage sustained in this action. But so that the reader may not be left to trust to his imagination, I will anticipate, and give a short description of it.

A 10-inch shell had hit the ship's side under water on the starboard side, at a very acute angle, in the direction from forward—aft, and from up—down. The hole was just between the edge of the armoured deck, where it curves down, and the ordinary steel deck above, on which stood the dispensary, sick-bay, and ship's office. The shell had torn open the ship's side in a fore-and-aft direction, and had made a hole about 17 feet long and 5½ feet at its greatest width. It was thanks to the fact that the shell was travelling nearly parallel to the ship's side, that its whole force was expended in tearing open the ship's side. The armoured deck only leaked very slightly. But, above all, the light steel deck above the armoured deck had stood. This saved the ship, as it prevented water from penetrating into the inner spaces. Certainly this light deck could not resist the pressure of the water from outside for long. It had already begun to buckle and to open out in the seams. Still we gained a few precious minutes during which we were enabled to strengthen and support it. We thus succeeded in confining the dangerous enemy, who had got in—the water—to a small space.

The first thing I saw below were the sick and wounded. The doctor and the sick-berth staff were carrying and leading them out of the threatened spaces. How great the damage was could be seen at a glance. The wooden planks forming the deck in the sick-bay and the adjoining dispensary were bursting with loud reports and the water was squirting up through the openings. The seams of the steel deck underneath might give way any moment and open up the deck to the sea completely. The carpenter and such of his party as were stationed in the after part of the ship had at once started wedging down the deck. Some of the men who were only slightly wounded had assisted. When the boatswain's party arrived the work went on briskly.

Need I say how these men worked, with what care and with what zeal they handled the heavy hammers with which the struts were wedged up? Those wedges which were preventing the deck from bursting, were working directly against the sea, the mighty pressure of which had already opened the seams. It was a life and death struggle. The water-tight doors were closed, there was no exit upwards. If the sea should get the upper hand, then we should be the first victims. The starboard after 6-inch gun, just overhead, disturbed our labours a good deal. Every time it was fired the deck vibrated so much that the wedges became displaced. Repeatedly the struts threatened to snap, and we had to give them lateral support. Unconsciously one formulated the criminal wish: "If only this infernal gun were shot away." Suddenly it ceased, and our work proceeded more rapidly.

We succeeded.

"That will hold now!" exclaimed the carpenter in triumph, and tapped the deck with his foot, and the boatswain also said: "It's all right now."

I stopped their jubilations. "Don't say that, for Heaven's sake!" I cried. "Don't tempt fate! You will only spoil everything by boasting."

How long had we been at work? The first impression was a few seconds. When I looked around, saw all we had done, and thought of the different episodes, I fell into the other extreme and thought we had been half an hour or more. I looked at my watch. It had got wet and had stopped.

The sick-bay, its bathroom, the dispensary, and the office presented a sorry spectacle. We stood on the bare steel deck. The wood planking had been split and torn away in the process of securing down the seams underneath. It lay about in untidy heaps. The water reached to our ankles, but what still came in could be kept under with such primitive means as buckets and swabs. It only trickled through the openings between the bent plates and through rivet holes where the rivets had been loosened or had dropped out. Some of these rivet holes were closed up with wooden plugs. Where there was a whole row of these rivet holes, we laid a cushion or a mattress over them, a plank over this, placed a strut between it and the beam above, and wedged down. This part of the work was not so bad. It was no longer a case of fighting the inrush of water, but merely keeping under what still found its way in. I left this part to the engineer in charge of the hull and ordered him to flood some of the port wing-passages, so as to get the ship upright. I myself inspected the neighbouring compartments, asked those stationed there whether everything was in order, and then went on deck to make my report to the captain.

When I reached the upper deck I chanced to pass the starboard after 6-inch gun. Now I saw why it had ceased firing, so opportunely for us. It was being unloaded from the muzzle. The crew were trying to push the projectile out again. In the heat of the action it had been rammed in too hard and had stuck in the grooves of the rifling.

"What's up?"

"A projectile that hadn't been gauged, your honour," replied No. 1, almost crying with rage.

"It's an ill wind that blows nobody any good," I thought, and went on. Without this accident we should hardly have been able to do that business down below. I found the captain in the conning tower. My report, which was of course full of technical terms and explanations, would not interest the reader, nor be understood by the majority. I therefore omit it.

On the bridge I asked what time it was. It was 7.40 p.m. We were steering N. 30° W. I went to the end of the bridge and looked round. We were in no regular formation. It was neither single column nor two columns in line ahead. The *Retvisan* was the most advanced ship and we were the rear ship. Ahead of us were the *Pallada*, *Retvisan*, and another ship astern of the latter (perhaps *Pobieda*). Our ships were firing slowly at the hostile cruisers making off at their best speed to the N.E.

I pulled out my notebook and began making notes by the evening twilight.

"*Now* it is certain, quite certain," someone near me was saying. His voice shook with rage.

I looked round. A group of officers was standing on the bridge.

"What is it? What is so certain?" I asked,

"We are returning to Port Arthur. We are to make a solemn entry, to bury the squadron."

"Silence! The men can hear it." I said in a low voice, then added aloud: "To do what? What nonsense! We shall fill up with coal, ammunition, and stores, repair our damages, and then go out again. Can't you see how undecided the enemy's movements are? He has probably not fared any better than we. We have only 100 miles to go to Port Arthur, whilst he has 500 and more to Sasebo."

I need hardly say that I did not believe any of this myself. For me, too, this retreat looked like a funeral.

"Hold hard!" "Stop!" "Wait a bit!" came from all sides. In their eagerness the one was ever taking the words out of the other's mouth. "If our damages are unimportant, then there is no need to return. If they are serious, how are we to repair them at Port Arthur? It is being bombarded from the land side and we should get fresh damages every day. Shall we ever get there at all? The enemy's torpedo craft are everywhere. But that is not all. We are now heading straight for Port Arthur, right through our own mines as well as those laid by the Japanese. God won't help us like on the 23rd of June. With us it is always St Nicholas [15] who is to do everything. We are to fill up with stores? Not only will they not give us any stores, but they will make us give up to the fortress what we have on board. We shan't be repaired in any case. We shall all be simply turned into marine infantry. Our guns will go into the batteries; and the ship—why, she will be handed over *gratis* to the Japanese as a present, when the fortress surrenders. She will yet sail under Japanese colours. *With compliments.*[16] Ha, ha!"

The officers laughed nervously and spoke very loudly, quite clearly for the captain's benefit.

The captain came out of the conning tower and stepped on to the bridge. His face, as usual, had a calm, almost indolent expression. Every one became silent, there was the stillness of the grave around us.

"Our late admiral," the captain began to say quite slowly, as if he were reading it out, "informed us by signal that *His Majesty had ordered us to proceed to Vladivostok*. The cruiser *Admiral* has gone south, flying the signal: 'Keep in my wake.' As soon as it is dark we shall separate from the squadron, and, if it be possible, go to Vladivostok. We must now lay off the courses and find out from the chief engineer how we stand for coal."

No one dared express his approval aloud, but it was plain how pleased everyone was.

The courses were laid off at once. The intention was to go round the south end of Quelpart Island and at such speed as to bring us to its eastern end by sundown. From there we were to proceed at our utmost speed, run through the Straits of Korea by night and by the shortest route. If this succeeded we should be in the Sea of Japan at daylight, out of sight from the coast of Korea and from Tsu-shima. Then, by the grace of God, we should go on to Vladivostok. The chief engineer assured us that going at full speed for twelve hours and the remainder of the time at economical speed (10 knots), the coal would last, in fact, there would even be something over for an emergency.

---

15. Patron of sailors.—Trans.
16. In English in the Russian text.—Trans.

CHAPTER 11

The End of the "Diana's" War Services

Towards 8 p.m. we saw once more, though indistinctly, several small Japanese cruisers to the south-west, two armoured cruisers to the southward, the main fleet steaming away to the eastward, and to the northeast the *Chin Yen* with her consorts.

To the south-east, precisely where we wanted to go, were numerous destroyer flotillas.

A species of council of war was held on the bridge. It voted in favour of breaking through to the south-east. At first sight this seemed a strange proposal, but it proved to be right in the end. We reasoned as follows:— Probably the Japanese destroyers would not expect us to do such a mad thing, and would therefore not be prepared for it. Moreover, they might easily take the *Diana* for their *Yakumo* in the dark, and think that the latter had been sent with despatches to Japan. If we chose another course on which we might meet Japanese cruisers or battleships, our identity would be quickly revealed. If we became involved in a night action, they would all go for us. There remained the question, how we should act towards hostile torpedo craft, so as to prevent their recognising us and attacking us.

I made a proposal, which at first met with general opposition, and nearly raised the suspicion that I was not in my right mind. I proposed simply to do nothing. If, for instance, we were to light up any destroyer with our searchlights and fire at her, we should bring the entire flotilla down on us. Against an attack in numbers we were powerless. Our after 6-inch guns we dared not fire, for fear of loosening the supports over the damaged deck below. Consequently we were practically undefended against attacks from astern. But on each beam we only had two

6-inch and ten 12-pounders available. That was very little.

"But are we not even to light up and fire on a destroyer actually firing a torpedo at us?"

"Certainly not! A destroyer would only be able to make us out at quite short range. She must adjust her director, after estimating our course and speed, in a few seconds, and that is no easy job. Is it likely that she will hit us? Do you think that a destroyer, which has once shot past us, can turn round, chase and overtake us and attack anew? In the dark she would simply not find us. But when once we begin to light up and fire, in the first place, any destroyer can find us, in the second place, more destroyers will approach from all sides. With our big hole we can't stand a hit from a torpedo. If we are unlucky and get hit, we shall go down, and then, we can have a parting shot at the boats, to wish them farewell."

The captain entirely agreed with me and issued orders accordingly.

"We'll do it," he said, smiling, "although it is quite a new method of repelling torpedo attack. We are probably the first to try it."

"I am confident that it will succeed."

"If we remain alive we shall prove it, and if not the opposite."

Soon after 8 p.m. the *Diana* put her helm a-port and separated from the squadron on the course which had been determined upon.

A destroyer joined us. We asked her for her name. She replied *Grosovoy*.

This circumstance was specially favourable for our plans. Every Japanese might think: there is a cruiser which looks like our *Yakumo* and she has a destroyer in company—they are sure to belong to our side.

Towards 9 p.m. we reached the part of the sea where hostile torpedo craft were swarming, and steamed through it until 10.15 (the time of meeting the last Japanese destroyer). There was no moon, but the night was not very dark. The sky was not over-cast, but only showed here and there light semi-transparent clouds. The stars showed faintly through these and just gave enough light for trained eyes to see a big ship at a distance of 1½ miles, and a destroyer at 5 to 6 cables (1,000 to 1,200 yards). To "see" of course only means to make out something vaguely.

During this hour and a quarter we "saw" nineteen shapes, which we took to have been hostile destroyers. Every time we sighted such a shape we at once altered course largely and endeavoured to prevent the distance being decreased sufficiently for us to be made out. In the nineteen cases we succeeded in this thirteen times. Only six destroyers attacked us. They fired eight torpedoes at us, but not one of them hit us. (This last statement is really superfluous, for if any one had hit us, I should not be in a position to communicate my narrative to the reader.)

We never switched on our searchlights and we never fired.

I believe that this method of receiving torpedo craft was only possible with a reliable "fireproof" crew, such as we had on board. One only need think of the panic on April 13, and how we all fired into the water. It was very different now.

I cannot conceal the fact that two shots were fired. But the circumstances extenuated the offence of the gun-layers. They were as follows:—

Towards 9.30 the officer commanding the stern group, Sub-lieutenant Sh——, came running up on the bridge.

"Permission to open fire."

"In no circumstances."

"The two boats which have already attacked us once on opposite courses, are chasing us. They seem to be overhauling us."

"If it only seems so," interrupted the torpedo lieutenant, an authority in this case, "then there is nothing to fear for the present. Their excess of speed is not much. To fire torpedoes after us is useless. It is only when the boats come up abreast that the situation changes."

Suddenly there was a greenish golden flash right aft in the ship. The sharp report of a 12-pounder shot reverberated through the still night.—The same thing again.

"Your group is firing without you being there! What are you still standing about here for?" I shouted at the officer. But the fine young fellow had already jumped off the bridge at one bound and was tearing off to his guns as if the devil were behind him.

Once more the ship was hushed in utter silence, which was only interrupted from time to time by the voice of a signalman or lookout-man calling out: "Four points on the starboard bow, sir!"—"On the port beam, sir!" and the corresponding orders from the captain: "Hard a-starboard!"—"Hard a-port!"

A considerable swell was coming in from the south, making the ship roll from 5° to 7° both ways. The destroyers must have felt it still more, and of course this did not increase their chances of making good practice with their torpedoes.

Towards 10 p.m. a Japanese destroyer passed us on an opposite course and fired a torpedo at our starboard side from a distance of barely 11 cables (300 yards). We not only saw the torpedo fly out of the tube, but heard the characteristic sound which always accompanies the firing of a torpedo, like the snort of some big animal.

"He is running straight," said the torpedo lieutenant, and leaning over the bridge rails, followed the air bubbles which indicate the track of a torpedo, with a professional eye.

There were some moments of acute suspense.

"Missed!"—Our torpedo lieutenant appeared quite to sympathise with his brother torpedoist's failure.

Everyone heaved a sigh of relief.

"We don't seem to shine compared to the gunners," was the captain's jocular comment. He was a former torpedo specialist himself.

At about 10.15 p.m. we met an enemy for the last time. We nearly ran over a destroyer crossing our bows at full speed. We only just cleared one another. The boat evidently took us for Japanese. He showed a light signal, apparently a recognition signal, and disappeared into the darkness.

At 11 p.m. we sighted the northernmost light on Shantung. Half an hour later, having fixed our position by its bearings, we altered course to S. 23° W., which was to bring us, according to our plan, into the southern, less frequented, part of the Yellow Sea. We now only met some Chinese junks, and not many of those. It was clear that we had already left the waters in which the two belligerents were operating. We could now thinly of taking a rest. The men had in any case to remain in two watches, as regarded sleeping, and no one was allowed to leave his fighting station.

Many authors of narratives and reminiscences of war time describe the high state of nervous excitement which dominates all participants long after the battle. Many stories tell of disturbed sleep and wandering minds, and how easily one succumbs to any external impulse. Personally, I have never observed anything of the kind. Some facts which I had noted (in my diary) seem to prove the contrary, that is that after a battle sudden relaxation of the nerves takes place, so as to nearly amount to insensibility.

During the night of August 10-11 I have seen men who, on being relieved, quickly sought a snug corner near their fighting stations and at once went off into a deep, sound sleep.[1] All the same these men had

---

1. I can give the assurance that so long as I was at the theatre of war—that is in the first or second squadron—I never dreamed of the war at all. This only happened to me once, and under very peaceful conditions, for I was travelling from Saigon to Libau. It was at the Wirballen Station (Russo-German frontier), where we were spending the night. I dreamed of the *Diana's* sick-bay, of the deck buckling on which we were at work. I fell out of my bed shouting "Shores, bring more shores," much to the alarm of the other travellers,

previously done their work without showing signs of special fatigue, and had carefully passed on their orders.

One of the officers manifested such a degree of "insensibility" that the French looked upon him as one of the Wonders of the World when he reached Saigon.

Before the battle I had given orders that the bodies of those who might fall were to be taken up on the after-bridge. Until such time as they could be buried, they were to be laid down in a row on a tarpaulin, covered with a second tarpaulin, over which was stretched an ensign.

When the order allowing men to fall out for rest, but to remain near their stations, reached the commander of the stern group, he thought of the after-bridge as a very suitable place for him to rest. At that time there were seven corpses on it, laid out on a large tarpaulin, the unused part having been folded up several times. This would make a capital mattress. How delightfully comfortable! There really could not be a better place!

Towards three o'clock in the morning, one of the men who had been severely wounded died. The well-drilled sick-bay men carried the body up on the after-bridge. When they tried to place it in a row with the other corpses, they felt in the dark an officer's great-coat. They came to the conclusion that it would not be proper for the officer's corpse to be lying between those of two common sailors. "His honour" ought to be at one end. No sooner had they seized the presumed corpse by his shoulders and feet, when he offered desperate resistance and sat up.

"What's up? Have they sounded the bugle?"

"No!"

"Then what do you want with me, confound you! Can't you leave me in peace, you infernal—"

At first the men were staggered, for they thought that one of the corpses had come to life. But when they heard "his honour's" language, they realised that he must be quite well.

"We only wanted to make a little room, your honour. We have just brought up another body. He is only just dead."

"That is quite another story; you might have said so at once," the sub-lieutenant replied. He rolled the tarpaulin back a little, and moved further along on it. Then he looked on whilst the "new one" was laid out in the proper way, that is, on his back, with the arms crossed in front, then he once more curled himself up and slept soundly, side by side with his silent comrades.

I did not manage to get much rest that night. The swell was hardly perceptible, yet the ship was rolling 5° to 7° both ways. This must have been caused by the water which had lodged on top of the armoured deck. But it was not the rolling which kept me on my legs, but something much worse. The flooded compartments were in direct communication with the sea outside. Every time the ship heeled over to starboard the pressure in them became so great that the thin deck, which we had only wedged down temporarily, received a violent shock. The shores "complained" and the wedges moved. The water squirted up with a hissing sound from under the packing we had placed over the leaky seams, and the wooden plugs flew out of the rivet holes with a report like a pistol shot. We were continuously at work, and had constantly to place new shores or replace the old ones.

"You boasted! now we see the consequences. You old chatterbox, why couldn't you hold your tongue?" I said to the carpenter. I believe I really did not know myself whether I was blowing him up in earnest, or whether I merely wanted to cheer up myself and the others by putting everything down to this unlucky remark. The carpenter considered himself guilty in any case. He crawled about on all fours in the water,[2] which was washing about the deck, lamenting: "It was a sin—a great sin! God forgive me! If only the wind does not freshen!"

God forgave. It did not freshen up, and the swell even went down somewhat towards daylight.

I was just dozing a little in an armchair on the bridge when I was suddenly awakened. It was quite light, and absolute silence reigned everywhere.

"The enemy?"

"No, no," replied the navigating officer, who was shaking my shoulder not very respectfully. "The chief engineer has just been to see the captain. Our coal is giving out. We are going to Kiaotchou, and that means that we are going to be disarmed."

"I don't understand anything, my dear fellow. Give me one minute to recover my senses.—Now, let us have it all over again."

He told me again. It seems that there had been a misunderstanding—God knows by whose fault. The chief engineer, in speaking of economical speed, had counted on ten boilers (instead of twenty-

---

2. Another detail. Our armoured deck did not possess a single sluice valve with which the water could have been drained into the lower spaces, where the steam pumps could have reached it. We had to bail it out with buckets.

four), whilst the captain had thought that we could keep steam in all boilers so as to develop our full power any moment. But our coal would only last if we economised steam, that is, coal. It could not last under the captain's conditions.

I turned to the conning tower.

The navigating, gunnery, and torpedo officers—all the captain's chief assistants—were there. Only the chief engineer was absent. He had gone below again after having made his wretched report.

The captain expressed himself very categorically. This time he did not, as was his custom, give short, definite orders, but went fully into all the considerations of the case.

As we were unable to employ our stern guns the ship's only safety lay in her speed. He must be able to develop her full power at any moment. It was true, we had water-tube boilers, and when steaming economically with ten boilers we could raise steam in all the others in forty minutes and go on full speed. But the enemy (assuming that he also only possessed a speed of 17 knots) had half an hour, which sufficed to bring him up to effective range (30 cables = 6, 000 yards) from us. When the adversary had reached that point, he would be able, thanks to his superior speed, to choose his distance, and fight as suited him best. In another ten minutes we should be at his mercy.

Only the three bow 6-inch guns were available.[3] Even a ship like the *Niitaka* was more powerful than we. Moreover, in an action with her we should be practically standing still. The captain thought it would be criminal to expose his ship to such a situation. The ship would be doomed to certain destruction, without the least prospect of causing the enemy any damage.

We must unquestionably get more coal. Where from? At Kiaotchou? According to the German declaration of neutrality we could not stay more than twenty-four hours in that port. Though that would be time enough for coaling, should we, in that time, be able to make the hole watertight? For this we should have to rely solely on our own means. According to the German declaration of neutrality, if we were repaired by the dockyard we should have to disarm. Could we carry out these necessary repairs at all with our own means?[4] What was the nature of the hole? We only knew that the water-tight bulkhead at

---

3. The *Diana* carried eight 6-inch guns—five forward and three aft. The latter could not be fired, and of the former, two had been landed at Port Arthur.—Trans.
4. It was afterwards found that we could not have done so, even in more than twenty-four hours.

frame No. 103 was destroyed, and that the ship leaked heavily between frames No. 98 and 108—that was all. Should we only go in and coal? The telegraph would at once have told the Japanese of our arrival. On going out again we should at once come upon the enemy, and "the ship would be doomed to certain destruction, in a criminal manner," as the captain expressed it.

If we allowed ourselves to be repaired we should be disarmed. Apparently there was no possible way out of the difficulty.

Suddenly the paymaster, who happened to be on watch, made a proposal, which at first seemed to us all quite mad.

"All that is left for us now is to go to the nearest French port," he said. "According to the French declaration of neutrality the belligerents are permitted to stay in their ports for an unlimited time. Furthermore, they permit the execution of all repairs, with the assistance of any local establishment, except an increase or any repairs to the armament."

"But, in the devil's name, the next French port is Saigon! Our coal won't take us there neither."

"Oh, bother your coal! Is there no such thing as a merchant steamer on the way? We stop any steamer we meet, and take out some of her coal. We only leave her enough to reach the next port. Our government will pay her for the delay and for all losses, and she will after all be pleased with making a profit. In the first instance, we must get to some out-of-the-way place. The Japanese would never discover our whereabouts. If we can get repaired we shall be in a very different position. The French are, after all, our allies. Perhaps we could even replace in some out-of-the-way bay the guns which we were made to land."

"Now you are allowing your imagination to run riot," broke in the captain, who had suddenly dropped his imperturbable calm, and even became quite cheerful. "But the idea is not bad! We will see at once whether our coal would last."

Calculations were at once made.

The captain explained that if we did not sight any enemy either today or tomorrow it would be very improbable that we should come across one south of the latitude of Shanghai. The need to keep steam in all boilers would then disappear of itself. There might be some Japanese in the Formosa channel, but that was also unlikely. Consequently, we should be able, for the remainder of the distance, to put out fires not only in fourteen but in sixteen boilers, and steam with only eight.

But even then our coal would only take us to within 500 miles of Saigon. If we took into consideration that we might meet with strong headwinds, it would be still worse. Our only hope was to meet one or two merchant ships. About the weather prospects we did not speak—as if by common consent. August, with its typhoons, is a very disagreeable month in the China Sea, September alone is worse. If we were to get into a typhoon with that hole in our side! !

At 9 a.m., whilst we were still debating and calculating, a ship hove in sight, which appeared to be chasing us. At first we went on full speed, hoping to get away from her. She continued chasing us at high speed. End on as she was, we could not make her out. Suddenly she seemed to have made us out and turned off short to the East. As soon as we saw the ship broadside on we recognised her at once. It was the *Novik*. There was not another little ship the least like her in the whole of the Pacific. We began making distant signals to her, but she would not look our way. The *Novik* evidently took us for a Japanese. We sent the *Grosovoy*, who had followed us faithfully, to her to clear up the misunderstanding, and to ask for news.

Whilst the *Grosovoy* was chasing the *Novik*, we moved ahead dead slow; in fact, we nearly remained on the same spot.

This delay we employed in rendering the last honours to those who had fallen. The whole eight were laid out in a row between the after 6-inch guns. Each body was sewn up in canvas with a weight at his feet. They all looked alike, except that of Sub-Lieutenant Kondratyeff, on which we had placed his sword and cocked hat. A short funeral service was held in the presence of the whole ship's company. Then the captain, the officers, and the oldest members of the ship's company lifted up the bodies. The guard presented arms, the drums beat a roll, and the funeral procession moved slowly on to the poop. From there one body after the other was allowed to slide slowly overboard along an inclined plank. Slowly they sank in the greenish sea down to the depths below, they who had once been our shipmates.

I remember well the beautiful words of our priest. He spoke of the dead with so much heartiness and fervour, and never became sad or lugubrious. He conducted the service with as much love and warmth, as if he were celebrating resurrection instead of death. How full of love and faith was his voice, as he leant over the poop-rails, blessing the dead for the last time, and praying: "*Take, O Lord, thy servant, fallen in battle.*"

I don't know if these words form part of our Liturgy, but they were certainly very appropriate.

I watched our ship's company carefully, and tried to guess their feelings. I confess that I had feared that this ceremony would have a depressing effect on them. Our men don't like burials at sea. How often, in my long sea service, have I not heard men who were dangerously ill begging the doctor to keep them going till the ship got to Russia. If that were impossible, they wanted at least to live until the next port was reached. Everyone wants to have his modest grave, even in foreign soil.

Many were moved, but none of them were strongly affected or depressed. Of course, habit had much to say to this. They were accustomed to funerals from Port Arthur. Still, I think that our priest had the greatest merit in this.

As it was quite calm, and there was no suspicious smoke in sight anywhere on the horizon, we stopped engines and sent over our best divers to examine the underwater damage. We were in hopes of perhaps being able to make it water-tight from outboard, as we could see that the shoring up from inboard was insufficient. When we had got the dimensions of the hole, we had to give up this idea. The dimensions were such that it would have been impossible to bolt on a wood casing, filled with bedding. It was not even possible to place a collision mat over it, as the hole reached aft beyond the "A" bracket of the starboard screw. Whilst steaming ahead, if one of the lines securing the collision mat in place were to carry away or become shifted (and that could always happen), it was bound to foul the screw shaft and perhaps bring Up the engine.

The *Grosovoy* returned at 1 p.m. She reported that the *Novik* had not been damaged in the action. The ship was going to Kiaotchou to fill up with coal and stores, and then meant to go to Vladivostok, steaming round outside Japan.

Unfortunately, we did not get into direct communication with the *Novik*. Perhaps there was something not right between the two captains.

Our captain did not approve of the *Novik'* s plan.

"If I had his speed I should go through the Straits of Korea, "he muttered to himself. "Outside she'll probably be discovered." [5]

The *Grosovoy* received orders to join the *Novik*, and place herself at her captain's disposal.

---

5 Unhappily, this prediction came true.

The *Diana* proceeded south.

The news of the *Novik*'s decision perturbed me very much. Reason here was in opposition to the dictates of the heart. I knew only too well how justified the captain's doubts were. I also quite appreciated that the wounded *Diana*, with her 17 knots, was not to be compared with the *Novik*, which was quite intact, and had absolutely no rival as to speed in the whole Japanese Navy. And yet down in my heart I felt the tantalising thought: the *Novik* is going to Vladivostok, and we are not.

I was not the only one who suffered under these contradictory feelings. Towards three o'clock, tired and in ill-humour, I sat down in the mess and, quite mechanically, drank a glass of our hot, but absolutely tasteless tea [6] (the concoction of this beverage was one of the secrets of the pantry), when the first lieutenant sat down near me. He at once began to speak of what was so much on our minds.

"Kindly tell me, quite openly, as a messmate—what do you think of this? Everything hinges on that decision about putting out fires in fourteen boilers. It is not yet too late to carry out our original plan. Can't we risk it? Tell me openly."

"You know my persistent attitude towards our old maxim: '*Be careful and risk nothing*.' Come what may, I should risk it."

"Well then!" my messmate exclaimed, his face literally beaming with pleasure.

"The captain has decided differently. What can we two do? There are only two of us."

"No, no; we are also on your side," a number of officers suddenly broke in. They had evidently been awaiting the result of our conversation from a distance, and were now coming across to us. I turned round and counted them. They were five (I was the sixth)—just half the mess. Without another word I took up my cap and went straight to the captain, this time not in my capacity as his second-in-command, but as the officers' representative and spokesman.

I began by opening my heart to the captain. The *Novik* was going to Vladivostok, the *Diana* not. What did our pride and the good name of our ship alike demand? Of course it was a risky undertaking, even desperate. But if it succeeded? If we did not try, who would ever enquire about our reasons? Everyone would say at once: "They have turned tail." Rather go down than face such disgrace.

The captain shrugged his shoulders angrily and pulled at his beard,

---

6. In Russia, tea is usually drunk out of glass tumblers in metal stands.—Trans.

but he replied in the tone of friendly conversation. He repeated what he had already said once, and pointed out the great difference between the situation of the *Diana* and that of the *Novik*. He ended with the words: "Now, listen! When you made me the suggestion last night of breaking straight through the torpedo craft, without lighting up searchlights or firing, even when attacked by them, I agreed. It was bold, not to say rash, but expedient in our special case. We might hope to save the ship by risking that much. But now you are proposing to me to destroy the ship, without doing Russia any good and without any hope of damaging the enemy! When we have repaired her, and once more made a sound ship of her in one of the ports of our ally, we can order a collier (or as many as we like) to any rendezvous we may choose. Then we can go to Vladivostok—such is my intention—or, if ordered from St Petersburg, commence independent cruiser operations. And we are to give up all these prospects and expose the ship to destruction? Why should we do this? Only out of personal considerations? From fear of what others may say? No, and again no! I have come to a decision and don't mean to depart from it."

Strange to say, I could not bring forward any very plausible arguments against this; still, the more the captain said, the more I pressed him. "But the *Novik* is going to Vladivostok—why should not we risk it? We still have some chances in our favour." At last I brought up my big guns.

"I am not merely giving you my personal and private opinion, but that of the majority of the officers, who—"

"I have not called together a council of war, and have not charged you to collect the votes," the captain broke in sharply. "I have to request that you will see that my orders are carried out." With that he turned short round, and went into the conning tower.

Our voyage to Saigon does not offer anything of special interest, from the military point of view. I shall therefore not give a detailed account of it.

On the evening of the same day (August 11) we buried yet another bluejacket, who had died of his wounds. The doctor was now only anxious about one of the remaining nineteen wounded. The others he hoped soon to have "off the list," as the phrase goes. As the sick-bay was completely destroyed, all those who were at all seriously wounded had been put into officers' cabins.

When we had passed the latitude of Shanghai we put out fires in sixteen boilers and began to economise coal. The weather was favourable. Only in the Formosa channel we had a fresh breeze. Luckily, it was a fair wind, so that the sea was on the port quarter. We again had to work below, but this time we had plenty of time, and it was no longer a case of "bending or breaking." In the spaces concerned there stood a whole forest of spars and shores.

"A regular Acropolis," was one of the jokes.

"Not the Acropolis, but 'The Last Days of Pompeii' by Brüllow."[7]

They might look as they liked, these spars at least stood the weather.

But there was a danger approaching us in a totally different direction, and, moreover, a danger which we could only overcome by luck—and that we had had luck up to now no one could deny. Our coal was running out.

The hopes of falling in with a merchant steamer were not fulfilled. Up to now we had seen nothing.

"Very stupid," said the captain, when the chief engineer reported early on the morning of August 15 that our coal would not last quite twice twenty-four hours more. "Of course I mean our fate," he added quickly.

Our situation was beginning to be unpleasant. Should we go to Hong Kong, to the allies of our enemy? A most unattractive idea!

A sudden reminiscence of a former cruise of the captain's saved us from this situation. He remembered having called at a small port called Kwantshau about two years before the war with a cruiser (*Sabyaka*, I believe). Kwantshau is situated on the peninsula which stretches out from the mainland towards the island of Hainan. The French had acquired some territory there from the Chinese, to be used as a small base for their navy.

Could we get there? If the naval base has been ,completed, then it is sure to contain some coal. If it never got beyond the mere project, then at least we can obtain wood. The French are, after all, our allies.

On the evening of August 16 we entered the mouth of the Kwantshau River just before sunset. We anchored for the night, and proceeded 25 miles upstream next day to the French colony.

The French received us with cordial friendship and were ready to do anything in their power for us. The naval base had unfortunately never got beyond the project stage. The colony at the time only possessed 200 tons of coal, and this was not intended for ships that might call, but for their own requirements. The French let us have 80 tons

---

7. Russian painter of historical subjects, born 1799.—Trans.

out of these 200—just the amount we required for twenty-four hours' steaming. We were indeed grateful, even for that amount. These good people had shared with us like brothers. Between what we had left in the bunkers and what they gave us here, we could reach Haiphong, and there we should find as much coal as we wanted.

On August 19 we left Kwantshau and anchored in the Bay d'Along next day. Here we found lighters with *briquettes* waiting for us. We filled up our bunkers to full stowage.

On August 25 the *Diana* arrived at Saigon.

The captain had already sent off his telegraphic report to St Petersburg on August 20. Consequently, we thought that as a matter of course the first person who should set foot on our deck would hand the captain a cipher telegram signed by one of our principal home authorities.

Neither that day nor the next did anything of the sort take place.

The local authorities had been informed about us by their colleagues at Kwantshau and Haiphong. But now they began to feel uncertain. Why was there no telegram from Paris?

"Haven't you informed your government?" asked Admiral de Jonquières. "And why is our government acting as if it knew nothing?"

Who could answer that? We did not understand anything ourselves.

Instead of the expected instructions from St Petersburg the Saigon newspapers brought telegrams of the "Havas Agency." These stated that the Russian Government had decided to disarm the *Tsesarevitch*, *Askold*, and *Diana*, which had reached neutral ports.

As regarded our ship we did not believe this. What possible grounds could there be for voluntarily disarming a ship which had entered the port of an allied power in need of repair? This power did, after all, permit the ships of both belligerents to remain in her ports for an indefinite time, and to make use of all its appliances for the repairs of hull and machinery.

The eager sympathy shown by the colonial authorities at Saigon was in marked contrast to the cold reserve of Paris, and to the ominous silence of St Petersburg.

On the second day after our arrival constructors from the dockyard came on board. They asked for our ship's plans, so as to prepare the dock for her. Moreover, they examined our damaged bottom as far as possible, and promised to have it put to rights within ten days or a fortnight.

"What nonsense!" exclaimed the admiral, when we expressed to him our apprehensions in connection with the obstinate silence of the two capitals. "Don't these people out there understand that it is your turn first and then ours? We must hold on to our declaration of neutrality with both hands. If we get involved in war, we should be in the same situation as you now, and have only Saigon as a solitary naval base."

Meanwhile, time was passing.

The chief constructor of the dockyard came on board nearly every day to ask if we had any reply from Europe.

"Just wait," he said; "I suspect that the reason why they don't like letting you go into our dock is that in that case they would have to do the same thing for the Japanese. The dock is right in the centre of the depot of our submarines. But then they ought to send a reply of some kind! We can repair you without docking. Of course not here in this strong current. Here it is impossible; but you might go into some sheltered anchorage like Kamranh Bay or Port Dayotte. We should build a cofferdam as in Port Arthur.—You know the kind of thing.— Workmen and material shall be there. Why, the devil take me if I don't go there myself, as a stranger in want of amusement! We'll make that damaged side stronger than it ever was. But a reply—a reply! Get us a reply!"

Whence were we to get this reply? I ran about as distracted as all the others, anxiously awaiting the reply which was to decide our fate.

Through our agents and consuls we had ordered a number of colliers to different ports. These were ready to go to sea on receipt of a prearranged telegraphic order, and to meet us at certain rendezvous. All we now wanted was some kind of reply, some definite order from St Petersburg, even if it were merely the information that we could not be docked, but that we could otherwise do what we liked. We should have done something fast enough. (Of course, with the assistance of our good friends, who would not have refused.)

At last the reply came. It was such as neither we nor the local Frenchmen had thought possible.

On this fatal day my diary merely contains this entry:—

September 4.—It is all over! This morning at eleven o'clock the telegram came to disarm.

The text of this telegram I did not note in my diary, but I can still see the rag before my eyes. The telegram was not even in cipher.

By order of the General-Admiral [8] the ship is to be paid off, to strike her colours, and to be disarmed as directed by the French authorities.

(Signed) Avelan.
Minister of Marine!

What went on on board was not far removed from open mutiny.

"We won't allow the colours to be struck! We won't allow the ship to be disarmed! We'll go to sea!" were the shouts to be heard in the mess.

It was impossible to stem their outbreak of rage. I let them shout themselves hoarse, and then begged to be heard.

"Gentlemen, the fate of our ship is sealed! All our protests cannot revoke the General-Admiral's orders—"

I was interrupted by murmurs.

"Allow me to finish! The ship is ordered to be disarmed, but this can. only be done officially in a few days. But half an hour suffices for the captain to order us all out of the ship for insubordination and improper criticism of our superiors, during a state of war. Whilst the ship is still in commission and he is not obliged to give any account of his actions to the French Government, the captain would be absolutely justified in this. But when once we are ordered out of the ship, we scatter to the winds—possibly to the Second Squadron."

The captain approved of the idea, only, of course, he did not wish to leave the ship quite denuded of officers. I received my orders separately, the remainder drew lots. Chance decided that the commander, one lieutenant, three sub-lieutenants, and two engineers were to leave at once. There remained on board two lieutenants (one as executive officer), two sub-lieutenants, and two engineers. The doctor and the priest were not considered. They could not leave in any case. Meanwhile, I telegraphed to Admiral Rojëtvensky:—

> Our ship is being disarmed. I beg that, in view of our former services, we may be appointed to the Second Squadron. We cannot remain idle when our brother officers are fighting.

I received a reply in the affirmative.

Soon after there appeared in the various hotels of Saigon a number of *étrangers de distinction*, who were waiting for the next opportunity of

---

8. "Lord High Admiral," usually held by a Grand Duke.—Trans.

returning to Europe.

When the *Diana* had been officially disarmed, the captain handed to the French governor-general a nominal list of the officers and men actually on board the ship, on which it was declared that the persons named thereon would no longer take part in the war. Such a declaration was synonymous with being a prisoner on parole. It relieved the French authorities from the obligation to watch the "interned" Russians, so as to prevent their escape.

Of course we were not on that list.

On September 13 the first section of the "Excursionists" (three in number) sailed on board a freight and passenger steamer,[9] and on the 15th Messrs Bernard Christian, author (I had kept the initials B. C. [10] on account of the marking on my linen), Frederick Schoeschling, engineer, and two mechanics, who had been employed at Dalny, Meier and Schulz, left Saigon on board a steamer of the Messageries Maritimes. The two last named even travelled second class. They did not wish to arouse any suspicion, as they only knew Russian.

---

9. These three were unlucky. They did not get home in time for the Second Squadron.
10. The Russian letters W. S., Wladimir Semenoff.—Trans.

PART 2: THE VOYAGE OF ADMIRAL ROJESTVENSKY'S FLEET

CHAPTER 12

From Saigon to Libau

Thus M. Christian (a Swede, and naturalised French subject), M. Schoeschling (German by birth), and the two Russians from the Baltic provinces, Meier and Schulz, started successfully from Saigon on September 2, on board a "Messageries Maritimes" steamer.

Unfortunately, none of them kept a diary on the voyage home, consequently I do not propose to give its detailed description, as I have promised the reader to keep strictly to documents.

As in this case I can only base my account on reminiscences, I shall be brief.

The danger which threatened the "travellers" consisted in the fact that any Japanese auxiliary cruiser, which had received information on the subject, could stop our steamer and demand the handing over of any "contraband of war." Naturally, the identity of the persons affected would have to be determined first. Unfortunately, this would not have been difficult, as the involuntary "travellers" had repeatedly been photographed at Saigon before they knew what was in store for them. Moreover, the French declared that the town contained a large number of Japanese spies; whilst from Singapore a report had been received to the effect that Japanese cruisers were watching the Straits of Malacca.

The large majority of the passengers were naturally French, but we also had representatives of other nationalities on board. There were several Englishmen travelling in the first-class saloon, whilst amongst the second-class passengers there were, in addition to Europeans, a number of Asiatics, Anamites, Malays, Chinese, and two Japanese.

Chiefly for the benefit of the latter, a certain comedy was enacted on board, in which not only the "travellers" took part, but also the captain of the steamer, numerous French officers going home on leave, and M. Deloncle, the French deputy for Cochin-China, who was returning to Paris.

These had all been repeatedly on board the *Diana*, but they evidently had a very bad memory for faces. We only made their "acquaintance" some time after sailing, and our relations with them remained quite formal—at least outwardly. Our kind travelling companions almost overdid the thing in trying to preserve our secret; still, they attained great perfection in this. No sooner did a "suspicious person" appear anywhere within earshot than they changed the subject and tone of the conversation so rapidly, and in doing so cut such unexpected "capers," that we were often tempted to laugh aloud and express our admiration. Thus one day the French captain was criticising Kuropatkin's dispositions at Liao-yang, speaking with much animation, but in a low voice.

Suddenly, he pointed at "M. Meier," who was walking up and down the deck (he was short and very dark), and continuing to speak in the same tone, but still more mysteriously, he said: "This Baltic-Russian appears to me very suspicious—possibly a Japanese spy. They seem to be swarming everywhere." It turned out that one of the Englishmen had approached, and had sat down not far from us. An officer of the Foreign Legion, who spoke Swedish fluently, never lost an opportunity of practising this language. He used to tell M. Christian how he had once spent several years in Sweden. The latter used to feel very uncomfortable on these occasions, but replied boldly, mixing up Danish, Swedish, and German words, and trying to give the impression that he was anxious, from sheer politeness, to carry on the conversation in French. Needless to say, all conversations in our inner circle, and whenever there was no danger of their being overheard by others, were on the war.

Unhappily, though as was to be expected, our friends had no more information about the later events than we. The two newspapers which were published at Saigon did not regularly take in Reuter's telegrams (for the sake of economy), and consequently did not reproduce them textually. And with the Havas agency they had also only a very limited agreement. Telegrams therefore only occupied a few lines in their columns, and that not even daily. Their news was generally extracted from the home papers, which arrived once a week, and were from twenty-two to twenty-five days old. As regarded the Second

Squadron, its composition and the period of its sailing, the French were not able to give us any information; they even asked us our opinion on it generally. One of our fellow-travellers told us that he had heard privately from Paris that Russia was negotiating about the purchase of certain armoured cruisers—four Argentine ships (*Kasuga* type) and two Chilians. It was, however, uncertain whether there were any chances of a favourable settlement. Besides this, there was much talk of armed merchant cruisers.

We had already heard about these cruisers at Port Arthur. There we were told—Heaven knows on what this was based!—that the best steamers of the Hamburg-Amerika Line had already been bought, and might appear any day on the trade routes leading to Japan, in the China Sea, and in the Pacific. The mere rumours of the possible appearance of these steamers produced a tremendous effect on the rate of freight. Soon, however, all these rumours vanished.

It is interesting to note that the French anticipated just the same activity from our auxiliary cruisers as our officers in Port Arthur had pictured to themselves.

"*Tenez, mon commandan!*" the first officer once said, in conversation with me. "I am a seaman of the Merchant Service. I would gladly undertake to bring everything, which might be required to Vladivostok and to Port Arthur. But I should not be such an idiot as to have my papers made out for blockaded ports on leaving Marseilles. Is there no port in the neighbourhood with an agent to whom the cargo could be consigned? Not a soul on board, except me, would know the ship's real destination. My officers, my crew, could take an oath, with a perfectly free conscience, that we had no contraband of war on board. And as to papers—there would not be a single document in the least compromising. You may object: 'But how about the cargo? the guns?' What nonsense! Why should I not put all this down to the account of the German Government at Kiaotchou? (of course, assuming that the German Government gave its consent).

"I am sure this is what those do who take contraband of war out to Japan.... Ships carrying contraband of war should be caught in the latter part of their voyage, on their way to the final port of destination. Then there can be no excuses, the facts are dear. But to stop them thousands, yes, tens of thousands of miles from their goal ... that is nonsense. This is simply an offence against the most elementary principles of cruiser warfare.... It only leads to misunderstandings, and especially, if you will forgive me for saying so, such as are prejudicial to Russia.[1] Who has charge of these things with you? *Surtout, qui tient les cordons de la bourse?* . . . In my opinion, there are only two explanations possible—either it is a case of *sancta simplicitas,* in presence of which one forgives everything (but then the choice was bad), or *cest de la trahison.* . . . I go further. Your steamers *Terek, Kuban, Ural,* which on being turned into auxiliary cruisers would, in the German Navy, have been armed with fourteen 6-inch guns, have received from you a toy armament, and any despatch vessel of 2,000 to 3,000 tons of equal speed can destroy them. What does it mean? How is this to be explained? *C'est de l'ignorance, ou la bourse."*

I became quite enthusiastic over this sunburnt "sea-dog," ever calm and cool, who could get so keen, who could take to heart so much the faults of those who directed the operations of the naval forces *de la nation amie et alliée.* It was especially characteristic of him that he never even attempted to criticise the actions of our fighting fleet. As to the latter he only asked questions, but as regarded the operations of the auxiliary cruisers, the field of activity which might be his in time of war, there he felt himself to be an expert, and expressed his views without reserve. He did not understand. . . . No! He could not understand. "But was there no one, *le plus ordinaire des vrais marins,* who was bold enough to say to the emperor himself: '*Sire, ce n'est pas comme cela qu'il faut faire?*'"

Touching simplicity!

"*Et puis ces bruits qui courent sur cette affaire? Ces pots de vin? Que ce passe-t-il? Que fait on? Est-ce vrai? Voyons, mon cher commandant, dites le moi!*"

What could I tell him? . . . I myself did not know anything very definite, but after I had read the newspapers and had heard of the rumours, a vague feeling of doubt as to the future crept over me.[2]

At Suez, Bernard Christian received a telegram (in French):—

To Libau by the shortest route.

We consulted friends, we searched the guide-books—the longest route, measured by distance, but the shortest by time, was the one *via* Marseilles.

We decided upon taking it.

---

1. This was actually the case with the Malacca.
2. I will not anticipate, and therefore abstain from giving from my diary any news which I only received later.

At Port Said, where the steamer stopped some time for coaling, we saw the *Petersburg* and *Smolensk*.³ Only from a distance; they would not let us come near. There they lay, as if infested with the plague, cut off from the rest of the world by cordons by land and water.... It was the first time I had witnessed such degradation of the Russian flag. . . Thanks be to the French, they organised a regular watch to prevent our getting sight of the English local papers, in which the *Petersburg* and *Smolensk* were styled pirates pure and simple; moreover, it was suggested in solemn earnest (so as to prevent their ever again being tempted in the same way) that these vessels should be driven out to sea, fired into, and sunk with all their crews, without giving quarter, in satisfaction of the just indignation which all civilised nations felt, and as a warning to any other barbarians.⁴

We only remained a few hours at Port Said (so far as I recollect, from 9 p.m. to 2 a.m.), and then steamed on.

In the Mediterranean we were unlucky. The next day our engines broke down. They were repaired with the ship's own resources, but henceforth we were only able to steam 12 knots, and had to stop several times for adjustments. The result was that we reached Marseilles a good twenty-four hours behind time. Here we were met by a fresh difficulty. The *Mistral* was blowing its worst. It was therefore impossible to enter the inner harbour, and in consequence of a strike of dock labourers, the Steamer Company could only beat up two small steam launches, manned by non-strikers, with which to land the passengers and their luggage. We ourselves and our handbags got on shore the same day, but we could not count on getting our baggage, which had been stowed away below, for another twenty-four hours.

And yet we had orders to go to Libau by the shortest route. Certain travellers, known to the reader, who now no longer attached much importance to preserving their *"incog.,"* were tearing about in the steamer, and were nearly involved in a serious quarrel at the last moment.

"This is not a passenger steamer! It is a man-trap!" B. Christian hurled at the captain. "Can I start by the express tonight? *Dites, mon commandant?*"

"*Ah—la—la!*" replied the captain. "*Suis-je le bon Dieu? Dites mon*

---

3. "Volunteer Fleet" steamers, escaped from the Black Sea.
4. It would be interesting to know what paper, printed in English, could have published such an article.—Trans.

autre commandant!"

"Peace, peace!" With these words M. Deloncle intervened between the disputants. "*Voyez bien—dest la force majeure!*" he said to the one party. "*Pour ces braves, des heures, des minutes perdues—c'est la question d'être en retard pour la Seconde Escadre!*". . . thus he pacified the captain, who had already spoken of obtaining satisfaction.

We went on shore, and straight to the Consulate. In consequence of the *Mistral* the temperature had fallen considerably, and the thermometer showed 60° F. The ladies we saw in the streets had wrapped their fur boas round their necks. Our tropical costume therefore attracted a good deal of attention. Little boys made remarks about it and dogs barked at us. At the Consulate the reception was cool, but when I had explained who we were and whence we came, this changed at once,

"Where is the Second Squadron?"

"I don't know. But probably still in Russia."

"When does it sail? Shall we get to Libau in time if we start *via* Paris-Berlin tomorrow evening?"

The consul-general (a very sympathetic and amiable old gentleman) only shrugged his shoulders.

"Very well. Then we'll manage it like this. Please send off at once a telegram which I am going to write to the Chief of the Naval General Staff. Tomorrow evening we start—it is impossible to do so sooner—and the day after tomorrow morning, at the Embassy in Paris, we shall be told by what train to proceed and for what place."

"Capital! Just you write the telegram, and I'll see to all the rest." The telegram was despatched and all necessary directions given.

"And now, sir, tell us kindly where we can get some ready-made clothing, more suitable for October than these."

"Yes; I confess, I did not know . . . in fact I was rather astonished," the consul-general said with a smile. "Of course you must first of all get more suitable clothes."

With the kind (one may say, truly friendly) assistance of the consul-general's secretary, who had long been a resident in Marseilles, we first found a good hotel, and then "clothed" ourselves so expeditiously, that by dinner time (that is, in about two hours) we no longer aroused the suspicions of the peaceful citizens by our outward appearance.

Meier and Schulz suddenly—I don't know why—exhibited an unwonted degree of independence, declared that I was no longer their superior, and started next morning by the Vienna express.[5]

We, the remaining two, stuck to our plan and started north in the evening. At 9 a.m. next day we arrived in Paris and at once went to the Embassy. Our reception by the officials was decidedly cool (they probably thought we were countrymen of theirs, who had gambled away their fortune in Monte Carlo); they said:—"His Excellency does not receive any one so early...."When, however, I had written on the back of B. Christian's card—"A commander and a sub-lieutenant of the *Diana*" all doors opened wide for us.

The ambassador—Nelidoff—received us very amiably, but as to the Second Squadron he was unable to give us any definite information, although his own son was serving in the *Ossliabia*. The telephone was worked, a messenger despatched to the general post and telegraph offices, and at last I got a telegram, addressed to B. Christian:—

To Libau as quickly as possible.

At 1 p.m. we started by the Nord express for Berlin.

At 10 p.m. on October 12, twenty-seven days after sailing from Saigon, B. Christian and F. Schoeschling, *étrangers de distinction*, stood behind their luggage at the Russian frontier station Wirballen, patiently waiting for their turn to have it examined by the customs' officials, when suddenly a colonel, booted and spurred, entered the room.

"The officers of the *Diana*?—Let me introduce myself. I hope you will have some supper with me. You have time—What? Your luggage? Just hand over your keys and everything will be seen to. They won't take anything away from you. Anyhow, you are not likely to have anything which could be confiscated."

There was no hesitation on our part, and, sick of the railway fare, we tackled the "*Sakuska*" (Russian *hors d'œuvre*) and the chicken *à la polonaise* so determinedly that the colonel, who had evidently hoped to get much news out of us, was visibly disappointed.

"You are going straight to St Petersburg?"

"No, to Libau."

"To Libau? Then you need not hurry at all. If you go on in the train you have chosen you will have to wait nine hours for the Libau train, and that too at a miserable station, where you will not even be able to lie down and sleep. You had much better spend the night here and leave by the early train, which has direct communication."

---

5. They arrived too late. Meier later joined Nebogatoff's squadron.

"But where can we spend the night here?"

"Don't let that worry you. I will make them open the guest rooms. You'll sleep there as you haven't done for a long time."

"But we are in a great hurry. Couldn't we get a special? We are quite ready to pay for it."

The colonel whistled. "In the first place, you would have to obtain the permission of the Minister of Communications by telegraph; secondly, it would cost over 2,000 *rubles* (£200). Is money a matter of complete indifference to you? My advice is to spend the night here. However, I don't know. . . . What is your attraction at Libau? If you were going to St Petersburg, that would be quite different."

"Why, the Second Squadron sails either today or tomorrow. I have got a telegram about it."

"You want to join the Second Squadron?"

"Of course."

"After six months at Port Arthur?"

"We don't want to sit still, twiddling our thumbs, whilst others are fighting."

The colonel was on the point of replying something, but merely cleared his throat, and ordered: "Champagne."

At two o'clock next morning we arrived at Libau. Here an agreeable surprise was awaiting us. The assistant chief of the General Staff (Rear-Admiral N——)had found time and opportunity to let our relations know the probable hour of our arrival, and consequently they were awaiting us. During the remainder of the night, of course, we never closed an eye, and by the time colours were hoisted (8 a.m.) we were already down at the harbour. An incredible hubbub was going on there. We obtained a boat with great difficulty and pulled out to the outer harbour to the battleship *Knias Suvoroff*, where the admiral commanding the Second Squadron had hoisted his flag.

The staff received us with some coolness; on the other hand, our reception by the admiral was extremely cordial. My companion, the sub-lieutenant, was at once appointed to a destroyer, but in my case the thing was not so simple, on account of my rank. However, the admiral promised that he would settle the matter one way or another, and directed me to join the *Suvoroff*, for the present as a passenger (*i.e.* "borne for passage").

In the squadron, which was preparing for its long voyage, stores of all kinds and coal were being shipped, and there was such "feverish activity" (as it is called in the navy), that I had no leisure for any thorough conversations, for any detailed enquiries, or for reflection. I employed my few remaining hours of liberty in buying a few necessaries on shore. A few things my brother had brought with him from home (St Petersburg) when he came to meet me, others I had been able to take with me from the *Diana* [6] but this was not nearly sufficient.

Notwithstanding the assurance of the commander of the *Suvoroff* that the last boat would be on shore at nine o'clock the next morning, and although I was at the landing-place a quarter of an hour before the time, and waited there half an hour, no boat appeared. I did not lose my temper over it; it was the old business—"feverish activity." No doubt some one would get me off. I went in the *Alexander III.'s* boat, and got on board by 10 a.m. The departure, however, did not take place that forenoon. The water was so low that several ships touched the bottom; they were "stuck in the mud," and could not get off.

"An infernal harbour! Just look at this!" the admiral called out in ill-humour, as he passed me.

Luckily, a light south-west wind had been blowing since early morning, which drove the water into the harbour. The *Suvoroff* was not afloat Until 4 p.m.

I remember very accurately all the incidents of that day. Low, grey clouds; half fog, half icy drizzle; dark faces, hands buried in overcoat pockets; heads drawn well into the turned-up collar, into which streams of cold water were trickling steadily; general nervousness and irritability—be it in consequence of the weather, or of annoyance at all the small mishaps, or ... from anxiety due to ill omens.

"Libau won't let us go!"—"Not Libau, but the makers of the port!"—"Weather fit for a funeral!"—"Rain at starting is a good omen!"—"Friday into the bargain!"—"Besides that, it is the feast of the intercession of the Holy Virgin!" was heard here and there.

I don't know whether those who declared the omens to be favourable were sincere. Their appearance was anything but cheerful.

I was astonished at this. But then I did not yet know all that they did; and I had not yet been able to enquire as to the composition of the squadron, and had not the least conception of its state of preparation for war. I was happy in having reached the squadron before its de-

---

6. These latter things, that is, my uniform, were embarked in our steamer as goods consigned by Messrs Morthe at Saigon to some firm at Marseilles; they were packed in cases, suitably addressed, and had no outward connection with the "travellers."

parture from Russia. What doubts could there be? Since the squadron was being despatched, the presumption was that it was strong enough to meet the enemy! Otherwise its despatch would have no sense! The future lay in our hand! But notwithstanding the dull weather, and the dark faces around me, there was sheer joy in my heart.

I distinctly remember one episode.

The *Suvoroff* was already steaming out between the mole heads of the outer harbour, when Sub-lieutenant Prince Z—— rushed up to me. "Here are your people! Come quick—quick!" he called out, and dragged me towards the port side by my arm. I stepped out on to the port ladder platform.

Not far off a small grey steamboat, flying the flag of the Harbour Works Department, was being tossed about on the waves, burying its bows deep into the sea. On her deck, and holding on to the rails, stood my brother and his wife. He called out something (I could not make out his words in the strong wind), and waved his cap; she was holding high over her head her small dog "Temika," as if she wanted to show that this small creature was also interested in my fate and wanted to wish me farewell.

These are mere trivialities, but how deeply they engrave themselves in one's memory! . . . The ship increased speed. The grey steamboat returned into port. The open sea was ahead of us.

We did not get far that day. Something was wrong with the *Sissoi*, which had remained behind in port. She had apparently lost her anchor and was looking for it. We waited for her. With our departure the great activity on board slackened somewhat. It was possible to sort one's gear, which had simply been pitched into the cabin, to have a look round generally, and occasionally to ask a question. Amongst the officers of the staff I found that there was no old friend with whom I could have a talk, such as my heart was yearning for. It was true that the senior flag lieutenant, S——, had been in the same term with me as cadet (he remained behind though, when I left), but after that we hardly met for twenty years, and though acquaintances, we were hardly friends. . . . Moreover, all the members of the staff always looked so busy that I could not make up my mind to engage any of them in a private conversation. On the other hand, I found amongst the ship's officers two, the gunnery lieutenant and the chief engineer, with whom I had been long together in the *Donskoi* and the *Rossia*. I therefore turned to them to clear up my doubts.

"Why did you take the *Sissoi?*" I asked. "Your division can do 18 knots, but she, when all goes well, only 14."

The chief engineer gave me a questioning look, as if he wanted to make sure whether I was joking or speaking in earnest. At last he understood.

"Ah! Of course you come straight from Port Arthur! You see, speed really plays no part here. The *Sissoi* goes her 14, and of our lot, the *Borodino* gets heated eccentrics even at 12 knots. As to the *Orel*,[7] she never had time to get through her trials, so that we have no idea on what speed we can rely with her for any length of time and without complete breakdown.... *Suvoroff, Alexander, Ossliabia*—they can probably all do their 15 to 16."

"Well, and the *Navarin* and the *Nakimoff*, with their thirty-five calibre guns and their obsolete mountings? And the *Donskoi*—that old 'tub'? I love her, as I have gone many a mile in her . . . but how will she fare in action?"

"But what other ships were they to take? If they could have got them ready, they would also have taken the *Monomach* and the *Korniloff* and any other old 'warjunk'! These are all ships which count in the active fleet. In the war on paper, which our strategists play at in the privacy of their offices, they all figured in accordance with the data of the Naval Pocket Books! And of course, now that real war has begun, they can't admit that they are only fit for the 'scrapheap.'"

He gave a bitter laugh.

"But the *Slava, Oleg, Isumrud?*—Where are they?"

A look full of doubt.

"Of the *Slava* there can anyhow be no question; she'll hardly be ready in a year's time. The *Oleg* and *Isumrud* have not even begun their trials; they are, in fact, not yet completed by the builders. They were sent to Reval, but in such a condition that the admiral positively declined to tie such logs to his feet. They say that they are to catch us up somewhere on the way out."

"And the Chilians and Argentines?"

"That will all come to nothing," he said with a hopeless expression. "We are only wasting hundreds of thousands, if not millions, on all kinds of adventurers, who vainly promise to conclude the purchase."

We were both silent. I no longer felt the joy in my heart; my spirits sank, and my mind was troubled. I would not believe it; and yet the

---

7. Pronounced *Ariol*.—Trans.

pitiless reality was so plain before my eyes. I knew my old messmate well, and had no cause to doubt his truthfulness.

"Of course," I said after a pause, "if matters stand like that, then we must take all there is. But will it fulfil our object? If those old ships had been out there when war broke out, then they might have been of use, with a good naval base at their back. They might have accepted battle with their equals in strength, but would have avoided those that were stronger. But to make them steam 12,000 miles merely to let them fight their way through to their base at the end of it, and to send them into action, when the adversary dictates the conditions, when he goes into action with possibly his best ships, which are fully up to the mark and have just left a dockyard . . . such an enterprise does not offer many chances of success."

"I think so too."

"What a pity that this detachment returned to Cronstadt in 1901!"

"That's just it!" the chief engineer went on excitedly. "It makes me feel quite ill when I think of it! What, in the devil's name, was the object in bringing them back? Perhaps on the pretext of saving the expense of keeping them in commission. Surely it is immaterial where they pay off, where they lie, housed in—at Cronstadt or Vladivostok. It was said that they required a thorough overhaul, which the Vladivostok dockyard was not equal to. Well, look here; I have calculated the cost of only coal and lubricants for the passage from the Pacific to the Baltic—without any other expenses—over half a million! (*Rubles*= £50,000.) If this half million had been spent on improvements in Vladivostok dockyard it could have carried out these repairs! And the old ships, rejuvenated, would have hoisted the pendant at the sound of the first guns! And they would have done something. We could have made up two squadrons, one at Port Arthur and the other at Vladivostok. And how do we stand now?

"But this is not the whole of the outstanding account! This passage to the Far East of ships hastily equipped, this passage in times of war, when we have to pay double, yes, quadruple prices for everything, what will that cost? Merely the passage—half a million? No; at least two! They wanted to economise indeed! It was simply habit—that damned routine: 'The ships of the Pacific Squadron which require a thorough overhaul return to Cronstadt.' Of course another consideration may play a part in this. At Vladivostok nothing comes off the new contracts for material and the wages' vote, etc., etc. The 'percentages' are lost.... But now—now nothing is lost. Perhaps the ships will go to the bottom, but the 'percentages' have been pocketed. O Lord!" And as usual, when he had worked himself up, he snatched up his cap and rushed down into the engine room.

"I wonder if the 'General'[8] is not exaggerating a bit. Is it really as bad as that?" I thought when I was left alone in my cabin.... I went into the ward room. Here, with the exception of a few green youths, they were nearly all friends of mine from the Pacific Squadron. I could not help thinking what a promising lot they were.

The conversation did not exactly flag, but I had to admit that my efforts to hear a candid opinion as to the condition of the Second Squadron were not crowned with success, whilst questions about Port Arthur, the Japanese methods of fighting, the action of August 10, etc., etc., were showered upon me. My shipmates remained silent as to the former subject; they would not touch upon it. Not that they tried to hide anything from me. By no means. But on that day and the succeeding ones, they simply declined to discuss what each thought in his heart.

I remember that the Admiralty had been flooded with applications for appointments to the Second Squadron, and consequently had been forced to refuse these to a good number of thoroughly capable officers. The complements had all been exceeded, and yet there were officers on board the different ships in excess of even these increased complements. They had persuaded the authorities that an additional man on board was not a superfluous weight, but, in battle, a useful substitute for such as fell out. Generally speaking, one can say that the squadron was replete with volunteers. But then, whence this mysterious mood?... I soon understood and became contaminated by it.... But I will not anticipate. I will keep strictly to the notes of my diary.

During the night, the *Sissoi* got over her troubles, and on October 15 the squadron started on its voyage, in four detachments. The weather was calm and dull. Every now and then there were light showers.

I remained a passenger.[9] There were no vacancies, and it would have been a great hardship to turn someone out for my sake. I never

---

8. "General" was the nickname which had been bestowed on the chief engineer, in all kindness, when serving in the *Rossia* many years ago.
9. What in our service would be called "supernumerary borne for passage."—Trans.

suggested such a thing, and even if it had been offered to me, I should have declined. I was thoroughly satisfied with my lot, for it gave me the possibility of playing an active part still, instead of being obliged to sit still at Saigon whilst others were fighting. Nor could these say: "He has had his small share in the war, but now he is taking a rest." No—a thousand times No! I should have been unhappy for the rest of my life under such a suspicion. It would have been all the same to me if I had embarked as a historian, as a newspaper correspondent, as a passenger, even as a hired steward, but I was bound once more to risk my life, I was bound to prove by my acts, that for me there was no fate worse than that which befell the *Diana*.

I beg my non-professional readers not to imagine that I use the term "passenger" in an ironical sense; this position for naval officers is regulated by the instructions. When an officer is embarked, from whatever cause, without filling one of the regular positions in the ship's complement, he is termed "passenger." He draws the pay of his rank, and in lieu of messing allowance, his "passage allowance," of about equal value. At the same time, the admiral or captain may, if it be desirable, assign him some work, or some special duty; but, generally speaking, he has no fixed occupation—a passenger, in fact.

"There is no harm in your having no regular occupation. You will assist us with your accounts of the events of the war generally, and at Port Arthur," the admiral told me. He added jokingly: "We shall ply you so much with questions, and you will consequently have to work so hard with your mouth, that you won't be able to think of any other work."

In this respect he was under a considerable misapprehension. I have already mentioned that my reception by the staff was cool, not to use a stronger term. In part this was only natural. They, the select of the whole body of naval officers, had drudged, worked, prepared for the departure of the squadron, drafted orders and circulars, drawn up instructions, had exerted to the utmost all their capacity, all their knowledge, all their experience, so as to foresee and provide for every contingency. Finally, they had had the co-operation of the General Staff at the Admiralty and the Technical Committee,[10] infallible authorities both—and there suddenly arrives, owing to a whim of the admiral's, some senior officer from some cruiser, simply because he had spent six months at Port Arthur, where of course people knew

---

10. Corresponds to our department of the "Controller."

nothing of all these things, and *he* was to give them advice and directions! *him* they were to consult! ...

Of course no one asked me anything. If at any time I started a conversation with one of the specialists as to the many things we should have to alter and to make more "war-like," he would, at the most, listen to me graciously, but sometimes he would show his irritation. "Based on our experiences at Transund ... the experiments of Björko ... the trials at Reval ... the ranges at Cronstadt ... the results of the proving ground ... the Technical Committee ... the General Staff. . . ." A kind of Polynesian Taboo seemed to be placed on every word, every act which was "alive"!

The following lines are neither meant to condemn those who have gone down, nor to reproach those who have escaped the trial of Tsushima.

As regarded the large majority, these men were merely the product of the general conditions of their time. Can one reproach the more senior officers who served in Admiral Alexeieff's fleet with not being the equals of a Nakimoff's[11] companions in arms?

I am not speaking of individual members of Admiral Rojëstvensky's staff, but only of the general impression which I received in the early days of my presence in the squadron. On the one hand, there was the admiral, whom nothing escaped, who remembered everything, who thought of everything, who gave himself up entirely to the one idea—the successful prosecution of the war—and who aroused the general desire to co-operate with him. On the other hand, the staff gave one the impression of the typical staff in times of peace, an accurate copy in small of the General Staff, which flourished—and still flourishes—at the Admiralty, with all its high-and-mightiness, its exclusiveness, with its petty intrigues, and with that peculiar anxiety to preserve its field of activity against any outside interference, which is the fundamental characteristic of officedom.

It was not at all necessary to submit an independent report. The mere expression of an opinion in the admiral's presence, or suggestions made as to any measure in contemplation, quite sufficed to arouse the strongest displeasure of the specialist concerned. In such cases it could be anticipated with certainty, that no pains would be spared to prove the impracticability of my proposal, by all the teachings of that par-

---

11. Admiral Nakimoff (1803-55) fought at Navarino and was killed during the defence of Sebastopol. A ship is called after him.—Trans.

ticular science. Even if the business was approached in the most diplomatic manner, by previously discussing the subject in private with the members of the staff concerned, one was met by almost insurmountable difficulties.

"Certainly, but I don't know how it could be carried out ..." was the usual formula which met a suggestion. "In connection with this very thing we have already drawn up an order which has been approved and signed by the admiral."

"But, after all, he only approved what you submitted to him. Why could you not report to him now that, in consequence of information received since, such and such a modification is necessary?"

"You see, that is very difficult. . . . The admiral does not at all like changing anything when once it has been promulgated."

"Well, you might at least try! Is this the time to consider anyone's likes or dislikes? It is not a case of Chile waging war with Argentina, but of ourselves with Japan!" Thus I would urge, as I saw clearly that this exaggerated respect for the admiral's signature was merely a mask to protect the speaker's own *amour-propre* against any possible censure.

Sometimes I succeeded, sometimes not.

I don't like reviving the memory of all these trivialities, to rake up all this rubbish— but what is one to do? Out of these trivialities history is made.

What I have said here of the staff of the Second Squadron does not by any means represent any peculiarities of this particular staff. These are characteristics of every admiral's staff, of the general staff itself. Here there was only one peculiarity which up to then I had not met with elsewhere: the duality and the anonymity of reports. Anyone (and of course this only refers to members of the staff or junior flag officers and captains, not by any means to ordinary mortals) who wished to make a suggestion or submit his views in any way, had, in the first instance, to give the chief of the staff ample and detailed verbal explanations on the subject. If the latter had no material comments to make, or only desired some modifications in matters of detail, a short exposition in writing had to be drafted; this was then typed and added to the chief of the staff's report, but bearing no signature.

The subsequent fate of such a suggestion varied: either it immediately had the desired effect, or it was referred for remarks to the specialist concerned, or a decision was come to, which in no way corresponded with the author's intentions, or it remained barren of all results. In the two last mentioned cases it depended upon the author's importunity, whether he managed to have a personal interview with the admiral, although there was not much promise of success in this, since the first failure had undoubtedly been the result of the adverse opinion of the specialist concerned or of one of the senior members of the staff. It then became necessary to fight against preconceived notions, without knowing what these were based upon, and what arguments the other party had adduced against the proposal.

I do not think that this system was of use to the service. I do not know who invented it. Anyhow it enclosed the admiral like a wall, which it was not easy to penetrate! The only opportunities for breaking this wall could be found in the three meals at the admiral's table,[12] during which it was possible to lead the conversation on to the desired subject. These conversations were invariably led by the admiral himself, with much animation; he never curtailed them, but, on the contrary, his replies were such as to force the disputant to be most explicit. On the other hand, all the members of the staff were not embarked in the *Suvoroff*, so that those who were on board other ships were deprived of the possibility of resorting to the above-mentioned method. On the pretext that the flagship was overcrowded, an attempt had been made to shift me elsewhere, and I only remained on board by the admiral's personal order.

When I took stock of the internal economy and general arrangements in the squadron, I was astounded at the almost total disregard of the experiences of the war, that bitter experience, which we had gained during the course of eight long months of active service, at the cost of failures and reverses. I would not believe that no account was taken of them, nor that they had remained unknown in this squadron, itself going out to the war.

This could not be, since Commander K———, who had been sent home from Vladivostok by Admiral Skrydloff, expressly for the purpose of assisting at the fitting out of the Second Squadron, had now been over a month on its staff.

It was true that this officer had held a shore appointment at Vladivostok, had taken no part in any action, and had never heard the whistle of a hostile projectile, but he could at least have collected the necessary information from eye-witnesses, and finally, in his position (head of the war section in the staff of the Commander-in-Chief of

---

12. The whole of the staff messed with the admiral.

the Pacific Fleet) he had before him all reports of proceedings, both from the Vladivostok Cruiser Division and from Admiral Vityeft. Was it conceivable, that all these truly valuable reports had neither reached St Petersburg nor Vladivostok, but had remained in the viceroy's office, for "further consideration"? This appears simply monstrous.

Be this as it may, the experiences of the war were *not* utilised, as they should have been. Now, what was the cause of this? Was it due to the meagreness of the reports from the Far East, or to the ignoring of these reports by the home authorities, impressed by their own infallibility? It is hard to say; it might be the one or the other. It is, however, as well to state that Admiral Skrydloff's envoy was always guided by the views of these patent wiseacres. He himself did not take part in any fighting, but he openly expressed the opinion, that exaggerated hopes were placed on war experiences, that any such experiences acquired at first hand had to be met with scepticism, that they would not produce any revolution in naval warfare, etc., etc. To me these opinions appeared to be criminal heresy, and they troubled me much. If our wiseacres, who are now prophesying after the event, had foreseen everything, why did they keep silence?

Why did they not foretell our failures? And, finally, if the experiences of the war only verified their prophecies, only confirmed their theories, then they should have made more ample use of them, instead of discarding them! Would that not have been the right course? But in reality things fell out differently. In the course of a conversation I had with the torpedo lieutenant of the *Suvoroff* (an old acquaintance from the China campaign), on the day of my joining the squadron, I discovered that on board all ships the mining rooms had not only not been emptied, but that they contained, in addition to the regulation number of loaded mines, a number of countermines, which were intended for the destruction of hostile mine-fields; this meant that on board the *Suvoroff*, for example, we had over three tons of *pyroxylin*.

At first I tried to discuss this point with those on the staff who were responsible in this matter, but of course without any success. On my representing that these loaded mines should be transferred to the ammunition ships, that battleships should not be permitted to harbour such volcanoes in their storerooms, I was met by a condescending smile; I daresay they pitied me on account of such gross ignorance. However, the question appeared to me to be so serious and urgent, that, without troubling myself as to any unpleasant consequences, I introduced the subject of the blowing up of the *Petropavlovsk* after dinner the same day, gave a detailed description of the event, and also mentioned the blowing up of the *Hatsuse*, which disappeared below the surface of the water in fifty seconds.

"So you are of opinion that the cause of the sinking in both cases was the explosion of the mining charges carried on board, which in turn had been caused by the blowing up of a mine outside?" the admiral asked.

"Beyond any doubt, your Excellency! This is not only my own conviction, but it is shared by all."

"Quite impossible!" broke in the staff torpedo officer, with much excitement. "So I am to go back and be taught, now, such elementary truths as the conditions necessary to cause an explosion: the actual contact of the materials concerned, or their separation by a metal partition, with which the material is in direct contact on both sides. An air-cushion between them removes all possibility of explosion. The Technical Committee has come to this conclusion as a result of the scientific experiments it carried out both in the Baltic and in the Black Sea. However, this is nothing new, it was all known long ago! But after the disaster to the *Petropavlovsk* fresh experiments were carried out to confirm these old truths, so as to refute completely any silly statements to the contrary which might crop up here and there!"

"Whatever the experiments may have been, of which you speak, *I*, with my own eyes, saw the blowing up of *Petropavlovsk*, and I remember as distinctly as if it had only just happened, the enormous cloud of smoke, of that characteristic dark reddish-brown colour, which enveloped the entire fore-part of the ship, and in this cloud the mast coming down. . . . One does not forget a sight like that! And so violent an explosion, such quantities of smoke, dark reddish-brown, moreover, could only come from the loaded mines. The clouds of white steam only appeared later, and we all knew clearly that this meant the bursting of the boilers and the end of the ship! . . ."

"I can only repeat to you that, provided all the precautions prescribed by the Technical Committee are carefully attended to, *such a thing is impossible*. If the disaster did really take place in the manner you describe, it can only mean that on board the *Petropavlovsk* these precautions were neglected. The loaded mines must have been touching the ship's side; there was no isolating aircushion between!"

"Almost the same opinion was held by a portion of the committee of torpedo officers, which was assembled at Port Arthur directly after the loss of the *Petropavlovsk*. But we must surely assume that the Japanese, who had observed this catastrophe, at once carried out on board their ships the complete isolation of the mining charges, according to every scientific precept. They always pick up everything as quick as lightning. None the less, one month later the *Hatsuse* was destroyed in the same way as the *Petropavlovsk*. I was not an eye-witness of this event, but I heard the description which was given of it by people who had seen it from Golden Hill. I did not hear this as recollections of passed happenings, but as the description of an event, which had just taken place before their eyes.

"They related how a gigantic column of smoke and fire rose up in the air near the mainmast—like the eruption of a volcano; fifty seconds later there was nothing to be seen of the ship. The interval of time mentioned is quite accurate. It was taken with the second hand of a watch! After this all doubts were removed. Only the cruisers, which were stationed in the entrance, kept (either on board, or on shore near their berth) each three mines, in readiness to supply them to destroyers, which went out at night to lay out mines. On August 10, before sailing, the admiral expressly asked by signal: 'Has any ship got any loaded mines on board? If so, they are to be landed at once, or if there is no time, simply sunk.'"

"And I can only repeat that the Technical Committee, based on its scientific and exhaustive researches . . ."

"What can be better than the experience which we gained as eye-witnesses? Two battleships!"

"The results of scientific experiments should not be lightly discarded. In the first instance, the Technical Committee . . ."

"Above all let me beg of you not to mix up science and the Technical Committee; secondly, I should like to point out that not one of the sciences has spoken its last word. Every day brings new revelations. Astronomy was a science even before the days of Copernicus, and mechanics before Newton! When facts for once run counter to rules which by all appearance seem to be well founded, then we must not shut our eyes to the facts, so as to uphold the latter."

The admiral now interfered in the dispute, trying to reconcile the widely divergent opinions on the subject and to soften the asperities.

I fully realised the difficulties of his position. On one side was the statement of an eye-witness, as to whose truthfulness and powers of observation he could have no doubt. On the other side there was the decision of the committee, which was looked upon officially as final and irrevocable in all technical matters. I did not succeed in obtaining a complete victory: the mines were not transferred to the ammunition ships; but on October 20, a circular was issued containing special regulations for the proper isolation of the mines. These were not only to be carried out with reference to the ship's side itself, but also as regarded any metal fittings connected to it, so as to avoid any concussion being transmitted by these to more distant places. Between the mines wood "dunnage," felt padding, etc., were to be packed. How far these measures would have proved effective, there is no actual war experience to tell, as none of the ships of the Second Squadron were struck by a mine anywhere near the mining room.

All these technicalities do not, of course, possess any special interest for my readers, and I only dwell on this episode at some length, in order to bring out clearly the relations which subsisted between the central authority and those who did the fighting. If a live man, speaking a living language, who was in a position to reply at once to any objection raised, to stand up for his views, to vouch for what he had seen with his own eyes, found it so difficult to bring about the discarding of the infallible rules and regulations laid down by the magicians and necromancers who were sitting in the shadow of the Admiralty, what value would possibly be attached to reports from the Seat of War, which were necessarily brief and perhaps not sufficiently reasoned out? No doubt, they were generally endorsed "Record Office."

Although of course this, my "first appearance in public," was hardly calculated to reduce the coolness with which I had been met by the staff, I ventured all the same to enquire from the chief of the staff what steps had been taken to ensure the safe passage of the squadron through the Belt. He replied that all necessary measures had been taken; irrespective of the supervision by Danish men-of-war, which had to safeguard the neutrality of their territorial waters, a special service had been organised on our side, both on the coast-lines and afloat, the latter by means of special steamers, which were to cruise in the narrow waters and to keep a good look-out for any suspicious vessels which might be laying out mines on the squadron's line of advance.

Relying on my recent experiences, I began to broach the subject in all humility: Since such a danger existed, would it be considered superfluous to let a mine-sweeping detachment steam ahead of the squadron, as was done at Port Arthur? No doubt the steps taken were sufficient to meet the case, but an accidental oversight was always possible, whilst the water in rear of a sweeping party was safe beyond any shadow of a doubt.

The chief of the staff did not gainsay me, but suggested my speaking to the staff torpedo officer, since the decision and any report thereon was his special business.

I applied accordingly, and expressed ray views in a thoroughly friendly, conciliatory manner. I was received fairly graciously; at any rate there was no open hostility. "This is rather a large undertaking," the officer said. "Of course mine-sweeping is an additional guarantee against any accident. But judge for yourself the time we should take to get through the Belt—a week or more."

"Why?"

"Because, on an average, we should not be able to sweep more than 8 or 10 miles of Channel per day, and if you allow for bad weather ..."

"It is evident that we do not understand one another. I am speaking of a mine-sweeping detachment steaming ahead of the squadron. The second destroyer flotilla of Port Arthur, which used to precede the squadron on its departures as a sweeping party, consisted of boats, built in our home yards, of the *Sokol* type, of 220 tons. A pair of these, towing a heavy sweep, 100 fathoms long, used to steam 5 to 6 knots without any difficulty. Our destroyers are of 350 tons, so that they would be able to do this all the easier. If you were to place five pairs in two indented lines abreast, you would have a perfectly safe channel 600 yards wide immediately ahead of the squadron and on its line of advance. By starting at daybreak, the Belt would be passed by that evening."

"Indeed we don't seem to understand one another," was the irritated reply. "To say the least of it, this proposal is so—unexpected, that there is really nothing more to be said about it. The *destroyers* are to do the sweeping!—the destroyers of which we have so few, which we have to guard more carefully than the apples of our eyes!"

"But we must look after the safety of our battleships with still greater care."

"You are new to all this; you have been here just forty-eight hours, and are evidently ignorant of all that has been done. Here are the directions as to clearing narrow passages of mines, which were approved by the admiral and issued as far back as July 21. Read them through, that will be quicker than my explaining it all to you."

I buried myself in this document.

Has it ever happened to you, respected reader, to return home from a distance, convinced that dear relatives and friends would have made preparations and put everything in order in accordance with directions, which you had sent in advance, and then suddenly to realise that your letters either miscarried or had not been attended to? My feelings were something of that kind when I read through the *Directions for clearing a Minefield*, which had been so kindly placed at my disposal. Here were careful instructions, worked out in minute detail, which were bound to prove quite invaluable for the purposes of an inspection of mining drill in the peaceful waters of the roads of Transund.

Everything was provided for, down to the smallest detail in the outfit of the boats, even "Dry cotton waste, two pounds." But the 100-fathom sweeps, specially and cunningly constructed, were to be towed by *steamboats!* Pulling boats were to assist these when sweeping at especially suspicious localities. *Pulling launches were to keep handy with divers, which were to go down to the mines*, if these could not be made innocuous by any other means! *That!* after the bitter experiences of six months outside Port Arthur! That! when it had been recognised so far back as in April, that for the proper sweeping of a roadstead or passage communicating with the open sea, not only pulling boats, not only steam cutters, but even the picket boats were too weak.

That! when for the last six months special mine-sweeping flotillas had been organised both at Port Arthur and at Vladivostok! After the Port Arthur squadron had twice gone to sea, preceded by these flotillas! And then the pattern of sweep which we had finally adopted, after trials costing so many lives, the shedding of so much blood! Of this they (here) had not heard anything, or—they did not wish to hear anything.

What was agitating my mind must have been expressed pretty plainly in my face, for by the time I had returned him the paper after skimming through it, the staff torpedoist had pretty well lost his self-confidence. With evident hesitation he said something about "You see, we did what we could.... Trials.... Technical Committee ... the special Commission ... of course one can't foresee everything ... the admiral approved of it."

I felt like someone who has just been knocked down. However, I restrained myself. I did not become excited and I did not protest. I only began very quietly to relate everything in order, and to explain it with sketches. I urged him, I entreated him, for the sake of the thing itself, for the sake of the fleet, for Russia's sake.

He gave in, but not completely. It was quite clear that the chief difficulty lay in the fact that a "submission" would have to be prepared, setting forth the necessity for cancelling instructions which had been approved of three months ago, whilst new instructions, having nothing in common with the old ones, would have to be prepared for the admiral's approval.

CHAPTER 13

The Passage Through the "Belt"

On October 16 occurred our first mishap, which was reported to us by "wireless." The destroyer *Bystry* rammed the *Ossliabia* through being badly handled when closing her to convey a message; she bent her stem, as well as the stem torpedo-tube, and had a hole knocked in her side, above water, 4½ inches in diameter. The constructor on the staff gave it as his opinion that the damage might be made good next time we were at anchor.

On October 17 at 7.15 a.m. the first division of battleships anchored close to Fakkjeberg light, at the entrance of the Belt, and towards nine o'clock, with the arrival of the last detachment, which was a little belated, the whole squadron had assembled. Coaling was started at once, but soon after noon it came on to blow hard from the south and it had to be discontinued.

The idea of organising a mine-sweeping flotilla for the squadron met with the admiral's full approval, and its realisation at *some future time* was recognised as being urgently necessary, whilst almost insuperable obstacles (it was said) stood in the way of an *immediate* execution of the plan; in the first place, there were no sweeps of the Port Arthur pattern in the squadron; secondly, the destroyers had never practised anything of the sort, consequently nothing but mishaps were to be expected from their first attempt in that line, especially without adequate preparation, and, moreover, when trying it at once on so large a scale.

As regarded the first objection, I pointed out that at Port Arthur the sweeps had never been made in the dockyard, but on board the ships of the squadron with our own material and our men. Moreover, the reports as to the carrying away or the total loss of sweeps generally only came in towards evening, and as they had to be replaced by the morning, the new ones had to be made during the night. As regarded the second objection, I could not admit its validity. I knew very well what difficulties we had had at Port Arthur, how many sweeps were carried away, how many propellers got foul, until the officers commanding these vessels had acquired the necessary practice. The thing had to be learnt first, for without practice no satisfactory results could be expected from our novices, otherwise the business might end, not in small mishaps, but in serious accidents. The scheme was evidently on the point of being pigeon-holed, when I was suddenly supported in my efforts by the second torpedo officer on the staff (there were two), who, from want of room on board the flagship, had been quartered on board the *Borodino*. On his report the admiral gave orders that in any case an attempt was to be made at once.

Although the safety of the squadron might not at once be ensured thereby, it was pointed out that there was an advantage in having a practical demonstration of the business. It was all the more worth while to make the trial as the strong winds which were still blowing prevented coaling, and consequently our departure had been postponed to October 19, which gave ample time for preparing a suitable sweep. As sweeping vessels, the icebreaker *Yermak* and the tug *Roland* were told off. Pushkin, (the Russian poet), already had said "*that the fiery steed and the trembling doe should not be yoked together to the cart.*" This comparison, though, is still too weak. One should say: "*An elephant and a pony.*" However, there was no choice, and we had to take what there was.

For the purpose of making the sweep, a special circular was issued, in which it was laid down precisely what stores each ship was to send to the *Yermak* by the morning of October 18. The repair ship *Kamtchatka* was ordered by "wireless" to make at once fifty small grapnels,[1] which formed an important part of the Port Arthur sweep.

I endeavoured to obtain a hearing for my view, that although such a collection of component parts showed good organisation and no doubt was fully justified, it might perhaps be more expedient *if the flagship* were to supply all the stores required, and then to let the other ships replace these.

However, this was purely a question of staff-routine, and I only got snubbed for my pains.

On October 18 the two staff torpedoists and I went on board the

---

1. Small anchors with 4 arms. In this case they were not more than 8 inches long.

Yermak. My presentiment came true. Many of the ships (and for very good reasons) had either not supplied what was required of them at all, or had not been able to do so. This entailed signalling and writing. Chits were sent backwards and forwards. Amongst others the *Kamtchatka* had made no grapnels. Asked "Why not?" she replied: "As no written orders were received to that effect, the work was not taken in hand."

Is this not truly characteristic?—It reminded me of the state of affairs in the dockyard at Port Arthur during the first weeks of the war. There also one could not get anything done without the "necessary formalities," and an old friend of mine, *apropos* of this, once raised his hands solemnly towards heaven, saying: "A bit of paper like this, my dear fellow, is something sacred!"

However, we managed somehow, and after we had worked well into the night, the sweep was ready—not exactly the same as at Port Arthur, but somewhat after that pattern. In consideration of the fact that all hands in the *Yermak* had become sufficiently familiar with this manoeuvre after all my explanations, whilst the master and crew of the tug *Roland*, which had only just been chartered, had not the faintest conception of what minesweeping meant, it was decided that I was to go to her with one of the torpedoists, whilst the other remained in the *Yermak*.

As soon as it was light the two vessels steamed up to the entrance of the Belt and began paying out the sweep. Contrary to my apprehensions this was carried out without the slightest hitch. We neither fouled anything, nor got kinks in. By 7 a.m., when the squadron began to weigh, we were all ready to move ahead in front of it. And then....
It must be perfectly obvious to every one that in an operation such as this, a vessel towing a sweep will be manageable in direct proportion to its size and the power of its engines. It follows that in a sweeping couple the bigger ship must regulate its movements by the smaller. On board the *Yermak* this had apparently not been thought of, for she turned short to the new course and went ahead, without giving time to the *Roland* to take up her appointed station.

The little vessel, which was now practically tied up by the stern by the sweep, became quite unmanageable, and made a despairing signal: "Stop your engines. What are you doing?" It must be owned, in justification of the captain of the *Yermak*, that he recognised his mistake at once. He not only stopped, but went astern. But it was too late. To stop the *Yermak*'s movements when she had once gathered headway could not be done easily or quickly. The sweep taughtened out and—parted!

Meanwhile the squadron was coming on. When the *Yermak* reported by signal what had happened, the admiral made back: "The passage is to be considered as having been swept," and continued on his course. The *Yermak*, which had to accompany the squadron as a powerful tug, made to us by wireless: "Haul in the sweep and follow," and then joined the battleships. Hauling in the sweep took an hour and a half. Then we tried to overtake the squadron.

This failure made me very sad. The thing in itself was a trifle. One need only remember how many sweeps we carried away at Port Arthur until we got it into working order. When I was asked: "Whose fault was it?" I could hardly name anyone. It was simply want of experience, nothing more. But this first utter failure—what a trump card this might prove in the hands of the defenders of the "Transund Scheme"!

At 10 a.m., just as we were joining up with the squadron (we had cut off a corner), we received orders by wireless: "Go to the *Orel*." About noon we came up to this battleship, which was at anchor right in the centre of the Belt.

When we were close I hailed the captain by megaphone: "This vessel is placed at your disposal. Request instructions."

"I require no assistance. I shall get clear with my own means. Anchor near me."

"Very good, sir."

As it turned out, we were to be of use to him, but in a very unexpected manner.

On board the *Roland* a somewhat feeble Marconi apparatus had been installed, and no sooner had we anchored than this apparatus began to register messages which were addressed to the *Orel*, or, to be more accurate, the *Orel* was being called up by the *Suvoroff*, but did not reply.

We semaphored to her: "*Suvoroff* is calling you up." Our apparatus then at once passed on the *Orel's* answer, and then received the *Suvoroff's* further question: "How soon will you be ready?"—No reply from the *Orel*. After the flagship had repeated her question twice, without getting anything out of the *Orel*, we passed it on to the latter by semaphore. She at once replied: "In about two hours."

Further conversations took place in this original manner. The *Roland* received the *Suvoroff's* messages, and passed them to the *Orel*, which for some reason or other was unable to take them in, but was able to make the replies direct.

As I am not a specialist in this branch of the service, I asked the staff torpedoist, who had remained behind with me on board the *Roland*, for an explanation.

"Evidently the *Orel's* receiver is not in order," he said.

"I thought so too, long ago, but tell me how it is that one cannot find out the error and rectify it. The *Orel* carries two torpedo lieutenants, both wireless specialists, and yet a tug like this has to come to their assistance, with a weak little apparatus, which has had no expert supervision for some years, and which yet works so well."

"It is a Marconi apparatus. They are much more simple."

"Then what system have we got in the squadron?"

"We carry apparatus made after the patents of the German firm Slaby-Arco."

"I suppose that means that this is the best system in the market? Has it been adopted universally?"

"No ... not as yet ... nowhere, in fact, but the firm made such advantageous offers, it guaranteed such extraordinary ranges, such as no one had yet succeeded in obtaining, that. ..."

"And so the Russian battle fleet, the last card in our game, was placed at the disposal of Herr Slaby-Arco for experimental purposes, for the acquisition of more extended experience? Suppose all this is merely an advertisement?"

"I have had nothing to do with it, absolutely nothing," the torpedo officer hastened to assure me (apparently he thought I intended "going for" him). "I protested as much as I could ... I stood up for the Marconi system, which has been tested for years ... but, you will admit yourself, what more could I do? ... The Technical Committee considered it the best. The Central Administration made the contract. There was nothing more to be done. Even the admiral could not have done anything to prevent it, if he had tried! ... Might as well run your head against a brick wall!"

"Very well, and now tell me what your own opinion is of all this. There are none but Germans around, who don't understand what we say—tell me frankly what do you think of this system?"

"It is hard to say how it will turn out. ... Perhaps we shall yet get it to work. On board several of the ships experts from the firm have been embarked. Possibly they may manage to get the instruments to take in as well as transmit messages. Meanwhile, to be quite candid, it is not worth much...."

At 2 p.m. the *Orel* weighed and steamed after the squadron. We followed astern. From the wireless messages which passed between her and the flagship, we gathered that her steering engine had broken down, and that apparently the damage had not been thoroughly repaired. The ship had considerable difficulty in keeping her course, and was yawing about a good deal. We steamed like this all night. At eight in the morning we sighted ahead the *Aurora* and the store-ship *Meteor*, which had dropped astern of the squadron. About 11 a.m. on October 20, we four ships, almost simultaneously, reached the squadron's anchorage, south-west of the Skaw.

On my return to the *Suvoroff*, on coming over the side, I ran into the arms of an old messmate and friend of mine, who had left the service long ago, and—as it was called afloat—had "devoted himself to foreign branches of industry." I was in a hurry to make my report. He wanted to get back to his vessel quickly. Still we just stopped a moment to exchange a word of greeting.

"How do you come to be here?"

"I am in command of a destroyer."

"But what the devil brings you here? Did they send for you? What are you doing here?"

"And what do you want to do here? For the second time too! Didn't you have enough of it at Port Arthur?"

"With me it is quite another thing. I am on the active list."

"No, my friend. We are all tied by the same bond: I wore the uniform so many years, I was shown in the Navy List so long as a naval officer—no, I must meet my engagements. We now have to pay the reckoning!"

"Why not? But why this tragic air?"

"I've got no time now. Some other time we'll talk about it! .... Just look around, and then you'll understand. . . ." These disjointed sentences were pronounced as he was rushing down the ladder and jumping into the boat, which had just come alongside. From there he once more shouted back: "Remember my words—The reckoning! The reckoning!"

From the Skaw we had to send the destroyer *Prosorlivy* back to

Libau, as her condenser tubes leaked so badly that the defect could no longer be made good on board; also the *Yermak* which had something wrong with her tubes. A bad beginning!

So far as I could learn, it was intended to remain here two days for coaling in anticipation of the long run before us. Where did this run take us? What route would be chosen for the squadron? All this remained hidden from me.

Towards me the staff maintained absolute silence; they looked upon me as an "outsider."[2] I confess I did not complain in the least; thank God, they had learnt to keep secrets! Meanwhile a certain amount of information leaked out to the mess, by some inexplicable means. For instance, about midday, it became known that our agents had reported that fishermen had seen four torpedo-boats of unknown nationality, cruising about on the further side of the Skaw; a balloon had also been sighted which had passed over the squadron at anchor from S.W. to N.E.; the master of the supply ship *Bakan*, which had just returned from the Polar Sea, had reported to the admiral that some suspicious-looking vessels were hiding in the bays on the coasts of Norway. Possibly these reports were inaccurate. As I was not initiated into the secrets of the staff, I had, in making my notes, to be satisfied with what I picked up in the mess, and also in part with what the flag captain, an old messmate of mine from the Pacific Squadron, told me.

In any case, something clearly was up, for the squadron sailed as early as October 20, without completing the coaling.

At 3 p.m. the destroyers and the fleet auxiliaries weighed, the former having been attached to the latter. After these, the first division of cruisers (Rear-Admiral Enquist); then, at 5 p.m., the second cruiser division (Captain Schein); about 7 p.m. the second division of battleships (Rear-Admiral Fölkersam); and at 8.30 the *Suvoroff, Alexander III., Borodino, Orel*, and the fleet auxiliary *Anadyr*. It was a moonlight night, clear and calm.

Towards morning, on October 21, with a light S.W. breeze, a fog came on, which was so thick, that we could hardly make out the *Alexander*, only 2 cables astern. Towards noon the fog lifted.

The navigator told me that we were going through the English Channel. I could not help endorsing this bold decision of the admiral's. If the reports of our agents were true, if, that is, the Japanese really had prepared a trap for the squadron immediately on its exit

---

2. English in the original text.—Trans.

from the Baltic, then with their character which mistrusted everybody, they could hardly count upon keeping their plans secret. They were therefore bound to assume that we should choose, not the usual much frequented route, but the one round the north of Great Britain, and that we should coal at the Faroe Islands—a route on which ships are seldom met with, where it is possible carefully to watch any vessel sighted, to make out the identity of any suspicious vessel, and either to keep out of her way or request her to keep away. It was not for nothing that all these alarming reports came from Norway, or from the north-eastern coast of England.

The day passed quietly.

At 9 p.m. the repair ship *Kamtchatka*, which, as we afterwards found out, had dropped astern of Admiral Enquist's division, owing to machinery defects, and was steaming along by herself, reported by wireless that she was being attacked by torpedo-boats. The news was so improbable that, at the outset, it only met with doubt.

If, indeed, the Japanese were already in our neighbourhood, they would have to be regular *clairvoyants* to identify the solitary *Kamtchatka* as belonging to the Russian Fleet. Her appearance was absolutely that of a merchant steamer—and a very misshapen one at that. And finally, supposing them to have had this happy inspiration, if they really had succeeded in unearthing this treasure, with what object were they now throwing themselves on her? Could the destruction of the *Kamtchatka* possibly delay the advance of the squadron? It was all absolute rubbish. Many of us expressed the fear that she might accidentally have come upon a division of German torpedo-boats. And supposing this had happened and she had fired on them?—then an "incident" was there ready made, and a very awkward "incident" into the bargain.

The wireless messages which now followed were still more strange and aroused the suspicions of a deliberate mystification.

The *Kamtchatka* reported that some of the torpedo-boats had come up within a few cables' length of her, that she had turned away from them, had fired on them, and had got away from them by frequently altering course.... And by now it was eleven o'clock!.... It was perfectly clear to every one that the *Kamtchatka*, with her defective machinery (without this defect she could not do more than 14 knots), with her armament of a few 12-pounders, could not have stood the attack of an entire division of torpedo-boats all this time. If the attack had taken place, as reported, she would long ago have been at the bottom of the

North Sea! These suspicions were nearly confirmed, when at 11 p.m. a wireless message was taken in, in which the *Kamtchatka* requested the *Suvoroff* to give her position (by latitude and longitude), and then asked for "the position of the squadron to be indicated by searchlight."

"Somebody is making a fool of us," was the verdict amongst the officers. "Who is it who wants to know our position?"

I suggested, so as to make certain who the author of the message was, to request him to give us the Christian and surnames as well as the birthday of the chief engineer of the *Kamtchatka*. No "practical joker" could possess these data.

My proposal was not accepted.

The admiral ordered the following reply to be sent: "If you have escaped the danger, steer west. Indicate your position, then the further course will be given you."

Upon this all wireless messages ceased.

This was still more suspicious.

Fresh S.W. breeze, force three to four, a good deal of sea; spray coming over every now and then; wet overhead, too, partly rain, partly sleet; the cold penetrated to one's bones. . . . I had nothing to do, and a happy thought suddenly occurred to me: Why stand about here for nothing? the happy thought dated from Port Arthur; when on guard out in the roadstead and one's watch was over, one called the captain, who was sleeping the sleep of the just, handed over the ship, and turned in, with the firm determination not to budge, unless there was an alarm—provided one had not been blown up in the meantime!

Many people laugh at omens, but I believe in them.

I possessed a photograph of Admiral Makaroff, which he had given me just before my departure for the Far East. Naturally I had no opportunity of getting it framed either on my journey or at Port Arthur, but I always carried it about with me, like something sacred, and often read the simple words, going straight to one's heart, which were written on the back of the portrait—almost like a legacy, like the last will of my dear master—I venture to say—friend, who had come to such an untimely end.

Of course this photograph was also in my small cabin on board the *Suvoroff*, standing on the writing-table, and leaning against the bulkhead. The edges of the photograph had a narrow strip of red paper (the photographer's taste) pasted around, and . . . when I happened to look down, I saw that from a little stream of water which was running down the bulkhead (there must have been a leak somewhere) a few drops had separated, and were falling straight on the centre of the upper edge of the photograph. These drops became stained with red from the paper edging, and in running down on to the table formed a narrow red streak across the admiral's face and breast. "That is a bad omen!" I said to myself unconsciously, and took up the picture to see whether there was any hope of making good the damage. No, the red colour had already eaten into the surface and begun to dry.... That boded ill.

All the same I slept soundly.

I was awakened, as it seemed to me, by the sound of the bugle "action."

"Am I awake or asleep?" was my first thought.

The tramping of the men's feet, who were running up the ladders, the rattle of the ammunition carriers in the hoists, dispelled any doubts instantly . . . and now the first gun had been fired!

I rushed up to the after-bridge and nearly knocked down Lieutenant B——, the junior torpedo officer, who was superintending the after searchlights, and Dr N——, who had come up, as he loved anything in the way of strong excitement.

"What's the meaning of this? What are they firing at?"

"Torpedo boats! A torpedo attack!" they both shouted. "There, there!"

As I had only just left my cabin with its bright lights, I had not yet got accustomed to the darkness and consequently saw nothing.

The searchlights were throwing their beams to starboard and ahead. The whole of the starboard guns were keeping up a heavy fire. There was no confusion. On the contrary. . . . Now and then I heard the gongs of the range and order transmitters. They evidently knew their business. This was very different from the panic which I had seen on April 13, when the ammunition was simply pumped overboard.

I now ran to the fore-bridge, where the admiral, captain, and staff were sure to be. As I passed the wireless office I looked at the clock: 12.25. I made a note of it.

From the fore-bridge the following picture presented itself to my eyes: To starboard of us and ahead I saw, several miles off, a number of lights, amongst which from time to time signals flashed out. Someone (I don't remember to whom I addressed myself) explained to me that this was Admiral Fölkersam's division. In addition to this I saw in the beams of the searchlights, on the starboard bow, but much nearer, only a few cables off, a small steamer, with one mast and one funnel, which had evidently crossed over ahead of us from port to starboard, and was now slowly moving away to starboard. A second vessel, which looked like the other one, was steering on an opposite course to her, and was heading straight for the *Alexander* (No. 2 in the line), as if with the intention of ramming her on the starboard side forward; that battleship was pouring a hail of projectiles over her.[3]

The steamer sank before my eyes. A third one, of the same type, crossed our bows slowly, also from port to starboard. The gun-layer of the port 6-pounder mounted on the fore upper bridge, fired several rounds at her as soon as she had been sighted, but the admiral personally seized him by the shoulder with his iron hand, and shouted furiously: "How dare you? and without orders! Don't you see —— fishermen!"

Suddenly away to port some searchlights flashed out, and lit us up with their rays; no one had been firing in that direction, and consequently these came out of an inky darkness.

One's first movement on such an occasion is to shade one's eyes with the hand, as one can positively see nothing. Without orders of any kind, without any word of command, a fiery belt was now formed around our port side. The battleships opened a furious fire on the searchlights—quite at random, as it was impossible to determine the distance. "The real attack is from there!" I heard someone shouting. Were the other side replying? I cannot say for certain, although I thought that my practised ear was able to detect, through the roar of our own guns, the whistle of projectiles fired at us. (This noise is very distinct from that of a shell travelling away from one.)

Almost simultaneously signals flashed out above the searchlights, which were lighting us up—signals, moreover, made by the Tabulevitch system, which, as was known, are only in use in the Russian Navy. "They are our ships! *Donskoi* and *Aurora!* They are making the challenge!" I cried.[4]

"Cease fire! Switch off searchlights! One beam up!" the admiral instantly called out, with a voice which could be heard above all the noise and din.

---

3. It turned out afterwards that this steamer had already been hit and had her steering-gear damaged, in consequence of which she was involuntarily heading straight for the *Alexander*, with the apparent intention of ramming her.
4. It was indeed the division commanded by Admiral Enquist, which should have been six hours steaming ahead of us, and which now appeared abreast of us. Moreover, its ships were steaming with all lights out.

The bugles sounded, the searchlights were switched off . . . only one, the foremost, turned its milky-white beam towards the sky; this was, the prearranged signal to the whole squadron: "Cease fire." Of course, quiet was not restored at once. Even after the signal a shot was fired here and there.

Probably the fire did not last altogether more than ten or twelve minutes, for when I went below again (I had forgotten to bring my watch when I ran up) I noted: "1.10 a.m. October 22."

This is all that I, as an impartial eye-witness, can tell of the "Hull Affair," which has caused so much excitement all the world over.

Amongst the officers, who had assembled in the mess, and eagerly discussed the incident, three different views prevailed. There were some who declared that they had seen with their own eyes torpedo-boats, rigged up like steam trawlers, which had attacked the squadron: one of these, they said, had been badly hit, another had been sunk. Amongst these was Lieutenant W——, a reliable officer, who had already "smelt powder" in the China campaign. The most excited of all these was the ship's surgeon, Dr N——, who specially pointed out that not being in a position to give any orders, or to direct anything, he had been able to observe very carefully through his binoculars what went on. He said that it must surely be admitted that he, who had been at sea so long, who knew the navy thoroughly, would be able to distinguish between a steam trawler and so characteristic a type of vessel as a torpedo-boat.[5] . . . Others were of opinion that there may have been torpedo-boats, but that, having been discovered prematurely, they had retired, and that the steam trawlers had been fired at in their stead. The third party, finally, feared that the whole business was nothing but a fatal misunderstanding.

If I am to adhere rigidly to the notes in my diary, I must confess that, at the time, I inclined towards the latter assumption. I myself saw no torpedo-boat, and from my experience at Port Arthur, I remember well many a fanciful report of night engagements, published both on our side and by the Japanese. My views underwent a change later on, in consequence of facts which came to my knowledge subsequently, but that I will deal with later. At the time I assumed that we had got ourselves into a bad mess. One man held this view, another that.

Towards 2 a.m. the *Aurora* reported by wireless that she had four shot holes above water caused by 12- and 6-pounder shell. Wounded

---

5. His report is probably amongst the records of the International Commission.

were:—the priest, seriously (he had lost his hand), and a petty officer, slightly.

"That is not bad by way of a beginning," the gunnery lieutenant of the *Suvoroff* said, adjusting his *pince-nez* nervously.

From 4 a.m. on we again had light fog. It was calm, and the air became warmer. At 7 a.m. the fog lifted, but a drizzle came on. Between 5 and 6 we were constantly altering course, as we had to wind our way through a perfect labyrinth of fishing-craft. The night of October 22-23 was calm, with a clear sky and full moon, and at the same time warm—a very rare combination at this time of the year.

At 3 a.m. we passed the Galloper lightship and entered the English Channel.

In the dawn of an uninviting morning we sighted to starboard the chalk cliffs of the coast near Dover.

About 11 a.m. (on October 23) we sighted Admiral Fölkersam's division on the starboard quarter. How was that? They ought to have been two and a half hours steaming ahead of us!

When passing Cherbourg at g p.m., where we expected our three destroyers and the supply ship *Korea* to be lying, we called these up by wireless. They replied that they had arrived all well, that the local authorities did not restrict the length of their stay, and that they had therefore arranged to take in supplies of all kinds, over and above the normal stowage.

By the evening of October 24 we were at the mouth of the Channel, and about to enter the Bay of Biscay (in the autumn a very disagreeable locality). The sky was of a whitey-blue colour, the horizon hazy. The coast was not in sight, though it should have been. We had not been able to fix our noon position by sights. We passed Ushant apparently S miles off, but without sighting it in the haze. We shaped course for Brest. At 1 p.m. a fog came on, white as milk.

To enter Brest roads in a fog was impossible. On the other hand, an October fog in these parts might last until the next gale? The admiral therefore decided, so as to lose no time, to take his division to Vigo, however desirable it would have been to fill up with coal now. He looked upon the delay of not only a day, but of every hour, as an irreparable loss. We therefore shaped course for Finisterre.

All these considerations I repeat here in the words of the flag-captain, who did not think it necessary to keep them a secret. In truth, on reaching Vigo, our arrival there would be instantly communicated to the whole of Europe, therefore what sense would there be in concealing our destination from the ship's company out at sea? To whom were they to impart this secret? In such circumstances it is obviously a mere "office secret," an opportunity for bringing it home to the "common herd" that they must not meddle with the concerns of "authority." The commander-in-chief gives the order, the staff issue the necessary detailed directions, and all the rest simply carry out what has been ordered. . . . A pernicious system, of which the late Admiral Makaroff had been a determined enemy. He was of the opinion that a sub-lieutenant, acting intelligently and sensibly, was more useful to the state than a flag-officer who was carrying out to the letter, an order which he did not clearly understand.

Towards evening the fog lifted. The night of October 24-25 and the whole of the following day were quite calm.

These days of quiet, undisturbed steaming were not time wasted for me.

Deprived of the possibility of penetrating the secrets of the staff, of studying the route, the plan of operations, the tasks which would be before the squadron in the event of it happily reaching the Yellow Sea and the Sea of Japan, I turned with all the more zeal towards making myself familiar with the squadron itself, by means of documents and thorough questioning of the officers—of course only my old friends. As for documents, there were the written orders of the commander-in-chief, and the circulars issued by the staff. Between the beginning of May and the departure from Libau there had been issued, of the former over 100, of the latter over 400. Included in these, there were voluminous instructions and rules for the various branches of naval warfare. Besides these there was a whole sheaf of "very secret" plans and instructions, access to which I had some difficulty in obtaining.

This was a very praiseworthy piece of work, which would have deserved the prize for "diligence," or perhaps for "science," if there had not been in it pearls such as the "plan for organising the service of clearing a channel through a minefield," or "organisation of the watch, for look-out and repelling of torpedo attack on board ships at anchor in an unprotected roadstead."

As I read some of these *Rules and Regulations*, I was several times on the point of losing all self-control and of running to their authors and exclaiming: "What are you doing? Do consider for a moment! Do you really imagine that your experiments in the ports of Cronstadt and Reval, or in the still waters of Transund Roads, are more reliable than the experiences which we gained at the cost of blood in fighting the enemy?"

However, I pulled myself together; I only entered these queries in my diary; at some suitable opportunity they shall reappear. I had already learnt to my cost what a too energetic attitude led up to, in existing circumstances.

Otherwise—I repeat it again—the work was thoroughly praiseworthy, and, with certain improvements, it would have been of value as a handbook to the personnel of a *thoroughly trained squadron*.

The only question now—and a very essential question—was: could one apply this term to the collection of ships with which I was now on my way to the Far East?

From the dates of the orders and circulars, I saw that the squadron left Cronstadt for the first time on August 25, and that it arrived at Björkö the next day. Here it remained two days, and carried out in great haste the various mining exercises. It then proceeded to Reval, where apparently some target practice took place, under weigh against a fixed target. By August 31 it was back at Cronstadt for the completion of the dockyard work and the preparations generally for its long cruise. From these papers it also appeared that telescopic sights (which have been in use in foreign fleets, including, of course, the Japanese, for many years) were only supplied to our guns at the end of July! On September 11 the squadron again left Cronstadt and went to Reval— for a further stay, as the work on board was by no means completed. During the night of September 16 night firing took place for the first time—at anchor and at fixed targets.

On September 19 and 20, torpedoes were fired. On September 22 and 23 the squadron went to sea, executed some of the simplest evolutions, and carried out further target practice, this time against towing targets. From the middle to the end of September, when it sailed from Libau, the squadron drilled with feverish activity. . . . But two weeks. Is that much? A "squadron" can only be considered fit after *years* of training at sea.

The deeper I plunged into these documents, the more I understood the reserve, the disinclination to discuss the theme, which the officers showed every time the conversation came round to the fighting value of the Second Squadron.

The picture was made still more complete by the various confidential talks I had with my friends, and again and again I recalled my old messmate's parting words, shouted up out of the boat: "The reckoning!"

"What is one to do?" I thought. "The reckoning! Very well, then let us meet it; but it is just as well that one should know it, instead of pottering about in the dark"—and I continued my investigations.

The crews of the squadron consisted as to one-half of recruits, who had merely been put through some squad and rifle drills, and received the most elementary general instructions ("What is an able seaman? What is the flag? etc. , etc."), but who had never been to sea; then there were reservists.

The gunnery lieutenant of the *Suvoroff*, who possessed a pretty sharp tongue, defined the situation as follows:—

"One lot have to be taught everything, because they know nothing, the other lot because they have forgotten everything; but if these do remember anything, then it is obsolete. Just think of your service as navigator: the time required to teach a good, willing, peasant lad how to look through a telescope. What does he see the first time, no matter how anxious he is to carry out the instructions received? Of course I don't want to say anything against the telescopic sights which long ago came into use in foreign navies. It is a devilish advantage if one can make out the enemy at 75 cables (15,000 yards) as clearly as at 10 (2,000 yards). In the same way a typewritten paper is preferable to one written by hand; still, if you have a good clerk, who can write neatly and quickly, and being in a hurry for the fair copy of some long paper, you put him in front of a typewriter for the first time in his life, what would be the result?—A mess. I fear it is the same thing here," he ended, quoting the words of a well-known *chansonette*.

"Oh, well, I know you. You always like to exaggerate a bit, to lay it on thick, in fact. The chances are that, in reality, you have already trained your boys so well, that for them a telescopic sight is a matter of pure joy."

"Don't you believe it," he replied in a very serious tone of voice, nervously shifting his *pince-nez*. "When could I have done this? Paper work—receptions; receptions—paper work. . . . Always at anchor. Only on very rare occasions a few hours steaming. I *am* training them. Of course I'm training them. But aiming drill, without firing—that's no use. And a few rounds does not mean regular target practice."

"But why was there no practice? Why was there no firing?"

"There were heaps of reasons to be found in ships which were hardly completed, or whose defects were not yet made good. You remember the old 'chestnut,' where the commandant of a fortress is asked why, on some solemn festivity, he had not fired a salute? He replied: 'I had eighteen reasons for this: firstly, I had no powder. . .' He was not allowed to enumerate the other reasons. It is the same thing here. We have got on board our full allowance of ammunition and 20 *per cent*, besides. But that is all! More than that we must never expect, even if we should have to fight ten battles. Our attempts to get something abroad always ends in failure. Why, I don't know. Possibly because our agents spend the money in advance. Probably these agents count firmly on being able to act with impunity, as they are covered by the high position of those called upon to preside over these commissions. For instance, there is just now a certain captain, known to you (specially promoted, a rising star), actively engaged in Paris on this business of the purchase of the South American cruisers, which long ago was made a hopeless mess of."

"How can one keep silence over all this?"

"Stop! Confound all your questions! In our hearts all these wounds are nearly healed up, and now you want to tear them all open again."

"For heaven's sake, abuse me as much as you like, but don't run away; tell me some more. You see, I don't know anything. How is this possible? If we are in such a mess, why was the squadron ever sent off?"

"*Armada*, not squadron."

"Well, let us say *armada*."

"What could we have done? Ought the admiral to have sent in a report: 'As I foresee with certainty that we shall all go to the bottom, and as I am frightened of this, I can't go out to the war?' Or what? Was he to state publicly that we had no fleet, but merely a collection of stage properties? No one would have believed him. Why, that is just the pity of it all! We should simply have been called cowards and traitors. Well, then, it is better to go to the bottom. Though, in faith, we are, through no fault of our own, accomplices in his guilt, and—we have to expiate these sins."

"We have to meet the reckoning, in fact?"

"Yes, yes; that is the right term. They always believed that it would last out our time, that there would not be war. And the reports: 'Everything in the best of order,' were the best means of advancement in the service. But let me go now. To speak of these things drives me wild."

I then tried to cross-examine the navigating officer as to the degree of preparedness for war with respect to the movements in close order, performing of evolutions, etc., etc. He did not resemble the gunnery expert in matters of temperament in any way, he did not excite himself, did not get furious, but his quiet replies sounded all the more hopeless.

"Moving in close formations, keeping station,—let us hope we shall learn all this during our long voyage. Time for practising changes of formation we shall, I dare say, find. That will be difficult enough! But as regards battle exercises with the whole squadron, or by divisions, the execution of different tactical plans, the practising of any tactical 'tricks'—that will have to be adjourned. That is a matter of years of preparation. With us an absurd idea—convenient enough from an economical and a routine point of view—has of late years cropped up, namely, that the art of naval warfare can be taught in the peaceful seclusion of an office, which converts the ships into floating batteries, and where, instead of holding manoeuvres and experimental cruises on a large scale, one is satisfied with carrying out whole wars and individual battles—on paper.

"The incontestable truth that, as faith is worthless without works, so is theory without practice, and that skill is the crown of the edifice where handicraft is the foundation, was forgotten. This also explains the neglect of actual war experience, which shocks you so much. Even in the Pacific we did not know how to create thoroughly trained squadrons. The Japanese have done it. The English, the French, and the Germans possess trained squadrons; we—possess none. You yourself have told us that the first cruise of the mobilised fleet at Port Arthur was spoken of as the 'Cruise of the Argonauts,' and how Makaroff had, on taking charge, to teach his ships, instead of battle tactics, the most elementary movements, in which, too, they rammed one another and got clubbed instead of forming line. Going into action, then, meant that one had not only to look out for danger from the enemy, but from one's neighbour in the fleet. This would be ludicrous, if it were not tragic.

"Meanwhile, a 'squadron' existed officially in the Pacific, and the viceroy himself was never tired of reporting on its absolute preparedness for war. What do you expect from the Baltic, where, officially for over ten years, but as a matter of fact ever since Admiral Butakoff's time, no squadron has existed? Our wiseacres pretend that by multiplication of the guns, the projectiles, the personnel, the speed, etc., and by summing up all these results, a battle-coefficient of the squadron is obtained which is not much lower than that of Admiral Togo's squadron. But this is simply nothing but fraud, practised on the mass of ignorant landsmen. An infamous fraud! These wiseacres must know that there the factors are totally different: other guns and projectiles, experienced seamen, actual speeds, etc. And the chief thing: *there* it is a real squadron; here—merely a heterogeneous collection of ships. This is sad, very sad, but, unhappily, true.—Now what do you think about Port Arthur? What is the state of affairs there? What can one hope for?"

"On August 10, the men of the garrison, together with those of the fleet, amounted up to about thirty thousand souls. What the amount of provisions and ammunition comes to is hard to say at all accurately. Even in the fortress this was a 'war secret.' The supreme authorities declared that these would last out, at least until February, and even beyond. According to private information—from the different forts as regards powder and shell, from the magazines and stores as regards the quantity of provisions—this would appear to be correct. As regards the squadron, there is, in my opinion, little hope. As soon as the bombardment from the land front begins, how is the damage caused by gun-fire to be made good if every day increases it? Moreover, a large part of the guns are undoubtedly on shore, and firing away their ammunition there. A large proportion of the crews are employed in the fortifications, and, of course, suffering losses there."

"Yes, yes. . . . All the same it would be a good thing if they could hold out until we arrive. It would always draw off some naval forces from us. By the time we meet, we shall have accomplished a long voyage, but the Japanese will have a long winter's blockade behind them. That is also not so bad."

The plan of the operations in store for us was neither known to the squadron in general, nor to me in particular. Of course, every one had his conjectures and made his proposals, but, as I have remarked before, no one was inclined to discuss these. And why not? Because, whichever way one looked at it, the natural result was utterly hopeless, and because such discussions in time of war had a still more depressing effect on our spirits, which were low enough as it was.

CHAPTER 14

Arrival at Vigo

On October 26, at 10.30 a.m., our division arrived and anchored at Vigo. Here we found five German colliers, but it turned out that we were unable to begin coaling at once. On board each collier there was a Spanish water-policeman, who had orders "to prevent any replenishment of stores by the ships of a belligerent in neutral waters."

This prohibition was even extended to the *Anadyr*, which was in company with us and flew the Russian naval ensign. She carried in her holds about 7,000 tons of Cardiff coal, sufficient to fill up the bunkers of all the ships. I repeat, the *Anadyr* flew the naval ensign, and the Spanish Government therefore simply forbade all communication, any exchange of stores, even between the men-of-war, which had entered her ports. These were quite new, unheard-of rules of neutrality, which had been prepared at the instigation of England, the faithful ally of our enemy. It was said, however, that England would hardly have been successful in this, if it had not been for the circumstances in which our auxiliary cruisers developed their activity; these were, as is known, simply "auxiliaries" for the—Japanese. I could not help recalling the bitter words of the French seaman about the personages who were directing our cruiser operations.

A lively interchange of telegrams with Madrid and St Petersburg now commenced. (See appendix "Hull Affair").

Next day, at 1 p.m., we received the much desired permission, and started coaling, which was completed in twenty four hours. Still, we did not continue our voyage. We had to wait and see what decision would be come to at St Petersburg concerning the "incident." The English press was somewhat less violent, but was still pugnacious. News came that the Home Fleet was to be mobilised and combined at

Gibraltar with the Atlantic (Channel) and Mediterranean Squadrons: in all, twenty-eight battleships and eighteen cruisers. Now, however, they were no longer demanding the return of the squadron, but only the supersession of the Admiral. Spirits throughout our ships were greatly depressed, for every one realised that our game would be up if St Petersburg gave in, since there was no one besides Rojëstvensky who could lead the squadron. As to that there was only one opinion.

The admiral was, as always, full of confidence and energy, and even more cheerful than usual. Some one read him an extract from a newspaper article, in which it was said that if he persisted in continuing his voyage with his division, the almighty British Fleet (twenty-eight battleships and eighteen cruisers) would have no difficulty in destroying him. The admiral only laughed. "A strange amusement, to keep on counting this up. If we were to come to blows, then all we should be concerned with would be the first four ships, with which we could fight; how many more there might be—twenty-four or one hundred and twenty-four—is all one to us."

Whilst the Spanish Government met us in this unfriendly manner on our arrival—whether of their own accord or under foreign influence, I will not enquire—the inhabitants of the place were entirely on our side. Evidently the people still harboured the feelings of ill-will which had been engendered by England's attitude at the time of the Spanish-American war, and the citizens of Vigo lost no opportunity of showing us their friendly sympathy. This was proved by a host of trifling incidents, which it would be difficult and tedious to enumerate.

When the admiral went on shore to discuss matters personally with the governor, the crowd which had assembled in the street gave him a regular ovation on leaving Government House. The local papers expressed in unequivocal terms the view that "one should look upon the opponents of the ally of one's own enemy as friends, etc."

On the evening of October 28, the admiral's well-known "Order of the Day" was issued, and read out to the assembled ships' companies.

Today, October 28, His Majesty the Emperor was graciously pleased to send me the following telegram:—
> In my thoughts I am with you and my beloved squadron with all my heart. I feel confident that the misunderstanding will soon be settled. The whole of Russia looks upon you with confidence and in firm hope.
> Nicolai.

I have replied:—

The squadron is with your Imperial Majesty with all its heart.'

"Is it not so, comrades? What the Emperor orders we carry out. Hurrah!"

This "Order of the Day" aroused much enthusiasm, but—I will be quite candid—not everywhere. The half-lowering looks, the expressions on some faces, a word spoken at random—all this showed that many a one would have welcomed the news of the enforced return with a feeling of relief, though not one of them would have turned his back voluntarily.

"Pity it did not come to open rupture with England," my old acquaintance, Lieutenant B———,said half-seriously, half-jokingly.

"Why?"

"Because then they would have scattered us directly we had got outside. Now we have got to go all that distance for the same object."

On the evening of October 29 it became known that an international commission was going to be appointed to deal with the "incident," and that each ship was to send one officer as witness.

On October 30, at 8 a.m., the witnesses left by train.

From the *Suvoroff*, Commander K——— had been sent. I confess that this selection astonished me. So far as I recollect, according to his own statement (others knew this as well), he came on deck after me, because at the moment when the first gun went off he was in his cabin, undressing, and on the point of turning in. He could hardly, therefore, have seen more than I, so that his evidence could not be particularly valuable. Besides this, he was the representative of the Commander-in-Chief of the Pacific Fleet on our admiral's staff, had only just arrived from the seat of war, and, although he had not himself taken an active part in it, he had been, as it were, at the very centre of operations.

"You will overtake the squadron again somewhere?" I could not help asking him as he left.

In the meantime the chief of the staff did not permit the cabin thus rendered vacant to be occupied by one of the ship's officers, notwithstanding the great want of accommodation. On the contrary, he personally locked up every cupboard and drawer in it, which still contained papers or other articles, then the cabin itself, and kept the key.

"Then he is coming back?"

The chief of the staff cleared his throat, but said nothing in reply. Lieutenant S——, who, like myself, had chanced to witness this scene, took my hand, and said with an air of mystery: "Do you know what that means? It is said that rats leave the ship before she sinks. They scent it. It is their instinct. They are wise animals; they thus preserve themselves against better times—for the benefit of the kingdom of rats."

On the evening of October 31 the desired reply from St Petersburg apparently arrived, for a general signal was made to prepare for sea, and at 7 a.m. on November 1 the first division of battleships sailed from Vigo on its way east. The Spanish cruiser *Estremadura* escorted us through territorial waters.

At 10 p.m. a man-of-war—two masts, three funnels—steamed up on our starboard beam at good speed. She looked like the English cruiser *Lancaster*, which had come into Vigo during our stay. After having proceeded a short distance ahead of us, she turned round, steamed down our port side, and disappeared. Soon afterwards we sighted, several miles astern, the lights of five vessels, which were apparently following us. From the way the lights were placed it was clear that they were men-of-war. They remained astern of us the whole night, but they did not steer a steady course; they moved about, sometimes steaming up on our starboard quarter, sometimes on the port, changing formation, dividing into two sections, etc.

At daylight we could see that we were, in fact, being convoyed by a division of English cruisers.

At 7 a.m. the *Orel's* machinery broke down. The squadron stopped engines. The constructor and the torpedo officer on the staff were sent to her. The Britishers, who had up to then followed in our wake, now became very busy: first they formed a line of lookouts on the horizon, then they re-formed. One cruiser then went off to the south-east at top speed, probably with a report; the others divided into two pairs, which scouted to the north and to the south of us, 5 to 7 miles off. All their movements were so regular, all manoeuvres were carried out at such speed and with so much precision, that they did not look as if they were due to unexpected orders, but as if a well-rehearsed play were being enacted before our eyes, in which neither the stage manager nor the prompter could be noticed. "Do you admire this?"

I turned round. Behind me stood the admiral, who could not take his eyes off the English cruisers.

"Do you admire this?" he repeated. "That is something like. Those are seamen. Oh, if only we . . ." and he ran down the ladder, without completing his sentence.

In his voice there was suppressed anguish; an expression of so much suffering passed over his face that I suddenly understood. . . . I realised that though he did not allow himself any hopes which could never be realised, though he well knew the true worth of his squadron, yet he was faithful to his trust, and would cede to no one the honour of being the first in the ranks of those who were voluntarily hastening to pay the reckoning.

By 8 a.m. the *Orel* had made good her defects and we proceeded. Towards evening the detached English cruiser returned, followed by a further division of four cruisers. They accompanied us all night, during which they carried out various evolutions, and only on the morning of November 3, when they had made sure that we were going to Tangier, did they turn off to the eastward, making probably for Gibraltar.

In the roads of Tangier, where we arrived at 3 p.m., we found the whole squadron assembled, with the exception of the destroyers and the supply ships to which they were attached. Those had gone ahead to the Suez Canal.

Tangier was the only place where we were not only not molested in any way, but where we were even received with a good deal of friendliness. The governor treated the admiral, who paid him an official visit, as an honoured guest, welcomed him in the name of the *sultan*, invited him to remain at anchor as long as it suited him, and to do there whatever he pleased. It was said that when our first ships arrived, the English Consul had tried to protest, as the representative of Japan's ally, but without success. He was told that His Majesty the Sultan of Morocco had not only not received any official intimation of a state of war between Russia and Japan, but that no relations had ever been established between him and the latter country; that he had hardly ever heard of this faraway empire, but that anyhow, according to the word of the Prophet, every stranger brought blessing upon the house which sheltered him, and therefore he was not asked who he was, whence he came, or where he was going, for there was no more sacred law than that governing hospitality. If ever the Japanese were to visit Tangier they could count with certainty on the same friendly reception.

How much more generous does this frank precept sound, which has been held sacred since the days of hoary antiquity, than all those declarations of neutrality, based on juridical considerations, which modern diplomacy has evolved.

At 9 p.m. the same day Admiral Földersam's division weighed and sailed on its way through the Suez Canal. (*Sissoi, Navarin, Svetlana, Jemtchug, Almaz*, and some auxiliaries.)

The east wind which set in that day freshened up so much during the night, that on the morning of November 4 coaling had to be suspended. The wind went down in the afternoon, when the work was resumed.

At 3 a.m. on November 5 an English squadron steering south-west passed in sight of Tangier.

During our stay here the hospital ship *Orel*,[1] and the provision ship *Espérance* (flying French colours), joined us. The latter carried 1,000 tons of frozen meat and other food supplies. Thus we were now well off as regarded medical assistance and provisions.

At 7 a.m. on November 5 we began to weigh. The ships (fleet auxiliaries), which were not accustomed to moving in company, steamed about all over the place for a long time, before they got into their places in the line. Signal upon signal was made. One was told: "Increase speed"; another: "Stop engines. Don't go over there"; a third: "Steer more to starboard"; a fourth: "Steer more to port," etc. The two flag-lieutenants were run off their legs. At last, soon after eight o'clock, some kind of order was established, and our squadron moved off. We steamed in two columns: the starboard one consisted of the battleships *Suvoroff, Alexander, Borodino, Orel*, and *Ossliabia*, the port one of the fleet auxiliaries, *Kamtchatka, Anadyr, Meteor, Korea, Malay*, and *Russ* (ex-*Roland*, which had been bought and re-christened under the Russian flag). In rear of the squadron the cruisers *Nakimoff, Aurora*, and *Donskoi*, followed in wedge formation (double quarter line). This division was commanded by Admiral Enquist, whose flag was flying on board the *Donskoi*, but which was shifted to the *Nakimoff* later on. I describe this "order of sailing" so minutely, as it remained the same until we reached Madagascar.

At 9.45 a.m. we had just got into the prescribed formation and had settled down to the normal speed when the steering engine of

---

1. Of the same name as the battleship.—Trans.

the *Suvoroff* broke down, after jamming the helm hard a-starboard. She narrowly missed ramming the *Kamtchatka*. Luckily, the captain of the former never lost his head for an instant; he at once stopped the port engine and went full speed astern with the starboard one. A collision was happily avoided, but the whole of the port column got into utter disorder, as the merchant steamers composing it fled in every direction when they saw this battleship, apparently gone mad, rushing straight at them.

At the end of a quarter of an hour the damage was repaired and order was restored.

The passage to Dakar was only disturbed by one mishap—during the night of November 8 we remained stopped for five whole hours, owing to the *Malay's* machinery breaking down.

The weather was glorious—warm, with a light trade wind (we were just on the edge of its zone). I must, however, state that these were my personal feelings. I, who after a summer at Port Arthur, after a stay at Saigon, and the passage from there to Marseilles, had felt frozen through at Libau, in the North Sea, and "the Bay," felt very comfortable here, but the officers and crews of the ships had already begun to speak of tropical heat on leaving Tangier. How much Seltzer water and ice, but, above all, cold "*Kvass*"[2] was drunk on board the *Suvoroff* could not possibly be calculated. Amongst our men there was a professional brewer of *Kvass*, so that this beverage was excellent. Our route was little frequented. We hardly saw any sail going in either direction. The English cruisers still showed us their amiable attentions for some time longer, but by day they kept a long way off, sometimes they were quite out of sight, though at night they closed nearer; when we were south of the Canaries, they left us for good.

I forgot to mention that at Tangier, before the squadron divided, a final effort was made to get rid of me. The chief of the staff asked me in a very amiable, though very decided manner, what the particular appointment was which I intended applying for to the admiral, offering me his support at the same time. I replied no less decidedly that at the time of my arrival in the squadron at Libau I had asked for any appointment (no matter what) on board any ship, and that I was naturally under the impression that if anyone vacated an appointment from whatever cause, I should have some claim to it. But I would in

---

2. The national beverage of Russia since the sixteenth century. It is a fermented drink made with yeast, water, flour or bread, also malt. In the services, each ship or regiment brews its own requirements.—Trans.

no case request that any one should be deprived of his appointment, or should be ordered elsewhere; I would never consent that even the shadow of an injustice should be committed for my personal benefit.

"If you consider my position here to be not normal, not right," I ended, "if you have any intention of improving, or regulating it, I should be very grateful to you, but I shall not apply for this myself, and prefer to leave the whole business in your hands, with the request for a definite settlement."

I do not know what report he made, but the result was that an order was issued that I was to be borne on board the *Suvoroff*, as head of the naval war section on the staff of the admiral commanding the Second Squadron. My official position was thus somewhat altered: I was no longer "borne for passage" only, but as a supernumerary to whom a special duty had been assigned. As a matter of fact everything remained as before. Not only was I not admitted to the "Holy of Holies," nor initiated in the plans of our prospective operations, but even the current business of the staff, the cipher telegrams which were sent off or received, were kept a secret from me. If I chanced to enter the staff office, where the chief and the members of the staff were eagerly discussing the latest news received, their conversation was broken off so markedly, that there was nothing left for me to do but to apologise and withdraw.

The position of head of the naval war section on the staff was not provided for in the establishment. It was created during the war, but only on the staff of the commander-in-chief,[3] and therefore the several departments and duties had been allotted amongst the specialist members of the staff and the flag-lieutenants.[4] At my first attempt, on taking up my new functions, at clearing up this or that point, which unquestionably concerned my special work, I at once saw that this was being met with the greatest hostility, and led to unedifying squabbles and discord, as an intrusion in another's domain, as a violation of some sort of rights.

I on my side considered it would be criminal, in view of the serious situation in which the squadron was placed, if I were to cause even a shadow of discord in this fully organised and trained staff, the solidarity and unanimity of which appeared to me to be indispensa-

---

3. Nominally still Admiral Skrydloff at Vladivostok.—Trans.
4. An "Admiral's Office," with a secretary and clerks (accountant officers), does not exist in Russia. All their work is done by executive officers.

ble conditions for any success. To drag the admiral into this squabble seemed quite inadmissible, seeing that he was already overburdened with work and cares, and that he alone would in that case have to be my support.

I do not know if I acted rightly then, but I decided to curb my ambition for the sake of our cause, to renounce my great aim of having a share in the conduct of the squadron, to make no attempt at penetrating the secrets it was desired to keep from me, outwardly to content myself with the part of the "passenger" and "expert," who was left on the staff by the admiral's desire. I intended only to assert myself independently in the case of dire need, but on the other hand to obtain due recognition of my ideas by influencing, in a diplomatic manner, the specialist officers and captains of my acquaintance, as well as the junior flag-officers. In the end it became evident that these channels were well chosen, for under false colours my proposals, in the majority of cases, did not meet with so much opposition, as if they had emanated from myself.

On November 12, at 8 p.m., we arrived at Dakar. Colliers were awaiting us here; still, we were not able to commence coaling at once, although we were in the territory of our good allies. No sooner had we anchored than the captain of the port came off to see the Admiral, but not—alas!—to welcome us and to offer us his assistance, but to propose that we should leave again at once. He informed us that Japan had protested against belligerent warships, on their way to the seat of war, being permitted to coal in neutral ports; that England had energetically supported this protest, and that the French Government had apparently not decided to reject this new principle in international law.

At least he had orders to find some way out of this difficulty, to select and indicate to us some spot for coaling outside territorial waters, but in any case not to permit this operation to be commenced, without having previously arrived at an understanding with Paris. Personally, he placed himself entirely at our disposal, and in this he was evidently quite sincere. (This was very much like the reception accorded to the *Diana* at Saigon: the warmest welcome on the part of the local authorities and cold reserve on the part of the home government.) The governor promised assistance of all kinds, offered to send us not only fresh provisions, but, if necessary, workmen—only we were to go.

Where to? To the Cape Verde Islands, for instance? There the depth of water made it possible to anchor outside territorial waters, that is, beyond 3 miles from the coast.

We who had just come in from sea, knew very well what a swell we should find there. Under these conditions coaling was not to be thought of.

The admiral stated categorically that since coaling in the open sea was impossible, and sailing without coaling was equally impossible, the prohibition to coal in Dakar roads was equivalent to a demand for the disarming of any of the vessels belonging to one of the belligerents which might enter a neutral port; that this, however, was contrary to all declarations of neutrality. This brought things to a head.

Telegrams flew to St Petersburg and to Paris.

By the afternoon it was announced that the negotiations were taking a favourable turn for us; we therefore took advantage of the great distance between our anchorage and the French settlement on shore, from where one could not "see clearly" what was going on in the squadron, hauled the colliers alongside, and started coaling.

The reception we met with at Vigo, and again here, in the port of an allied power, forced us to consider very seriously what should be done as regarded the voyage of the squadron round the Cape of Good Hope. Our next stoppage was to be at Libreville, a French colony, 40 miles north of the equator, situated at the mouth of the Gaboon River, in which water was plentiful. If we entered it we were as snug as in any secure port, but, unfortunately, the French local authorities had definite orders, according to information received thence, not to allow us to enter the river at all.

At the same time it was pointed out that the depth of water at a distance of over 3 miles from the shore (that is, outside territorial waters) was generally from 10 to 12 fathoms, and that if we were to anchor there (that is, in the open sea), we should not only not be prevented from coaling, but would receive every possible assistance. That was truly French—and amiable; at the same time, it did not commit them to anything. It was just as if one said to a hungry man sitting under an apple tree: "I have no right to pick even *one* apple for you, but if one should drop off, eat it by all means; I would even peel it for you."

It must, moreover, be pointed out that November is the month of the most variable weather at Libreville. Calms predominate, but from time to time there are violent storms, with lightning and thunder (tornadoes), which in strength are hardly inferior to the West Indian hurricanes, and which, though they do not last so long as these, are more frequent. Apart from the danger of the tornado itself a heavy swell continues for a long time afterwards. In short, coaling "at sea, near the Gaboon," could in no way be looked upon as a certainty.

The next stoppage (1,000 and odd miles south of Gaboon) was to be in Great Fish Bay—a very large bay, which offers perfect protection against the prevailing winds and the swell. Neither on the shores of the bay, nor for hundreds of miles around, is there a tree, or a bush, or a single fresh water spring—nothing but sand. Without doubt one could not imagine a better place for our squadron, hunted out of every port. But in our days no "no man's land" can be found anywhere on the globe, and this desert belonged officially to the Portuguese. If an English squadron were to appear in the bay, bringing a Portuguese official, from the neighbouring town of Benguela, who were to request us to leave, then, in case we declined, the English were undoubtedly entitled to place their forces at his disposal for action against us, as we should be transgressing the neutrality rules which had recently been formulated. How would this end ?—It does not pay to foretell the future. Come what may, this place, also, could hardly be thought of for coaling purposes.

On the entire west coast of Africa, there was only one spot on which we counted with certainty: Angra Pequeña, 700 and odd miles south of Great Fish Bay, the only harbour of the German colony on that coast. When it is considered that our coal was delivered to us by the steamers of the Hamburg-Amerika Line, we were surely entitled to count upon not meeting with any obstacles there (and in this we were not deceived).

After that, Madagascar. *Ni plus, ni moins*, as all other anchorages, which were suitable for our purposes, belonged to the English, whilst Delagoa Bay, which had been thought of when the route was being planned, belonged to Portugal, which came to the same thing.

The possibility of coaling at sea—in the regions of the south-west trades, south-east trades, and the westerly gales—was of course out of the question. The point to be decided therefore was: Should we turn back, or continue with the prospect of having to fill up the new battleships, with, say, 2,400 tons of coal each, as against the normal stowage of 1,100? Now the Technical Committee had found that these ships, which already drew 2½ feet more than was intended, gave cause for anxiety when their bunkers were filled up to extreme stowage, and had informed the admiral accordingly.

In consequence of this communication the admiral had issued on October 14 a general memorandum, in which it was laid down that "to ensure a safe metacentric height, the following was to be observed by the ships concerned: (1) To avoid stowing liquids in the free spaces in such a manner that these would be able to move when the ship rolled; thus, for instance, boiler water stowed in the several compartments of the double bottom should be used up in rotation, that is, no water was to be taken out of one compartment, until the preceding one was empty. (2) All objects of any considerable weight were to be securely lashed. (3) Coal was to be used in such a manner, that as it was taken out of the lower bunkers, a like amount was to be moved down from the upper to the lower bunkers. (4) In heavy weather all ports and other openings in the ship's side were to be closed."

I beg pardon of my "shore-going" readers for citing this order, which can hardly be either interesting or even intelligible to them, but which speaks volumes for those familiar with the sea.

Thus the question to be decided, put bluntly, was: "Either turn back, for there is nothing to be had here, or risk capsizing."

Turn back—easier said than done. How was such a thing conceivable, since "the whole of Russia was looking upon us with confidence and in firm hope."

Here the enormous difference which exists between a general commanding an army, and an admiral commanding a fleet showed itself clearly. In the case of the former there cannot, under any circumstances, be any question of his personal bravery. If he were to declare that he did not consider himself justified in sending the troops confided to his care to certain destruction, one could accuse him of anything one pleased, but never of personal cowardice. With the admiral it is just the opposite. He is on board his flagship, on which the adversary concentrates his fire, in the very centre of the danger, he is the first to risk his skin. . . . If he were to say that he did not want to lead his squadron to certain destruction, it would always be possible (whether rightly or wrongly is another question) to hurl at his head the terrible words: "You are afraid!"

Now judge for yourselves; when Russia was in this mood, when it "looked with confidence and in firm hope on the Second Squadron," would it have been possible for the officer commanding this squadron to have spoken of turning back? And so he decided to go ahead, and disregarding the warning of the Technical Committee, to fill up the ships with coal—as it was expressed in the mess—not only "up to the neck, but over the ears."

At Dakar the battleships of the *Borodino* type were ordered to take on board 2,200 tons of coal, which meant that not only the belt deck or flats, but the main deck as well had to be used as stowage places. The admiral signed and issued a general memorandum, drafted by the constructor on the staff, in which the manner of carrying out this unusual operation was laid down very precisely, and all precautionary measures, which were considered necessary, both in taking on board and in using up this "deck cargo," were prescribed.

The constructor on the staff, P——[5] (an excellent messmate, who enjoyed universal sympathy), was extremely busy, went from ship to ship, and finally assembled the other constructors for a consultation on board the *Suvoroff*.

"Well, and what do *you* think of it?"

"If there is no help for it, then we must manage it somehow," he said.

"Shall we capsize?"

"No, at least probably not, if the main-deck ports keep out the water. Let us hope we shan't get a strong head wind, for then things will be very bad for us. When the main-deck ports no longer hold and the water pours in—then goodbye."

During the night of November 12-13, the governor received instructions from Paris to permit us to coal, but only on condition that the operation was to be completed in twenty-four hours. As a matter of course, this period commenced with the moment of receiving this decision, that was 4 a.m.

November 13 was the first day of our "coal troubles." We afterwards went through many such days, but this first one was especially heavy.

In Dakar, as in the tropics generally, all signs of life ceases between 10 a.m., and 3 p.m. The government offices are closed; the shops do not sell anything; the troops don't leave their barracks; the European

---

5. E. Politovsky (author of *From Libau to Tsushima*). Every Russian ship of a certain size carries an officer of the corps of naval constructors, whilst a senior one serves on the admiral's staff.—Trans.

workmen interrupt their work; everyone not only seeks protection in the shade against the sun's scorching rays, but endeavours to move as little as possible in the shade, as every movement produces profuse perspiration. These rules were observed by people who, to a certain degree at least, had become acclimatised and accustomed to this life—but for us there were none of these conveniences. For us rapid coaling was one of the first conditions of life; every one took part in this, beginning with the captain; the ships company worked in two watches, night and day. In a flat calm, and with the thermometer never under 90° F., the *Suvoroff* was completely smothered in a cloud of coal dust for twenty-nine hours on end.

The sun's rays by day, those of the electric light by night, could hardly penetrate this black fog. From the bottom of the colliers' holds the sun had the appearance of a blood-red spot. Blacker than niggers, streaming with perspiration, lumps of cotton-waste between their teeth (it was necessary to breathe through the cotton-waste, to avoid getting the coal dust into the lungs), officers and men were at work in this hell. And nowhere could one hear the slightest grumbling, not even a hint that after all there was some limit to human endurance. Extraordinary-looking creatures—black and streaming with moisture—ran up to the bridge every now and then, "only for one minute, for a breath of fresh air," quickly asked the signalman: "How are we getting on? How much was it for the last hour? Are we ahead of the others?" and disappeared again below at once.

And what went on in the closed-in coal-bunkers, where the coal had to be stowed, as it shot down from above? Where the temperature was 115° F.? Where the strongest and healthiest could not stand it for more than fifteen or twenty minutes! No one enquired. It was necessary, there was no help for it. The work was kept at boiling point. It happened every now and then that one of the workers could no longer keep on his legs. He was then quickly carried out, the fire hose turned on him, and when he had recovered his breath, he returned to complete his task. There were many cases of light sun or heat-strokes, but happily they all ended well. Only on board the *Ossliabia* Lieutenant Nelidoff [6] died at 3 p.m. from heart failure. His funeral took place on November 14, just before sunset, after the heat of the day. All the officials of the colony were present; the garrison of Dakar took part in it and rendered the last military honours.

---

6. The son of the ambassador at Paris.

The whole of that day was devoted to washing down, cleaning, and resting.

The next three days (at sea) passed uneventfully; but then our troubles began. I will only enumerate the principal ones: on November 18, at 8 p.m., the eccentric strap of one engine broke on board the *Borodino*; until this was replaced by the spare one (a difficult job) the *Borodino* steamed with one engine only and was not able to do more than 7½ knots, the squadron meanwhile reducing to that speed. The damage was made good by 8 a.m. on November 20, when we resumed our normal speed of 9½ knots, but at 7 p.m. the cross-head pin of the air-pump broke on board the *Malay*. The tug *Russ* (ex-*Roland*) was ordered to take her in tow; they "backed and filled" for a long time, and what with their want of practice and the darkness, it was 10 o'clock before they were able to go ahead, but then only at 4½ knots. Towards morning the damage on board the *Malay* was repaired, and we once more went on 9½ knots.

On November 26, at 6 p.m., we anchored in the open sea, to the southward of the mouth of the Gaboon River. The weather was fine. On the two preceding days we had experienced a heavy swell, but now nothing moved. The German steamers and the *Espérance* (the refrigerating ship) joined us from the river. The lieutenant-governor also came out, bringing heaps of flowers and good wishes. He was apparently much pleased that we had not entered the river, as he possessed no means of preventing it, and as there was an English consul at Libreville, who would certainly not have let this opportunity pass without raising an outcry over such a breach of neutrality.

And these were our allies!

Nikolai Ugodnik and Seraphim Saroffsky [7] did all that was in their power. No tornado came to trouble us; there was hardly any swell from seaward.

We coaled almost as if in harbour.

On December 1, at 4 p.m., we weighed and proceeded—apparently just in time!

On December 2—the sky thickly overcast and a heavy swell in which the overloaded battleships staggered about badly; the same thing the next day.

---

7. Saint "Nicholas, the Just," patron of sailors, and Saint "Seraphim of Saroff" the new saint, canonised during the present reign, and hence frequently invoked.

CHAPTER 15

Off the Cape of Good Hope

If the time we spent at anchor could be characterised as the "black fever" or "feast of coal"—as it was called in the mess—the time at sea could also in no way be called a time of rest.

Apart from the fact that there was much which had been left unfinished when the ships were being built and equipped, and that in consequence there was work of one kind or another going on day and night in every part of the ships: this or that had to be taken to pieces, refitted or altered, put together again; the crews had to be trained; they had in fact to be put through the training which they had not received in time of peace, notwithstanding the reports as to "complete preparedness for war," the assurance that "everything was in the most perfect order."

Naturally our first object in our homeless condition was to get forward, but as the incessant break-downs, first in this ship, then in that, delayed us so much and forced us to spend our "elixir of life"—coal—to no purpose, the practising of tactical movements was out of the question, dependent as they were on the expenditure of time and coal. Even the admiral, who did not know the meaning of the word "impossible," did not risk tempting fate in such a manner. On the other hand, everything was done that was possible without materially retarding the progress of the squadron.

The personnel was kept hard at work. The daily exercises averaged about six hours; in the evenings the officers were kept busy in the mess, at night the bugle often sounded the alarm.

On November 22 the admiral issued an order which laid down that in each ship, on the day preceding any general battle exercise, a scheme for the same was to be worked out under the personal supervision of the second-in-command, according to the captain's general directions.

It was laid down that the scheme was always to represent a fleet action; it was further ordered that:—

> After the movements of battleships, cruisers and torpedo-craft on both sides during an artillery duel at medium ranges had been laid off on paper, it was to be stated which of the hostile ships employed in the scheme would be on the starboard side and which on the port side of their own ship during the forthcoming general exercise. Next, it is to be decided, according to the conditions of the scheme, what enemy's ships are to be considered as the opponents of the two broadsides; for each group of guns, as well as for each gun in the group, the times for opening fire, the bearing and distance of the object and the nature of projectile, are to be laid down beforehand. In more complicated cases, where both sides may be engaged, the precise time and locality where each hostile projectile is supposed to hit the ship and the damage done: losses of men, fires, damage to leads, connections, mechanisms, under water hits, etc., are to be indicated.
>
> In accordance with the general situation of the moment, orders are to be sent to the individual guns dealing with such losses in personnel and *matériel* as may hinder the due working of the gun or cause its temporary silence.
>
> *The details of the scheme must not only be known to the officers who worked it out, but also to all lower ranks who are concerned with carrying it out, such as gun-layers, all petty officers, electricians, torpedo men, magazine and shell room parties, etc., including the doctor's parties*

The order concluded as follows:

> The confusion which is bound to take place during the first exercises must not be minded, but the task completed and repeated. Exercises of this kind are to be started at once and the schemes executed sent in to my office once a week or on anchoring.

It is needless to say that this order was carefully complied with, that the crews made the greatest efforts to accomplish the task set them by the admiral. There was no lack of honest zeal. Every one did his best. But could such a battle scheme, worked out on paper, though admirably carried out during the exercise in all its details, make up for the lack of experience and give us that mastery of the craft, which, after all, can only be the result of years of practice at sea in a squadron, both as regards target practice and manoeuvring?

True it is always better than nothing. This reminds me of a pungent remark made by the admiral who commanded the Black Sea Fleet in 1898, when the staff gunnery officer reported that there was no more ammunition available for further target practice, as the regular allowance had already been expended, and all that could be done would be to fire out of rifle barrels fixed to the guns.

"Even this is always something," said the gunnery officer. "The gun-layer, it is true, only fires the rifle, but he has to work the gun. Always better than nothing."

"Then you are a believer in the saying:'*Better a louse in the soup than no meat at all,*'" replied the admiral, who was rather fond of quoting coarse proverbs. "I am not. Better nothing in the soup than such a substitute."

On December 4, 5, and 6, exactly the same weather; overcast sky and heavy swell. The south-east trades, which blow straight from the Antarctic Seas, produce a quite different climate on the west coast of Africa, south of the equator, compared to that in the torrid zone in the northern hemisphere.

On December 6, I wrote in my diary:

> Latitude 16°, temperature at 9 a.m. 63° F. Slept under a warm blanket. After three weeks of Turkish bath there is much grumbling at the terrible cold.

At about noon on December 6 we were off the entrance to Great Fish Bay. Here our colliers were already waiting for us, rolling about in the swell. Capital fellows, these Germans! They are as punctual as chronometers.

At 1.30 p.m. we anchored near the entrance of the bay, protected against the swell by a sandy spit, and more than 3 miles from the mainland. We did not steam in any further, because we had sighted a rather quaint-looking little vessel flying the Portuguese ensign, which was evidently on the look-out for us. It was clearly the river gun-boat *Limpopo*, built in the "'nineties," armed with one 3-pounder Q.F. and a few machine guns. That was not too alarming, and therefore when her captain came on board the *Suvoroff* and requested the admiral to leave at once, the latter pointed out quite calmly and amiably that we were more than 3 miles from any coastline belonging to Portugal, that is, outside territorial waters, and that therefore we were our own masters here.

"But you are anchored in the bay. That is the point."

"In this respect we can only thank the Lord that He made the entrance of the bay wider than 6 miles, and that between the two strips of Portuguese territorial waters, the neutrality of which is, of course, sacred to me. He has placed a narrow strip of sea, open and accessible to all."

The *Limpopo* was indignant, and steamed off to Benguela to enter a protest.

"Goodbye, little one! Pleasant passage!" we called out from the *Suvoroff* to the gunboat, which was slowly receding to the northward, rolling gunwales under. "By the time you crawl to Benguela across this swell, and get back with an ultimatum, not one of us will be left here."

Of course, if an English squadron had been here, and with it an official from Benguela, the conversation might perhaps have taken another turn.

International law, of which there is so much talk nowadays, is, after all, hardly more than an attempt to legalise that which is arbitrary, an endeavour on the part of learned lawyers to maintain their authority, to find a justification for the might which cares for no right.

The following day, December 7, at 4 p.m., we weighed and sailed for Angra Pequeña. As regarded the weather this passage was in marked contrast with the preceding ones. The south-east trade winds of the South Atlantic change to south-west along the coast, and then differ greatly from the mild north-easter of the northern hemisphere. At sunrise the sky was generally covered with low, fast travelling clouds, and the breeze freshened; about midday it cleared; in the afternoon the breeze lulled; by sunset the sky was again overcast and the breeze freshened up. From about midnight till sunrise it was nearly calm and clear overhead. In a word, the weather changed every six hours: now bearable, then again disagreeable. Even in the middle of the day the temperature did not rise above 68° F.

On December 11, at 1 p.m., we anchored at Angra Pequeña. We remained in the western part of the bay, which is separated by a narrow, rocky peninsula from the eastern portion, where the German settlement is situated. The colliers were awaiting us, but we were unable to begin coaling on account of the weather—it was blowing hard from the S.S.W., force 8,[1] and a heavy sea came rolling right into the bay. On the other hand, we received a warm welcome from the local authorities.

The chief of the staff, who had gone ashore to gather information (in the western part), reported on his return that the governor (whose military rank was that of major) had received him in a very friendly manner, and in reply to a diplomatic reference to possible difficulties which might be raised as to the stay of the squadron, merely opened his eyes very wide and asked: "What squadron? Where is it lying?" He went on to state very decidedly that as he could see no ships from the part of the bay where he resided, as he did not possess a fleet for the purpose of patrolling the coasts of the colony, and as he was a soldier, and as such it was neither his duty nor his intention to go cruising about in a native boat, least of all in weather like the present, he would be quite unable to take any action, even if a battle were being fought behind the next point of land.

On this occasion it was made more clear than ever that the very marked state of mental depression, which was general in the squadron, was not the result of fatigue after superhuman labours, of bodily ailments or privations. When the officers (and, of course, also the "lower deck," through the servants) heard of the major's answer, and realised that not only were we not hounded out, but not even rated for having come in at all, everyone revived and became cheerful—all the more when a rumour reached us that the major had merely used some very forcible German about our having snapped up under his nose a large supply of fruit and vegetables which had just arrived from Capetown, having apparently been ordered by him for his troops. Whole legends arose around the "Major," and the word became a generic name.

The torpedo lieutenant, B——, declared: "As soon as the 'Major' gets over his repugnance to salt water and pays his call to the admiral, I will undertake to introduce him into the mess and to welcome him with a beaker of the best in the name of the Russian Fleet. I hope, gentlemen, I may have your support."

"Of course—of course!"

"Don't make yourself too important, my friend. I am the mess

---

1. The strength of the wind is calculated according to a scale: 0 = calm, 12 = strong gale.

president, and as such it is my business to receive the major in the name of the rest," Commander M——, the second-in-command, broke in laughingly.

"So much the better, sir, if you will head the movement," B—— replied. "You may count on us. At last we have found a man who does not mean to put a spoke in our wheel. He must be duly honoured."

The major's goodwill was most welcome, as the weather was decidedly against us. Towards evening on the day of our arrival the force of the wind (as measured by anemometer) rose to 10 in squalls. Towards 3 a.m. on the 12th the wind began to go down. We risked it, and started coaling, but at six in the morning it came on to blow again so hard, that besides the swell rolling in from seaward, the sea got up in the bay itself.

The steamer from which the *Suvoroff* was coaling was nearly smashed up, notwithstanding all precautions taken, as our 12-pounders of the lower battery (main-deck), which were secured on the beam outboard, went into her side like needles into a cork. The loss would not have been great if the steamer alone had suffered—we should have paid him his damages, and that would have been all; but the worst of it was that the guns themselves suffered—one, for instance, which had hit upon a particularly strong part of the hull, was bent 5° out of the normal on coming out again on the return roll. Of course the gun could no longer be fired. Coaling had to be stopped.

On December 13 there was the same weather. We tried to coal in launches, but unsuccessfully. By 10 a.m. all boats had to be hoisted up or in. It came on to blow such a gale that they would have been dashed to pieces against the ship's sides.

During the following night the wind went down a little, and at 5 a.m. we recommenced coaling in launches; it was still dangerous to get the colliers alongside on account of the swell.

At about 11 a.m. the "Major" called on the admiral. Notwithstanding his military rank he was received like a regular governor. He lunched with the admiral. He was feted in the mess. On leaving the ship, he was saluted, and the band played the German national anthem.

The men were sent aloft to cheer. (I beg pardon for this incorrect sequence, but I am quoting textually from my diary.)

Throughout the day and the greater part of the night our coaling went on in hot haste. At 3 a.m. on the 15th the breeze suddenly freshened up. Many people thought it was only a squall, and kept their colliers alongside. A good deal of damage was the consequence.

At seven in the morning it suddenly fell calm again.

The chief of the staff and Colonel K——, ordnance officer on the staff, went on shore, as the admiral's official representatives, to return the governor's visit, and also to call on the senior military officer and the commander of an expeditionary corps sent here to fight the Hereros. Both these officers (again majors) came off about midday to return the call, and were of course received no less heartily than the governor had been.

On December 16 we had a flat calm all day, and a fog as thick as pea soup. Coaling was happily completed, the ships were washed down and prepared for sea.

A steamer arrived from Capetown. She brought newspapers and some verbal news. After repeated and determined attacks the Japanese had at last captured "203-meter hill"—called "*Vissokaya*" by the Russians.

"*Vissokaya?* Where is that? "I was asked in the mess.

"It is in the north-west corner of our land front," I replied, without going into details.

"*Vissokaya?* What is that?" the admiral asked me in a curious tone of voice, giving me a searching look.

"It may mean the end of the fortress, but certainly the end of the squadron. The hill overlooks the entire harbour and roadstead."

On December 17 at 9.30 a.m., full "over our ears" with coal, we left the hospitable but uncomfortable "Major's Bay" with the intention of getting to Madagascar somehow, without touching anywhere on the way.

It may be that until we reached Angra Pequeña the admiral had not given up hope of being able to look into Delagoa Bay, if only for a few hours, so as to take in a certain amount of coal from our own collier transports, whilst engaged in negotiations with the local authorities, and until an ultimatum had arrived from their home government. But the news which reached him at Angra Pequeña compelled him to give up this idea altogether. Our agents reported (I am quoting the flag-captain's words) that a flotilla of sailing schooners, of the type of fishing vessels such as were built at Bombay, had assembled at Durban; these were armed with torpedo tubes—even the name of the Japanese officer in command of them was given, Rear-Admiral Sionogu. By a singular coincidence the admiral received, together with the above news, a telegram conveying a friendly communication from the British Government, according to which there were extensive sea fisheries off Durban, and stating that numerous fishing vessels would be met with in that locality, and that a repetition of the "Hull affair" was highly undesirable.

To this telegram (of which I do not know the precise wording) the admiral sent a reply *en clair* (that is, one which could be read at all intermediate stations), to the effect that any Durban fishing vessels which might try to break through the squadron, or even approach it at torpedo range, would be ruthlessly destroyed; he requested that the British Government might be informed of this, so that the fishermen could be instructed accordingly by the colonial authorities.

I do not know what attitude our diplomatists assumed towards this telegram, but even if they suppressed it entirely, the admiral's decision was known in London earlier than in St Petersburg.

On leaving Angra Pequeña on December 17, we found the weather out at sea to be unpromising: heavy clouds, squalls, and swell from the S.S.W. Towards evening the swell had increased so much that even the battleships were dipping into it enough to take seas over. On December 19 there was the same weather: heavy, irregular swell, up to 20 feet in height. The battleships dipped deeply into it, but only rolled very little. On the other hand, the cruisers were a pitiful sight, being shaken to pieces.

Towards 11 a.m. we sighted Table Mountain, and steamed all day in sight of the coast. A glorious country, which reminds one to an astonishing extent of the other end of the Old World—the North Cape. At 4 p.m. we were 7 miles due south of the Cape of Good Hope, From there we shaped course for Cape Agulhas, on the meridian of which we turned to the north-eastward at 2 a.m. on December 20. We now entered the Indian Ocean: we began to make Easting and Northing.

During the night a fresh breeze sprang up from W.S.W. Towards morning the irregular, restless swell was replaced by a huge sea, which, luckily, ran in the direction of our course. At 4 p.m., with a clear sky, it was blowing with force 9 from W.S.W. The battleships pitched up to 7" and rolled 5½°. Occasionally the spray came over the bows.

Before sunset the squalls had the force of a gale. The sea got up steadily. About 8 p.m. we dipped bows under several times. The constructor on the staff was indefatigable in his rounds, holding consultations with the commander and the engineer in charge of the coal bunkers. Soon one heard blows of a mallet here and there; wedges were being driven under shores and struts, balks of timber and planks were being hauled about.

"Well, how goes it?"

"Oh, it is nothing at all. You remember, I told you: 'Only not from ahead.' From astern don't matter, we can stand that."

During the night there was an apparent improvement, but at sunrise on December 21 the breeze freshened up again. By midday it was blowing a whole gale.

I will not weary the reader with a description of the spectacle offered by the "elements let loose." The picture—thanks to the works of the great masters of the pen and pencil—is too well known for me to try and supplement it with my feeble strokes. I simply state: it was not "a fresh breeze," but "a whole gale," not as judged by personal impressions, but by the anemometer.

On this and the next few days I made so few notes in my diary, that I venture to reproduce these *verbatim*, without considering their incomplete literary shape.

21 Dec, noon.—Sea heavier than yesterday. Rolling up to 7°. However, 20 miles current with us,[2] instead of against. The gale sends us along. If it does not increase any more it is an advantage to us. In weather like this we need not fear any Japanese adventures, and if we don't develop any defects it will have been a very useful experience for the ships. Clear sky. Seas up to 25 feet high.

12.30 p.m.—Sea 35 feet high, possibly more. God help us! Can the ships stand this? Spray already over the upper deck.

3 p.m.—We shipped a sea over the stern. It filled the staff office, and the spray came over the upper bridge. One of the starboard pulling boats smashed,[3] but still hanging in the falls.

4 p.m.—The height of the seas has been measured—37 feet. Rolling up to 12° both ways. We are taking much water over the stern. And yet the wind seems still to be increasing.

5 p.m.—The *Malay* developed defects in her machinery. She signalled that it was trifling and would be made good in twenty minutes.

---

2. In twenty-four hours.
3. By the sea.

We continue. Stopping engines, waiting, is impossible. She will get on all right. Her machinery is poor, but the ship is an ocean liner which has weathered many a storm.

6 p.m.—The wind is not easing up, but the sea seems to be going down. We don't take over so much, but—or rather in consequence of this, the seas dash themselves against the ship's side like against a breakwater. P——[4] is looking anxious.

6.35 p.m.—We have lost our starboard seaboat.[5]

8 p.m.—The wind appears to be going down. *Russ* (*Roland*) reports by wireless that she can't keep the course[6] and is steering N. 56° E. (she is trying for shelter under the land). She was told to rejoin towards morning if the wind went down. *Aurora*[7] reported that she had lost sight of the *Malay* before sunset (apparently her engine defects not yet repaired). *Aurora* received orders to flash astern with her searchlight (the *Malay's* pendants) from time to time throughout the night.

11 p.m.—The wind is veering from S.W. to S.S.W. Squalls. Generally force of wind 6. Less rolling. Every now and then we get water over the stern and the starboard side.

22 Dec, noon.—Squalls, force 5 to 6, with rain, throughout the night from south-west, later south. Evidently the gale is abating. Sea rolling. Spray over from time to time. But how happy we are—how light-hearted we feel! One feels inclined to laugh. The ships had to pass through a bad time.

Thank God! all has gone off well, and probably Admiral Sionogu is in the bays along the coast with his flotilla of sailing schooners, foaming at the mouth with rage. They have waited in vain. It is all over; the gale has prevented it.

6 p.m.—*Russ* (*Roland*) has rejoined, and is now steaming along with us. Weather satisfactory.

23 Dec.—The wind fell altogether during the night, but in the afternoon it blew again from the south, force 5, with swell."

25 Dec.—Since yesterday morning fine weather."

---

4. The constructor on the staff—Politovsky.
5. It was washed away by the sea.
6. Apparently she shipped too much water over the stern.
7. The rear ship of the squadron.

Now more detailed entries appear again, and therefore I stop quoting my notes and resume my narrative.

Towards evening of December 24 the *Kamtchatka* kept dropping astern and was unable to resume her station in response to repeated signals. And yet the squadron was only steaming 9½ knots. Finally she received the peremptory signal:

> Report immediately why you can't keep station. Hold an enquiry and report who is to blame.

The reply was:

> Bad coal. Can't keep steam. Request permission to throw overboard 150 tons of coal. We shall be all right then.

The whole squadron was burning the same coal. Why was it suddenly so bad on board the *Kamtchatka* that she could not even keep up 9½ knots? Why was it necessary to throw 150 tons of coal overboard?

Only those who knew the admiral well were able to estimate at its true value the outward calm with which he read this astounding signal.

> Tell him that my orders are that only the culprits are to be thrown overboard.

The *Kamtchatka* at once increased speed. She was lucky besides, for at 9 p.m. the *Suvoroff's* steering-gear went wrong and for half an hour the squadron proceeded dead slow. The *Kamtchatka* therefore caught us up without having to throw overboard either coal or culprits.

On December 25[8] we entered the zone of south-east trades of the Indian Ocean, and next day, after passing the southern extremity of Madagascar, we reached the regions of summer gales[9] and calms, which surround that island. In time we became very familiar with this climate and did not suffer much under it, but at first it was extremely unpleasant: the sky is sometimes covered with thin clouds, sometimes hidden by fogs which have worked upwards; the sun neither burns nor blinds one through this veil of fog one can look into the sun with the naked eye; there is no great heat, 85° F. at the most, but a percentage of moisture up to 96°. One can hardly breathe. The lungs absorb more water than air. At 2 miles it is very difficult to make out the

---

8. This was really their 12th, as the Russian calendar is thirteen days behind.—Trans.
9. In the southern hemisphere December corresponds to our June.

colours of signal flags.

I forgot to mention that the hospital ship *Orel* had been sent on to Madagascar independently, so as to escape the trials which were in store for us; in doing so she called in at Capetown, where under the red-cross flag she was able to replenish all her stores of coal and provisions, and obtain all she required for the sick, untouched by the most Draconic rules of neutrality.

The southernmost point of Madagascar had been given her as rendezvous, so on December 26 we placed a cruiser on each bow as look-outs. The *Orel* was not seen. Evidently the gale was keeping her at Capetown.

Towards midnight on December 27 we experienced a violent squall from the north-east, accompanied by a gorgeous thunderstorm and a regular tropical downpour. At sunrise the wind went down. The atmosphere had been cleared a little. Breathing was easier. To the west we saw vaguely the jagged outline of the mountains along the coast (35 miles off).

When I greeted the admiral that morning his appearance caused me serious anxiety. He, who was so indefatigable, of such good cheer throughout this almost insanely risky cruise, suddenly "caved in" when we had nearly reached our goal; he had all at once literally aged by several years. The cause was not far to seek. A man of his age cannot with impunity spend ten days on the bridge, without losing sight of the squadron, and only snatching occasional moments of sleep in a chair—this was the reaction.

Be this as it may, it was not only I who felt anxious—the whole *Suvoroff* was in a state of excitement.

"Is the admiral well?" "What is the matter with the admiral?" These were the questions with which the doctors were being bombarded.

The doctors merely evaded their questioners.

About 11 a.m. there arose suddenly such a wild roaring and hissing in the ship, that it was only with difficulty one made out what one's neighbour was shouting into one's ear. I instinctively ran up on deck. The *Suvoroff* had left the line and was turning to starboard; the squadron was steaming along to port of her, the flagship flying the signal: "Disregard the admiral's motions." In everyday language this means: "Go on as you are and pay no attention to me."

Evidently the pipe which takes the steam from the boilers to the main steam pipe was damaged in one group of boilers.

By about noon the damage was made good; the flagship overtook the squadron and resumed her place at the head of the column. Happily there were no victims. Three men had been within an ace of being scalded to death. A lucky chance and the presence of mind of a leading stoker saved them. Close to the scene of the accident there happened to be an open manhole door leading into a coal bunker. No sooner had the pipe burst and the steam begun to escape, roaring and hissing, than the leading stoker pushed his men into the manhole, jumped after them, and closed the door. When, after nearly an hour, these men, whom every one believed to be long dead, emerged from their dark hiding-place into the daylight, there was general rejoicing. The admiral praised them before the assembled ship's company for having shown so much readiness of resource, called them fine fellows, distributed money rewards amongst them out of his own pocket, and ... in doing so suddenly lost the look of weariness and illness altogether, and appeared to be young once more.

"Did you see that? That stirred him up and he lives once more," the doctor said with a smile. "Such people only get ill and weary when their duties don't keep them busy."

December 28 passed uneventfully.

At 8 a.m. on December 29 we were up to the southern extremity of Isle Sainte Marie, and entered the straits between it and Madagascar. At 11.30 we came to an anchor.

The straits are over 10 miles wide; we anchored in the very centre, and could not therefore be formally accused of any breach of treaty.

About 4 p.m. the hospital ship *Orel* arrived from Capetown and brought a momentous piece of news: the Port Arthur Squadron had been destroyed by the fire of the Japanese siege guns.

This news did not seem to me to produce any particularly depressing effect on the squadron. Apparently it had been fully expected for a long time by a good many people, who, however, had made up their minds never to speak about it. Of course I only speak of the older and more experienced. The younger officers, intoxicated by Stoessel's bombastic reports, and especially the men, believed firmly that on our arrival we should continue to be the "Second Pacific Squadron," since the "First" not only existed, but would by then have repaired all damage received in action and join up with us as good as new. For these it was a bitter disappointment, but as ever, they did not ponder very deeply on the fate in store for them in a distant future. In this they were greatly assisted by their firm trust in the admiral, which found expression in the words: "Our man—he'll do it."

At daylight on December 30 the *Russ* was sent off to Tamatave to obtain more definite news about Port Arthur, but especially as to Admiral Fölkersam's division.

It was only then that I found out that according to the original plan the place of assembly for the squadron was to have been Diego Suarez, a first-rate harbour at the north-east corner of Madagascar, the principal base of the French ships-of-war and commerce in these waters.

Upon Japan protesting, supported by England, our good allies gave way, and declared decisively that they were unable to receive their dear guests in their own house. It turned out that the admiral received this intimation whilst we were still cruising down the west coast of Africa (I do not know exactly where). At the same time the Naval General Staff informed him that the French Government had no objection to the squadron assembling in the roads of Nossi-Bé, a suitable anchorage amongst the islands situated off the north-west coast of Madagascar; also that Admiral Fölkersam had already received orders to go there.

According to Flag-Lieutenant S——'s account to me, the admiral was very much incensed at this autocratic decision of our "armchair strategists." Quite apart from the fact that by going to Nossi-Bé the distance to be covered was lengthened by 600 miles, the approaches to it from a purely navigating point of view were by no means very safe. This little-used part of the Mozambique Channel is badly surveyed; even the sailing directions recommend navigating it with every caution, and not by any means to trust to the accuracy of the survey; on the contrary, they point out that there may be coral reefs, rising up sheer from great depths, not marked on the charts. It would surely be foolish to risk the grounding, or possibly the loss of one, if not several, of the ships which were on their way to the seat of war. The admiral replied that if Diego Suarez was closed to us, he intended to assemble the squadron in Sainte Marie Bay, to which place he requested that Admiral Fölkersam might be ordered.

We started coaling that same day, December 30. Unfortunately there were only two colliers present (the remainder were at Diego Suarez), so that we had to coal in turns.

About noon the *Malay* arrived, having weathered the storm all right.

At 10 a.m. on December 31 the *Russ* returned from Tamatave. From the telegrams brought by her we heard that on December 21 two Japanese armoured cruisers and six light cruisers had passed Singapore steering to the southward; that two armed merchant cruisers had lately left for Mozambique (quite near), and—the most interesting item—that Admiral Fölkersam had arrived safely at Nossi-Bé.

I must here point out that Isle Sainte Marie (on which there is a penal settlement) possesses no telegraphic communication whatever, nor does Nossi-Bé (only savage places like these were of any account for us). To despatch a telegram a vessel had to be sent to Tamatave or Diego Suarez; but of course not a man-of-war—that would have been looked upon as an awful breach of international law. As one of the colliers had meanwhile been emptied, she was sent to Diego Suarez, and in her went the staff officer in charge of supplies, Commander W——, with instructions to send us the remaining colliers which were waiting there, and to despatch a telegram to Admiral Fölkersam. The latter contained the order: "On receipt of this rejoin my flag."

I do not know if the admiral discussed with anyone the modifications rendered necessary in our plan of operations by the disappearance of the Port Arthur Squadron. Nor do I know if anyone had been initiated in such a plan. All the same, certain remarks of his, the sense of certain orders issued by him, certain information which the members of the staff did not consider it necessary to keep secret, showed pretty clearly the general trend of the decisions he had come to: immediate resumption of our voyage, so as not to leave the Japanese any time to replace guns damaged by erosion, to overhaul engines and boilers, to make good defects generally, to rest and refresh themselves after a severe campaign of eleven months; a "forced march" eastwards with all his best ships, stopping nowhere, leaving behind any damaged or otherwise hopeless units, so as to reach the Sea of Japan with a force, not, perhaps, very large in numbers, but consisting of picked and quite intact ships, having as their objective—"through to Vladivostok first" and from there to "threaten the enemy's lines of communications."

As I have repeatedly promised, I will be quite candid. In our detachment which went round the Cape, and which was under the immediate command of Admiral Rojëstvensky, under the influence of his iron will, the general feeling was good and hopeful. The success of the enterprise was not considered a matter of pure chance, nor were intoxicating ideas of a possible brilliant victory allowed to prevail; but there was a firm, almost cold-blooded determination to follow him unhesitatingly wherever he might lead us—even to certain destruction. On that score there was no difference of opinion. But as regarded both the expediency and the practicability of the plan itself, there were three divergent views. There were some who entirely shared the admiral's views; others still believed in the possibility of purchasing Argentine or Chilian ships, or of our being joined by the Black Sea Fleet: these considered it to be better for us to wait until we had amassed a force strong enough for the decisive battle with the entire Japanese Fleet.

The third party declared quite openly that now that the First Squadron—which at the outset had been considered (officially, that is) as superior to the Japanese Fleet—had been annihilated, the Japanese would only be given an opportunity for gathering cheap laurels, if the Second Squadron, weaker than the First, were also to be exposed to the blows of the victorious enemy; that we ought now to turn back, since the whole idea of breaking through to Vladivostok was mainly based on chance or good luck. But the latter had been on the side of the Japanese throughout the war.

So far as I was personally concerned the admiral's plan appeared to me extremely tempting, on account of its very audacity. Why not risk something for once in a way? (I had long ago got sick and tired of Alexeieff's maxim: *to be careful and to risk nothing*.) I had no belief left in the Argentines and Chilians, after the news we had received; and as to the Black Sea Fleet, I did not count on it, as I was to a certain extent familiar with our diplomatic methods. On the other hand, to declare ourselves to be incompetent, to turn back and run the risk of being branded as cowards—these ideas never entered my head. If however (and I mean to be ruthlessly candid about myself), at that time the authorities at St Petersburg had grasped how utterly hopeless—not to say criminal—our adventure was, and if they had sent us categorical orders to come back, I should by no means have been angry; on the contrary, knowing full well the preparedness for war of our "*armada*," I should have said from the bottom of my heart: "The Lord be praised! They have realised the situation whilst there was still time."

I dare not maintain that it was so, but I feel somehow that the admiral was, on the whole, of the same opinion. The fact that there was not one individual in the small circle of my brother officers who risked saying: "There is no more hope; to go on means to perish uselessly; we must turn back," was only because there might possibly have been some one amongst us—and even only a single one—who did not agree with this, and who might have looked askance at the speaker, saying to himself: "He seems to be a coward."

In these circumstances, could he, upon whom "the whole of Russia was looking with confidence and in firm hope," himself be the one to speak of turning back? In that case not only anyone who chanced to be present at such a conversation—possibly a quite insignificant person—but the whole of Russia could reproach him with not possessing the courage required to face death. No. He could not do this. He could—was even bound to—report truthfully on the entire situation, give an unbiased and candid opinion on the value of his forces and those of his adversary, submit his plans, say what his hopes were, without any concealment. *This he did.* The final decision had, however, to come from St Petersburg. Could he entertain the idea that "they" had not understood him or not wished to understand him? That these "armchair strategists" were incapable of grasping the situation, which was judged rightly, not only by himself, the flag officers, captains, and their seconds, but also by the younger officers?

To me and to many others it appeared as if the plan, as decided upon by him, had really been dictated by the hopelessness of the situation. It was the last attempt to snatch at least something out of the clutches of fate. Perish—even to no purpose! This plan reminded one of the desperate cavalry attack delivered by General Marguerite at Sedan. If there be no other way out of it, then let us go at it with the best of what we have.

Do you recollect the scene when the general, severely wounded in the head and sinking into the arms of his *aide-de-camp*, pointed out to his regiments, with his drawn sword, the way they were to go?

Do you recollect the scene when Admiral Rojëstvensky, severely wounded in the head, thrown half dead from the sinking flagship to a destroyer, still found the strength, during a short return to consciousness, to give the positive order: "Follow the squadron. Vladivostok. Course N. 23° E."?

Yes. If those who were no less than he in a position to judge of the situation did not order him to turn back, then there was only one course—forward, even if to certain destruction. And the quicker the better!

Flag-Lieutenant S——, whom I have already mentioned, filled at the same time the position of a kind of private secretary to the admiral. S conducted his most confidential correspondence, was initiated into all secrets, probably quite as much as the chief of the staff himself, and, above all, since it was he who handed the admiral the deciphered telegrams, and who put the replies, which were sent so frequently, into cipher, he was in a better position than anyone else to judge of the effect which this special correspondence produced upon the commander-in-chief.

As regarded keeping a secret confided to him, S—— was like the grave, and, needless to say, the information not intended for publication which he gave me in strict confidence, as an old messmate and friend, will never be divulged; with the exception, perhaps, of cases where the exposure of a lie may be necessary—of a deliberate lie spread by people who, personally interested in the affair, might be trying to clear themselves, in the belief that all reliable witnesses to the contrary are resting on the bottom of the Sea of Japan. Then it would be quite a different thing. And I trust that S—— himself will in such circumstances forgive my breach of trust.

He once said:—

> Yes, you may perhaps guess it, but no one really knows what the admiral has to go through. Sometimes I bring him a deciphered telegram. He reads it. He crumples up the paper in his hand. He looks as if he meant to tear it to pieces. But no. He masters himself. He begins to dictate the reply. Often he changes the form, makes improvements, gets furious with me. I hold my tongue. I know that his anger is not directed against me. I am indignant myself. Or he suddenly says, apparently quite calmly: 'Leave me alone now, by and by I will . . . I will write it myself'; and on going out I hear him breaking the pencil he has in his hand, grinding his teeth, and trembling with suppressed rage, calling someone 'Traitor!'

ALSO FROM LEONAUR
AVAILABLE IN SOFTCOVER OR HARDCOVER WITH DUST JACKET

ESCAPE FROM THE FRENCH by Edward Boys—A Young Royal Navy Midshipman's Adventures During the Napoleonic War.

THE VOYAGE OF H.M.S. PANDORA by Edward Edwards R. N. & George Hamilton, edited by Basil Thomson—In Pursuit of the Mutineers of the Bounty in the South Seas—1790-1791.

MEDUSA by J. B. Henry Savigny and Alexander Correard and Charlotte-Adélaïde Dard —Narrative of a Voyage to Senegal in 1816 & The Sufferings of the Picard Family After the Shipwreck of the Medusa.

THE SEA WAR OF 1812 VOLUME 1 by A. T. Mahan—A History of the Maritime Conflict.

THE SEA WAR OF 1812 VOLUME 2 by A. T. Mahan—A History of the Maritime Conflict.

WETHERELL OF H. M. S. HUSSAR by John Wetherell—The Recollections of an Ordinary Seaman of the Royal Navy During the Napoleonic Wars.

THE NAVAL BRIGADE IN NATAL by C. R. N. Burne—With the Guns of H. M. S. Terrible & H. M. S. Tartar during the Boer War 1899-1900.

THE VOYAGE OF H. M. S. BOUNTY by William Bligh—The True Story of an 18th Century Voyage of Exploration and Mutiny.

SHIPWRECK! by William Gilly—The Royal Navy's Disasters at Sea 1793-1849.

KING'S CUTTERS AND SMUGGLERS: 1700-1855 by E. Keble Chatterton—A unique period of maritime history-from the beginning of the eighteenth to the middle of the nineteenth century when British seamen risked all to smuggle valuable goods from wool to tea and spirits from and to the Continent.

CONFEDERATE BLOCKADE RUNNER by John Wilkinson—The Personal Recollections of an Officer of the Confederate Navy.

NAVAL BATTLES OF THE NAPOLEONIC WARS by W. H. Fitchett—Cape St. Vincent, the Nile, Cadiz, Copenhagen, Trafalgar & Others.

PRISONERS OF THE RED DESERT by R. S. Gwatkin-Williams—The Adventures of the Crew of the Tara During the First World War.

U-BOAT WAR 1914-1918 by James B. Connolly/Karl von Schenk—Two Contrasting Accounts from Both Sides of the Conflict at Sea During the Great War.

AVAILABLE ONLINE AT **www.leonaur.com**
AND FROM ALL GOOD BOOK STORES

ALSO FROM LEONAUR
AVAILABLE IN SOFTCOVER OR HARDCOVER WITH DUST JACKET

DOING OUR 'BIT' by *Ian Hay*—Two Classic Accounts of the Men of Kitchener's 'New Army' During the Great War including *The First 100,000* & *All In It*.

AN EYE IN THE STORM by *Arthur Ruhl*—An American War Correspondent's Experiences of the First World War from the Western Front to Gallipoli and Beyond.

STAND & FALL by *Joe Cassells*—A Soldier's Recollections of the 'Contemptible Little Army' and the Retreat from Mons to the Marne, 1914.

RIFLEMAN MACGILL'S WAR by *Patrick MacGill*—A Soldier of the London Irish During the Great War in Europe including *The Amateur Army, The Red Horizon* & *The Great Push*.

WITH THE GUNS by *C. A. Rose & Hugh Dalton*—Two First Hand Accounts of British Gunners at War in Europe During World War 1- Three Years in France with the Guns and With the British Guns in Italy.

EAGLES OVER THE TRENCHES by *James R. McConnell & William B. Perry*—Two First Hand Accounts of the American Escadrille at War in the Air During World War 1-Flying For France: With the American Escadrille at Verdun and Our Pilots in the Air.

THE BUSH WAR DOCTOR by *Robert V. Dolbey*—The Experiences of a British Army Doctor During the East African Campaign of the First World War.

THE 9TH—THE KING'S (LIVERPOOL REGIMENT) IN THE GREAT WAR 1914 - 1918 by *Enos H. G. Roberts*—Like many large cities, Liverpool raised a number of battalions in the Great War. Notable among them were the Pals, the Liverpool Irish and Scottish, but this book concerns the wartime history of the 9th Battalion – The Kings.

THE GAMBARDIER by *Mark Severn*—The experiences of a battery of Heavy artillery on the Western Front during the First World War.

FROM MESSINES TO THIRD YPRES by *Thomas Floyd*—A personal account of the First World War on the Western front by a 2/5th Lancashire Fusilier.

THE IRISH GUARDS IN THE GREAT WAR - VOLUME 1 by *Rudyard Kipling*—Edited and Compiled from Their Diaries and Papers Volume 1 The First Battalion.

THE IRISH GUARDS IN THE GREAT WAR - VOLUME 2 by *Rudyard Kipling*—Edited and Compiled from Their Diaries and Papers Volume 2 The Second Battalion.

AVAILABLE ONLINE AT **www.leonaur.com**
AND FROM ALL GOOD BOOK STORES

www.ingramcontent.com/pod-product-compliance
Lightning Source LLC
Chambersburg PA
CBHW031619160426
43196CB00006B/200